We Will Remember

The First World War sits firmly in our collective conscience as a period of terrible human suffering and the loss of almost an entire generation of young men. Yet, paradoxical though it may seem, from that death and destruction there was much to be proud of. Women found employment and earned wages on an hitherto unprecedented scale. Men displayed a willingness to support their country and make sacrifices for their fellow men-in-arms as never before.

The newly-independent countries of Australia, New Zealand and Canada forged their identities on the slopes of the Gallipoli Peninsula and Vimy Ridge. Many men found their voice through the graphic and evocative war poems that are still recited today.

There were also great advances in technology. Aircraft began to play an increasingly significant role in warfare and the lumbering, clunking tanks began to dominate the battlefield.

All these subjects are investigated in this commemorative issue from the *Britain at War Magazine* team. How the complex web of treaties and alliances led to a conflict that engulfed most of the developed world is explored, as is the rush of volunteers to fight for king, country and freedom.

Also explored is how the optimism of the early weeks, in which everyone expected to be home by Christmas, led to the stalemate of trench warfare and the realisation that the conflict was going to be a protracted war of attrition. Amongst the other subjects discussed are the attacks on the UK both from the sea and the air; the war in the desert and the exploits of Lawrence of Arabia; and the battle of the great Dreadnoughts at Jutland.

On 11 November 1918, the First World War came to an end. After all the fighting and the dying, the resultant peace agreement, the Treaty of Versailles, should have led to a lasting peace. It led only to resentment which exploded in an even more terrible conflict just two decades later.

Yet on 11 November every year we quietly state our resolve to remember the sacrifices of those men and women who lived and died 100 years ago. This is our first testament to them. Others will follow.

Over the course of the next five years, the *Britain at War Magazine* team will be producing a number of publications similar to this one, examining in detail the momentous events of the First World War. All the key battles, campaigns, innovations and personalities of that conflict will be highlighted in what will prove to be an exciting collection of compelling stories and vivid illustrations. Together, we will remember that heroic generation.

Martin Mace
Editor

www.britain-at-war-magazine.com

Editor: Martin Mace
Assistant Editor: John Grehan
Editorial Consultant: Mark Khan
Design: Mike Carr

Executive Chairman: Richard Cox
Managing Director/Publisher: Adrian Cox
Commercial Director: Ann Saundry
Production Manager: Janet Watkins
Marketing Manager: Martin Steele

Contacts
Key Publishing Ltd
PO Box 100, Stamford, Lincolnshire, PE9 1XQ
E-mail: enquiries@keypublishing.com
www.keypublishing.com

Distribution: Seymour Distribution Ltd., 2 Poultry Avenue, London, EC1A 9PP. Telephone: 020 7429 400
Printed by Warners (Midlands) Plc, Bourne, Lincolnshire.

Published by Key Publishing Ltd

KEY

A HISTORY OF CONFLICT BRITAIN AT WAR MAGAZINE

Contents

BELOW: **A panoramic view of the devastated city of Ypres as it appeared after the Armistice – an image which clearly shows the destruction caused during the First World War (the remains of the famous Cloth Hall are visible).** (US Library of Congress)

THE ROAD TO

FAR RIGHT: A cartoon on the Entente Cordiale as it was seen from a German perspective. It shows John Bull, stalking off with the harlot Marianne (in what is supposed to be a Tricolour dress), turning his back on the Kaiser. The tip of the scabbard of a cavalry sabre protrudes from beneath Germany's army overcoat, implying a potential resort to force. (HMP)

RIGHT: HMS *Dreadnought* pictured before the outbreak of the First World War. Dreadnought's entry into service in 1906 represented such a marked advance in naval technology that her name came to be associated with an entire generation of battleships, the "Dreadnoughts", as well as the class of ships named after her, while the generation of ships she made obsolete became known as "Pre-Dreadnoughts". She was the sixth ship of that name in the Royal Navy. (US Library of Congress)

War is often long in its gestation, its causes complex. So it was with the First World War. The growing might of Germany and the intricate web of alliances which it prompted were intended to prevent war. Instead they drew the nations of Europe into the most devastating conflict the world had yet seen.

Archduke Franz Ferdinand and his wife, Sophie, Duchess of Hohenberg, arrived at Sarajevo railway station on the morning of Sunday, 28 June 1914. Franz Ferdinand was heir presumptive to the Austro-Hungarian throne and Inspector General of the Austrian Forces. At that time Austro-Hungry was the second largest country in Europe after Russia and the third most populous behind Germany. Its empire encompassed the present-day nations of Slovenia, Bosnia and Herzegovina, Croatia, the Czech Republic and parts of a number of other countries including Serbia.

Since the early sixteenth century Serbia had been divided between Austria and the Ottoman Empire, but in 1835 the area occupied by the Turks had achieved independence. In the Balkan Wars fought against the Turks in 1912 and 1913 Serbia had considerably increased its territory and by 1914 sought to recover the territory still under Austrian control. Serbia was supported by Russia, which saw itself as the protector of the Slavic nations.

A covert group, known as The Black Hand, composed of members of the Serbian Army, hatched a plan to force Austria into invading Serbia, thus compelling Russia to intervene. The resulting conflict, it was hoped, would force Austria to relinquish its Serbian territory.

The plan devised by The Black Hand was to assassinate Franz Ferdinand. So, on that Sunday morning in the summer of 1914 a group of six Bosnian Serbs attacked Franz Ferdinand's car as he was being driven to the Town Hall. The attack failed but when the royal couple decided to visit those people in hospital who had been wounded in the bomb attack, another of the conspirators, Gavrilo Princip, was able to ambush the car.

Princip was standing near a bridge over the Miljacka River when he spotted Ferdinand's car as it drove past, having taken a wrong turn. After realizing his mistake, the driver put his foot on the brake, and began to reverse the vehicle. In doing so the engine of the car stalled and the gears locked. Princip seized the opportunity.

He stepped forward, drew his pistol, pistol-whipped a nearby pedestrian, and at a distance of about five feet, fired twice into the car. Franz Ferdinand and Sophie were shot dead. According to one witness, "the first bullet [fired by Princip] wounded the Archduke in the jugular vein; the second inflicted an abdominal wound on the Duchess." Just thirty-seven days later Europe was at war.

As expected, Austria responded by demanding a major change in its relationship with Serbia which was known would be rejected. This rebuttal of Austria's demands was all the justification it needed to allow it to mobilize its armies. Predictably, Russia was quick to demonstrate its support of the Serbs and it too began to mobilize.

Though mobilisation did not necessarily mean hostilities, a conflict between Austria and Russia would draw many other countries into war. This was because of the various treaty commitments which obliged signatories to support one another in the event of an attack.

Austria's principal ally was, of course, its fellow Germanic nation, Germany. Before 1870 there were as many as twenty-two independent German states in central Europe, excluding Austria. The largest of these states was Prussia and when these states amalgamated to form the German Empire on 10 December 1870, the Prussian king became the Emperor of Germany.

This new, powerful, energetic nation was determined to establish its position in the world. This manifested itself in Germany's bid to rival Britain and France as a world power with the creation of an overseas empire. In searching the under-developed countries of the world which they could conquer, the Germans looked to Africa, most of

which was not under colonial control. The result is what became known as the "Scramble for Africa".

Within just a few years of unification, Germany began its expansionist programme. Soon it had become the third largest colonial power in Africa. Nearly all of its overseas empire of two-and-a-half million square kilometres and fourteen million colonial subjects was found in its African possessions of Southwest Africa, Togoland, the ➤➤

This cartoon, entitled "The Boiling Point", was published in Punch on 2 October 1912. It illustrates the personifications of Germany, France, Russia, Austria-Hungary, and the United Kingdom attempting to keep the lid on the simmering cauldron of imperialist and nationalist tensions in the Balkans to prevent a general European war. (HMP)

"In the Balkan Wars fought against the Turks in 1912 and 1913 Serbia had considerably increased its territory and by 1914 sought to recover the territory still under Austrian control."

An image of a Territorial Army camp taken during the summer of 1914 – a camp which was held under the growing threat of war. Once Parliament had sanctioned the declaration of war that fateful summer, the administrative machinery required to mobilise the Territorial Army began to move, with the result that many of the men who attended camps such as this soon found themselves on their way to the front. (HMP)

"The Most Deadly Gun in History"

The Browning pistol that fired the bullets that killed Archduke Franz Ferdinand Archduke Franz Ferdinand and his wife, Sophie, Duchess of Hohenberg - deaths which ultimately sparked the crisis leading to the First World War - was discovered in 2004 gathering dust in a Jesuit community house in Austria.

For decades the murder weapon, more specifically a FN Model 1910 semi-automatic pistol which had been designed by John Browning and manufactured by Fabrique Nationale d'Herstal of Belgium and which has the serial number 19074, was in the possession of a community of Jesuits in Styria, southern Austria. They inherited it from a close friend of the archduke and his wife. A Jesuit priest, Anton Puntigam, gave the couple the last rites and later made public his intention of opening a museum in memory of the Archduke. But the chaos of the war foiled his plans.

On the priest's death in 1926, the objects were offered to the Archduke's family, which declined to take them. In 2004 the Browning was handed over to the Museum of Military History in Vienna.

The bullet fired by Princip which struck Archduke Ferdinand, sometimes referred to as "The bullet that started World War I", has also survived and is stored as a museum exhibit in Konopiště Castle, Ferdinand's residence, near the town of Benešov in the Czech Republic. (HMP)

RIGHT: **Archduke Franz Ferdinand of Austria. His assassination on 28 June 1914, set in motion a train of events that would eventually lead to the First World War.** (US Library of Congress)

MAIN PICTURE RIGHT: **A contemporary painting depicting Royal Navy warships in Scapa Flow being tended by picket boats and trawlers. The Anglo-German naval arms race of the early 20th century was one of the several intertwined causes that led to war in 1914. In 1914, the navies of Russia, France and Britain had a strength of 331,000 men and forty-three large naval vessels (Dreadnoughts), whilst those of Germany and Austria-Hungary were 95,000 and twenty-one respectively. Of all sides, it was the Royal Navy that dominated, with 209,000 men and twenty-nine large naval vessels.** (HMP)

ABOVE: **The assassin - Gavrilo Princip.** (US Library of Congress)

Cameroons, and Tanganyika.

As well as the prestige it sought in being a colonial power Germany's scramble for African territory also reflected a concern for the acquisition of military and naval bases for strategic purposes. With warships being seen as the arbiters of power, coaling stations were needed around the world. All this threatened Britain's and France's positions as world leaders.

The new Germany's growing industrial might also enabled it to build up its armed forces, including a powerful navy, which was seen as essential for the protection of its overseas empire. Britain saw the threat that Germany posed to its unrivalled supremacy at sea and responded by increasing its own production of warships, in particular the new class of battleships, the Dreadnoughts. An arms race had begun between the two greatest industrial powers on the planet. The result of this drive to create greater warships and armies meant that never before had the nations of Europe been so well prepared for war.

The new bold nationalism in Germany provoked similar sentiments in France and Briton. Increasingly the state and its people were seen as one. Therefore the state's achievements were seen to reflect upon the individual. "Thus, on behalf of the state," wrote C.R.M.F. Cruttwell, "the nation as a whole was prepared to make unprecedented sacrifices".

Such sacrifice saw the acceptance of universal conscription on the Continent of Europe. "It is an amazing paradox," Cruttwell observed, "that, in the very age when the working class were everywhere gaining power and increasing in comfort ... they should be ready, nay, often anxious, to impose upon themselves this tremendous servitude and potential risk."

By the beginning of the twentieth century the nations of Europe had created vast conscript armies that were armed to the teeth and imbibed with an aggressive nationalism. This naturally fostered great anxiety and led Britain to seek an alliance with

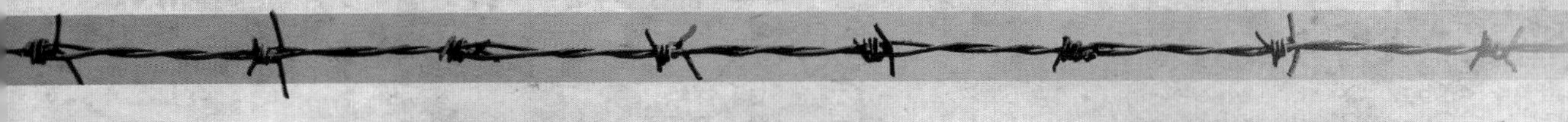

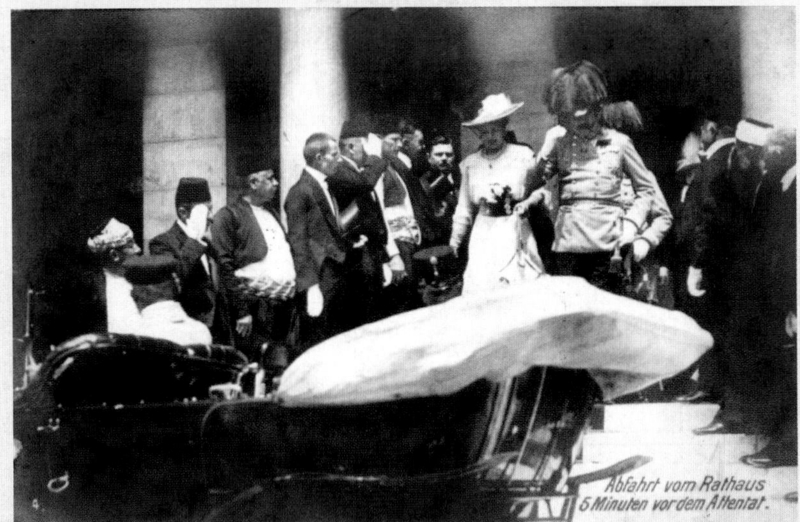

LEFT: **A postcard which shows Archduke Franz Ferdinand and his wife, Sophie, Duchess of Hohenberg, getting into a motor car to depart from the City Hall, Sarajevo, on 28 June 1914. As the original caption states, it would only be a matter of minutes before they were assassinated by Gavrilo Princip.** (HMP)

France. In 1879 Austria and Germany had agreed to support each other in case of attack. It only made sense for Britain and France, who had cooperated successfully together in the last great European War, the Crimean War, to re-establish their relationships. This took the form of the Entente Cordiale. Signed in secret in 1904, this committed each country to military support for the other in the event of war.

The other great player in Europe was Russia. The growing might of Germany and its alliance with Austria was of great concern to Russia which felt isolated. The result was the Triple Entente entered into on 31 August 1907 between Britain, France and Russia.

The opposing sides had thus been established. The massive strength of these great power blocks was intended to deter aggression. It had entirely the opposite effect. In 1914 the treaty obligations that bound these countries put them on the road to war.

On 5 July 1914, a week after the assassination in Sarajevo, the Austrian Emperor Franz Joseph wrote to Kaiser Wilhelm II, seeking his support for intervention in Serbia. The Kaiser quickly gave that backing, believing that Russia, the country most likely to oppose an attack upon Serbia, was not prepared for war. Two weeks later Austria delivered its ultimatum to Serbia, amongst the many terms of which was the demand that the Serbian government would have to accept an Austro-Hungarian inquiry into the assassination. As expected, the ultimatum was rejected. Austria declared war on Serbia and immediately began to bombard Belgrade.

Unprepared or not, Russia could not stand idly by and allow Serbia to be attacked. The Austrian ambassador was summoned to the Russian Foreign Minister. "This means a European War," the minister declared. "You are setting Europe alight."

For the next few weeks the people of Europe held their respective breaths. Despite all the treaties and promises there was no certainty that the Balkan conflict would lead to a wider conflagration.

Russia, however, had already begun to mobilize her forces and had called on France to comply with the terms of the Triple Entente and join her in opposing the Austrians. The question then arose in Britain of how it should respond if France was drawn into war. This was put to the Cabinet by the British Foreign Secretary, Sir Edward Grey, on 27 July 1914. Five ministers declared that if Britain went to war to support France they would resign immediately.

The other thorny problem was that of Belgium. Ever since the Treaty of London signed in 1839, Belgium's neutrality had >>

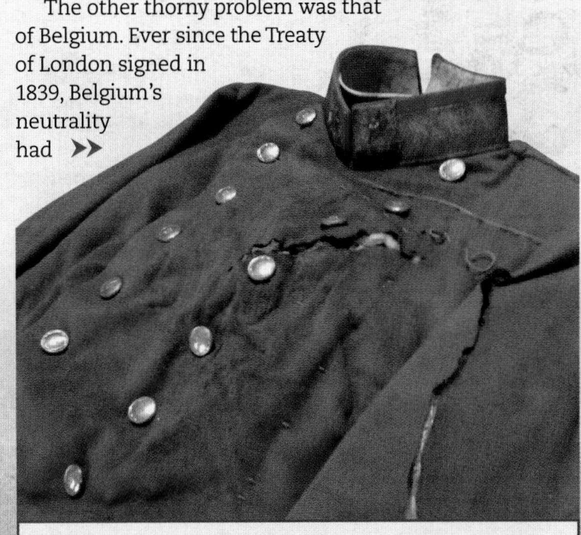

The blood-stained tunic which Archduke Franz Ferdinand was wearing when he was assassinated in Sarajevo. Along with a number of other items relating to the events of 28 June 1914, this uniform jacket can be seen in the Museum of Military History in Vienna. Other items that can be seen include the plumed cocked hat he was wearing at the time, as well as the chaise longue on which he died.

been guaranteed by the great powers, including of course Britain. If Germany and France did come to blows, Belgium might well find itself in the firing line. Could Great Britain, in all conscience, turn its back on tiny, innocent Belgium?

Understandably, Britain did not want to become involved in a European War and it would have been possible for her to insist that the affair in the Balkans was nothing to do with her. But the views of Grey's senior subordinate, Eyre Crowe, made Britain's position clear: "Our interests are tied up with those of France and Russia in this struggle, which is not for the possession of Serbia, but one between Germany aiming at a political dictatorship in Europe and the Powers who desire to retain individual freedom."

BELOW: **A plaque which marks the location of the assassination of Archduke Franz Ferdinand.**

SA OVOG MJESTA 28. JUNA 1914. GODINE
GAVRILO PRINCIP JE IZVRŠIO ATENTAT NA
AUSTROUGARSKOG PRESTOLONASLJEDNIKA
FRANCA FERDINANDA I NJEGOVU SUPRUGU
SOFIJU

FROM THIS PLACE ON 28 JUNE 1914
GAVRILO PRINCIP ASSASSINATED THE HEIR
TO THE AUSTRO-HUNGARIAN THRONE
FRANZ FERDINAND AND HIS WIFE SOFIA

TOP RIGHT: **The arrest of Gavrilo Princip in the aftermath of the assassination of Archduke Ferdinand. Princip initially attempted suicide with cyanide, then with his pistol, but he vomited the poison up. The pistol was wrestled from his hand before he had a chance to fire another shot. Found guilty at his trial, Princip was too young to receive the death penalty, being only twenty-seven days short of his twentieth birthday at the time of the assassination. Instead he received the maximum sentence of twenty years in prison. He was held in harsh conditions and, having contracted tuberculosis, died on 28 April 1918.** (US Library of Congress)

In blunter terms, he meant that Germany had to be stopped before she became too powerful to be prevented from dominating Europe, and it was in Britain's interests to do so. No-one really wanted war, but if Britain was to maintain its position as the world's leading nation, now might be a good time to inflict a crushing blow upon Germany from which she would be long in recovering.

Such sentiments were also being voiced in Paris. France had been beaten and humiliated in the Franco-Prussian War of 1870-1, losing its territories of Alsace and Lorraine to the fledgling German Empire. France could never hope to defeat Germany alone, but with the might of Britain and Russia behind her the opportunity for revenge, and to recover her lost territory, clearly presented itself.

Germany could see that a war with Russia, France and Britain might not be to her advantage and a frenzy of diplomatic activity ensued. Yet war is often harder to stop than to start and with the passing of each day the descent into conflict seemed to have developed its own momentum.

The next link in the complex chain of events was Germany's demand, late on the night of 31st July, that Russia should cease mobilisation or Germany would respond in kind. As Russia showed no inclination to stand its forces down, on 1 August 1914 Germany declared war on Russia. Knowing that France was committed to participating on Russia's behalf, on 3 August Germany declared war on France.

Germany had long expected to have to fight a great war against the other imperial powers and had planned accordingly. The Germans knew that they could not win a war fought simultaneously on two fronts, against Russia in the east and France in the west. Understanding this, General Count Alfred von Schlieffen, Chief of the German Great General Staff, devised a plan as early as the 1890s which would solve this problem. He knew that the ponderous Russian forces would take weeks to mobilise and that a comparatively small German army could be left to guard the country's eastern border. The vast bulk of the German forces would be free to attack France. Schlieffen expected to be able to knock France out of the war in just six weeks. Germany could then turn its full might against Russia. With the declaration of war, the Schlieffen Plan was immediately put into motion.

Everything now depended on how Britain would react. Even at this last minute there was still a possibility that Britain would not become involved. The Cabinet, and indeed Parliament, was split. The population was also divided. The *Daily Mirror*, one of the most widely circulated newspapers at the time, adopted a combative stance; "We could not stand aside", declared an editorial. For its part, *The Manchester Guardian* (now *The Guardian*) feared the country was facing "the greatest calamity that anyone living has known".

However, the Schlieffen Plan called not for a direct attack across the Franco-Belgium border, as that is where the main French armies were concentrated, but through Belgium, to fall on the flank and rear of the eastwards-facing French forces. For Britain this was the tipping point.

Immediately upon the declaration of war against France, Germany invaded Belgium. Britain demanded that Germany withdrew from Belgium and gave her until midnight, European time, on 4 August 1914 to comply.

Winston Churchill, the First Lord of the Admiralty, recalled the moment when the clock ticked towards the fateful hour: "The windows of the Admiralty were thrown wide open in the warm night air. Under the roof from which Nelson had received his orders were gathered a small group of admirals and captains and a cluster of clerks, pencils in hand, waiting. Along the Mall from the direction of the Palace the sound of an immense concourse singing 'God save the King' flouted in. On this deep wave there broke the chimes of Big Ben; and, as the first stroke of the hour boomed out, a rustle of movement swept across the room.

"The war telegram, which meant, 'Commence hostilities against Germany', was flashed to the ships and establishments under the White Ensign all over the world. I walked across the Horse Guards Parade to the Cabinet room and reported to the Prime Minister and the Ministers who were assembled there that the deed was done."

Timeline 1914 - Events that Shaped The First World War

June
28 Assassination of Archduke Franz Ferdinand in Sarajevo

July
23 Austria-Hungary sent ultimatum to Serbia
28 Austria declared war on Serbia

August
3 Germany declared war on France
4 Great Britain declared war on Germany
German forces invaded Belgium
7 British Expeditionary Force arrived in France
12 Great Britain declared war on Austria-Hungary
14 Battle of the Frontiers began
22 British cavalry engaged German units
23 Battle of Mons
The retreat from Mons began
26 Battle of Le Cateau
27 The Allies fell back behind the River Somme
Ostend occupied by Royal Marines
28 Battle of Heligoland Bight
31 Amiens captured by the Germans

September
5 Retreat from Mons ended
End of the Battle of the Frontiers
6 Battle of the Marne
Advance to the Aisne began
9 British passage of the Marne
12 Battle of the Aisne
13 Battle of the Marne ended
15 Battle of the Aisne ended
23 The Siege of Tsingtau commenced
25 The so-called "Race to the Sea" began

October
4 Royal Naval Division arrived at Antwerp
10 Antwerp surrendered to the Germans
Operations in Flanders started on this date
19 First Battle of Ypres began
29 Battle of Gheluvelt began

November
1 Great Britain commenced hostilities against Turkey
Allied invasion of German East Africa
Battle of Coronel off Chile
2 Royal Navy blockade of Germany started
3 Dardanelles forts bombarded by Allied fleets
Battle of Tanga, German East Africa, began
6 Operations at Basra commenced
7 British and Japanese forces captured the German-controlled port of Tsingtau
9 Battle of Cocos
22 Battle of Ypres ended
23 Defence of Festubert

December
8 Battle of the Falklands
16 German warships bombarded British East Coast
25 The Christmas Truce

Home

G. R.
YOUR KING AND COUNTRY NEED YOU
ENLIST NOW

RIGHT: **A British recruitment poster issued by the Parliamentary Recruiting Committee (PRC) in November 1914. The PRC was set up following the outbreak of war in August 1914 as a cross-party organisation chaired by the Prime Minister, Herbert Asquith. It utilised the party infrastructure in parliamentary constituencies to support recruitment - party activists were called upon to distribute leaflets and organise rallies, processions and public meetings. The PRC commissioned some 200 posters, most of which were published before the introduction of conscription in January 1916, though in July 1915 it had become the Parliamentary War Savings Committee. Entitled "Your King And Country Need You", this poster was the fifth issued by the Committee since the outbreak of war.** (HMP)

One of the great ironies of the First World War is that the philosophy of the military leaders, and the plans and training of the opposing armies, was almost entirely that of offensive action. What should have been a whirlwind campaign resulting in a rapid victory ground to a halt as both sides dug-in for a long war of attrition.

"Village folk used to turn out in force at the closing of the day to watch the Army go by – a long drab sequence of thousands of khaki uniforms, unit following unit with bands playing, some like ourselves with buglers and silver bugles, country regiments with drum and fife and the Scots with their droning pipes," recalled Bandsman Victor Shawyer of the 1st Battalion, The Rifle Brigade.[1] "Tired though I was at the end of many a long day, the sight of those swinging columns never failed to rouse me." The British Army was marching to war.

Down to the Channel ports marched the British Expeditionary Force (BEF), through the cheering, shouting, singing crowds. Civilian trains were commandeered to carry reservists to their units and civilian ships were pressed into service to carry the 80,000 men and all their equipment across the water to France.

With the news of the declaration of war with Germany, recruiting offices throughout the United Kingdom were inundated with volunteers. Aged sixteen at the time, George Coppard was typical of so many young men. "Although I seldom saw a newspaper I knew about the assassination of Archduke Ferdinand at Sarajevo," he recalled. "News placards screamed out at every street corner, and military bands blared out their martial music in the main streets of Croydon. This was too much for me to resist, and, as if drawn by a magnet, I knew I had to enlist straight away.

"I presented myself to the recruiting sergeant at Mitcham Road Barracks, Croydon. There was a steady stream of men, mostly working types, queuing to enlist. The sergeant asked me my age, and when told, replied, 'Clear off son. Come back tomorrow and see if you're nineteen, eh?' So I turned up again the next day and gave my age as nineteen. I attested in a batch of a dozen others and, holding up my right hand, swore to fight for King and Country." George Coppard had joined the Royal West Surrey Regiment.

On Saturday, 8 August 1914, the *Barnsley Chronicle* announced that,

> "The sergeant asked me my age, and when told, replied, 'Clear off son. Come back tomorrow and see if you're nineteen, eh?'"

RIGHT: **Recruits, in this case from the Honourable Artillery Company, begin their training at Fargo Camp on Salisbury Plain during August 1914.** (US Library of Congress)

by Christmas

LEFT: **Crowds gather near the House of Commons on the eve of war. The original caption states: "August 3, Bank Holiday, was a day of extraordinary national excitement. On Sunday the 2nd, a momentous Cabinet Council had been held, and on the afternoon of the Bank Holiday, Sir Edward Grey stated British policy in regard to the violation of Belgian neutrality and the German invasion of France. 'We cannot stand aside,' he declared. 'We cannot run away from our obligations of honour and interest with regard to the Belgian Treaty.' The mobilization of the Army immediately began, and so acute was the crisis that the Bank Holiday was extended for three days."** (HMP)

The German advance continues – enemy troops pictured marching through the Place Charles Rogier, Brussels, on 20 August 1914, the very day that they entered the Belgian capital. Richard Harding Davis was an American reporter who noted the following in the hours before the German arrival: "The boulevards fell suddenly empty. There was not a house that was not closely shuttered. Along the route by which we now knew the Germans were advancing, it was as though the plague stalked." The Belgians had taken the decision to not defend the city and the Germans marched through unhindered. (US Library of Congress)

"Such a noble response has been made for volunteers to go to the seat of war that the supply of documents used for this purpose gave out on Wednesday. The recruiting officer and the magistrates of Barnsley have been inundated with applications from willing recruits, and the signing on was temporarily postponed until the arrival of another batch of papers."[2]

By the fifth day of mobilisation, 9 August 1914, the advance parties of the BEF had landed secretly in France. The next day the first contingents of the main force set out to join them.

As the BEF disembarked onto French soil it assembled in an area between Maubeuge and Le Cateau. Just two weeks later the British concentration was complete forming part of the left wing of the Allied line.

This was all part of a plan that >>

ABOVE: **Elements of the British Expeditionary Force head across the Channel to France - the first of many millions who would make the same journey (sometimes never to return) over the next few years. Kaiser Wilhelm, who was famously dismissive of the BEF, reportedly issued an order on 19 August 1914 to "exterminate ... the treacherous English and walk over General French's contemptible little army". Hence, in later years, the survivors of the Regular Army dubbed themselves "The Old Contemptibles". However, no evidence of any such order being issued by the Kaiser has ever been found and it is now considered likely that the term was a British propaganda invention, albeit one often repeated as fact.** (HMP)

As they move towards the front near Mons in August 1914, the horses of a British Cavalry unit are rested and watered from a suitable canal. The cavalry's scope for movement was circumscribed by the availability of water for the horses. (HMP)

had been worked out years before on the French theory that the Germans would attempt to invade across the Franco-German border where the bulk of the French Army was massed. The British force, small in comparison with the 824,000-strong French Army, was merely to protect the Allied flank on the border with neutral Belgium. The invasion of Belgium by the Germans had not changed Allied strategy as the French considered it merely a feint to draw troops away from the main attack.

It was also French policy not to stand on the defensive. Fostered by the likes of General Foch, the young officers at the Saint-Cyr military academy were taught that battles were only won by offensive action. With the Germans also advancing, the two great armies were soon to clash in what was expected to be a series of decisive battles. One way or another, it was believed, the war would be over by Christmas.

The tiny Belgian Army delayed the German advance for eighteen crucial days, eventually being driven back to their National Redoubt built around Antwerp. With the Germans marching on Brussels, the French Commander-in-Chief, General Joffre, instructed his left wing, which included the BEF, to move into Belgium to confront the enemy.

By 20 August 1914, the leading columns of the BEF had started on their march into Belgium. On the men tramped, through a hot, but brilliantly clear, summer's day. Ahead went the Cavalry Brigade, the "eyes and ears" of the army, to seek out the Germans and to maintain contact with the French Fifth Army.

Ahead went the Cavalry Brigade, the "eyes and ears" of the army, to seek out the Germans and to maintain contact with the French Fifth Army.

The BEF continued into Belgium to come into line with the Fifth Army which had already experienced its first encounter with the Germans. The French advance was brought to an abrupt halt by the Germans and, without informing the British commander, General Sir John French, they began to retreat. Though the BEF should have still been behind the Fifth Army, it quickly found itself ahead of the French and directly in the path of the German First Army.

Early on 22 August 1914, 'C' Squadron of the 4th (Royal Irish) Dragoon Guards, advancing eastwards

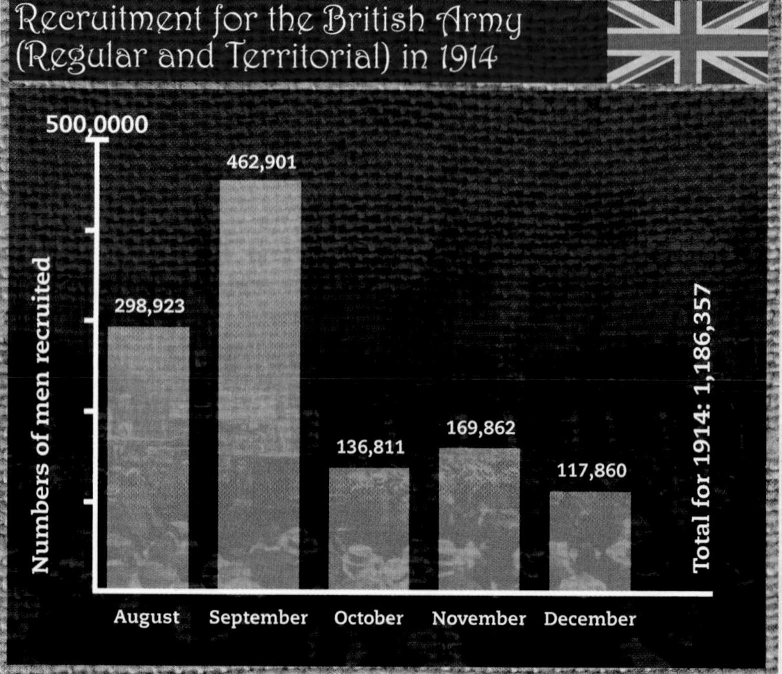

ABOVE: **Hot and tired, men of 'A' Company 4th Royal Fusiliers rest in the Grand Place at Mons. Not long after this picture was taken the battalion moved to positions on the Canal de Condé at Nimy where, on 23 August, they were attacked by the German 18th Division. The first two Victoria Crosses of the war were won by two men of 4th Royal Fusiliers at Nimy – Lieutenant Maurice Dease and Private S.F. Godley. Dease was killed during the action and Godley was taken prisoner.** (IWM Q70071)

INSET: **The same view today.** (Courtesy of Jerry Murland)

towards Obourg, encountered a patrol from the 4th (Westphalian) Cuirassiers "von Driesen".

"I saw a troop of Uhlans [*sic*] coming leisurely down the road, the officer in front smoking a cigar", recalled Corporal Drummer E. Thomas. "We were anxiously watching their movements when … they halted, as if they had smelt a rat. They had seen us!"

No.1 Troop was ordered to charge by 'C' Troop's commander, Captain Charles Beck Hornby. With sabres drawn, the Dragoons scattered the Cuirassiers left and right.

"Bullets were flying past us and all round us", continued Thomas. "I could see a German cavalry officer some four hundred yards away standing mounted in full view of me, gesticulating to the left and to the right as he disposed of his dismounted men and ordered them to take up their firing positions to engage us. Immediately I saw him I took aim, pulled the trigger and automatically, almost as it seemed instantaneously, he fell to the ground." It was the first British shot, fired in anger, of the First World War.

With this engagement, Sir John French knew that the enemy was close and the BEF took up defensive positions along the Mons-Condé Canal. It was ready to fight its first battle of the Great War.

When dawn broke on 23 August 1914, bringing with it a light drizzle that was soon banished by the strengthening sun, all was quiet. Then the first seemingly tentative movement of the enemy was detected, followed by a sudden great grey mass of infantry. The Battle of Mons, the BEF's first major action of the war, was underway.

"You couldn't see the earth for them, there were that many," exclaimed Corporal Holbrook of the 4th Battalion, Royal Fusiliers. "Time after time they gave the order 'Rapid Fire'. Well you didn't wait for the order, really! You'd see a lot of them coming in a mass on the other side of the canal and you just let them have it. They kept retreating, and then coming forward, and then retreating again. Of course, we were losing men and a lot of officers especially when the Germans started this shrapnel shelling, and, of course, they had machine-guns – masses of them. But we kept flinging them back."

Whilst it could be stated that both sides were victorious at the Battle of Mons, for the British, outnumbered by as much as 3 to 1, the battle was particularly important. The BEF had managed to hold off the German First Army for forty-eight hours, while inflicting significantly heavier casualties on the enemy, and was thereby able to retire in good order. It thus achieved its main strategic objective, which was to protect the French Fifth Army from being outflanked.

The Germans were also surprised to have been dealt such a sharp blow by an army they had previously considered inconsequential. "The men all chilled to the bone, almost »

RIGHT: **British troops facing the German onslaught in 1914.** (HMP)

BELOW RIGHT: **The "First Shot Memorial". On 22 August 1914, near this spot on the main Brussels road north-east of Mons, there was the first crack of a British rifle fired in anger during the First World War. Not since the Battle of Waterloo had British soldiers fired a shot, in action, on Continental Europe.** (HMP)

too exhausted to move and with the depressing consciousness of defeat weighing heavily upon them," wrote Walter Bloem, a Reserve Captain in the 12th Brandenburg Grenadier Regiment. "A bad defeat, there can be no gainsaying it ... we had been badly beaten, and by the English – by the English we had so laughed at a few hours before."

However, with the French Fifth Army having withdrawn, the British also had to pull back to prevent the enemy encircling them. The retreat

was a desperate affair, as Rifleman Gale of the 1st Battalion Rifle Brigade, described: "All night long, we never stopped all night. The Army Service Corps who had our rations, they couldn't stop. They just threw our rations on the side of the road and left us to pick them up."

With the Germans pressing hard on their heels, the British were forced to fight a number of rearguard actions before the commander of the BEF's II Corps, General Smith-Dorrien, turned and faced the Germans at Le Cateau on 26 August 1914. Though II Corps suffered heavy losses at the battle, the Germans were knocked back.

The consensus amongst military historians is that Le Cateau ranks amongst the most successful holding actions in British military history. Indeed, it allowed the BEF to retreat unhindered until it was able to join up with the French armies on the River Marne where they prepared to make their final stand in defence of Paris. Urging his men with the words that, "the battle upon which hangs the fate of France is about to begin,"[3] Joffre ordered the British and French forces to attack.

The Battle of the Marne lasted for a week (5-12 September), but the Allied counter-attack brought the Germans to a halt just thirty miles from the French capital. Whilst the battle of the Marne was an immense strategic victory for the Allies, the scale of the fighting can be gauged by the fact that over two million men fought in the battle, with, according to some estimates, as many as 500,000 killed or wounded. French casualties totalled 250,000, 80,000 of them dead, whilst the BEF suffered 13,000 casualties, 1,700 of them dead. The Germans suffered 220,000 casualties. No future battle on the Western Front would average so many casualties per day.

The Germans, though, were far from beaten. They withdrew to the River Aisne where they began to dig in, determined to retreat no further. The French, equally determined to give no ground also began to fortify their positions.

This marked the start of the static warfare for which the First World War has become synonymous. Yet the Germans still believed that they could by-pass the positions on the Aisne by outflanking the Allied left. As the Germans pushed their forces ever westwards, the Allies matched them. This was the famous "race to the sea" which saw the opposing trench systems eventually extend all the way to the Belgian coast.

British forces were moved rapidly to counter the German move to the coast, digging trench lines around the town of Ypres in Belgium, the French and Belgians holding the other parts of the long network of defences. It was clear that neither side would be able to achieve the rapid victory that they sought. As the trenches became deeper and stronger it was evident that the war would drag on for a very long time. No-one would be home by Christmas.

One Man Stand

In the retreat from Mons, on 23 August 1914, the 4th Battalion Middlesex Regiment was ordered to defend the canal railway crossing at Obourg. The positions they took up in and around the railway station, which commanded the bridge, eventually came under artillery fire and infantry. The rapid fire of the Middlesex held off the Germans all morning. Despite being reinforced by two companies of the 2nd Battalion the Royal Irish Regiment, the Middlesex were forced to withdraw shortly after midday. On the station roof one man remained alone, holding the enemy back whilst his comrades retreated. This unknown soldier fought on by himself until he was killed. The spot where this lone soldier carried out his gallant deed is marked by a plaque fixed to the front of this brick structure. (HMP)

NOTES:

1. Lyn MacDonald, 1914 (Penguin, London, 1989), pp.21-2.
2. Jon Cooksey, *Barnsley Pals: The 13th and 14th Battalions York & Lancaster Regiment* (Pen & Sword, Barnsley, 2006), p.21.
3. Ian Senior, *Home Before the Leaves Fall*, (Osprey, Oxford, 2012), pp.201-2.

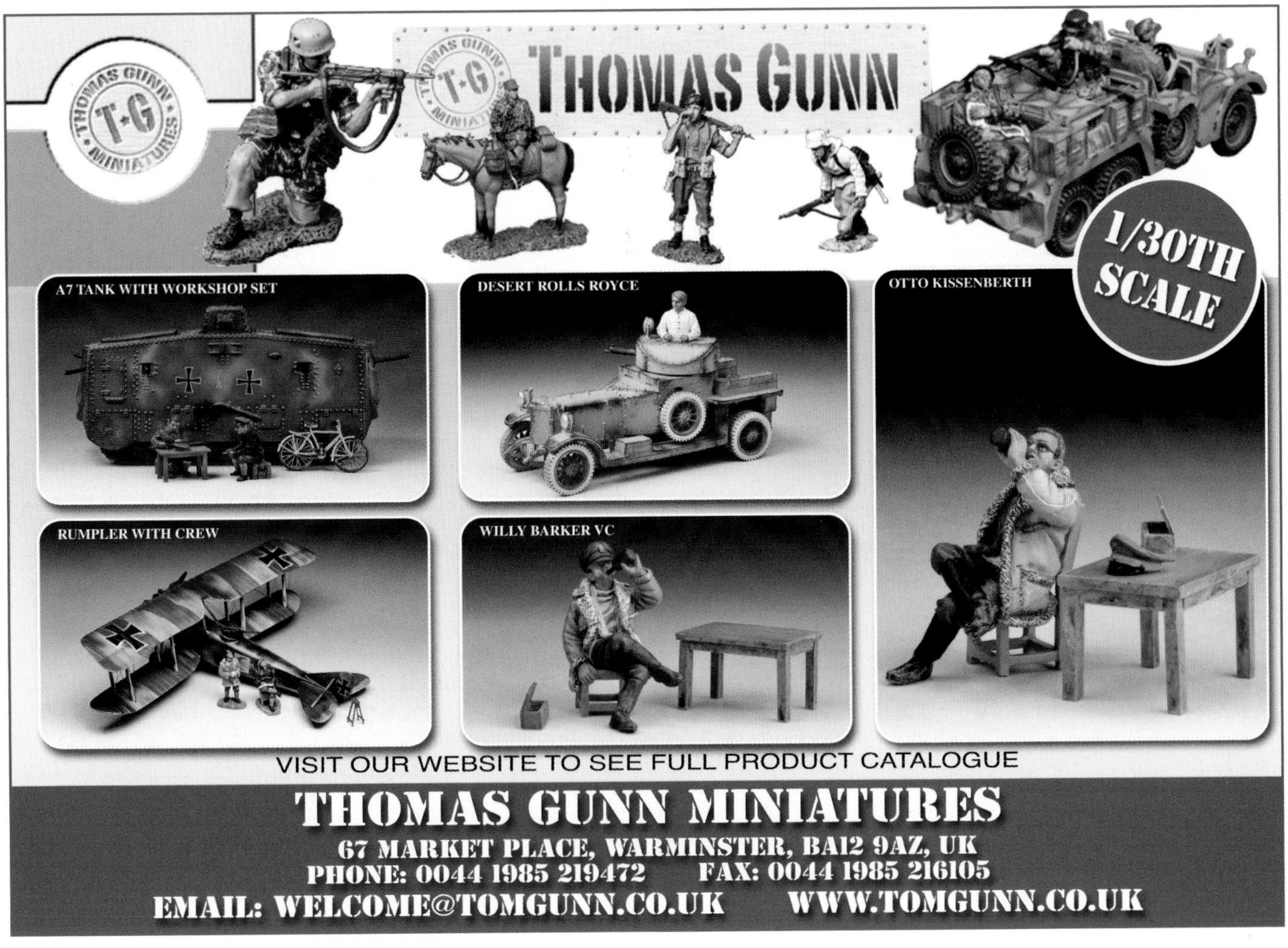

STALEMATE

RIGHT: **Men of the Northumberland Hussars sheltering in Sanctuary Wood, October 1914. It was about this time, and for the very reason that troops such as these had sought shelter there whilst being screened behind the front line, that Sanctuary Wood got its now famous name. It is stated that the Northumberland Hussars was the first British Yeomanry regiment to go into action in 1914.** (Imperial War Museum; Q50708)

ABOVE RIGHT: **The remains of an original shell-blasted tree which stands in the grounds of the Sanctuary Wood (Hill 62) Museum near Ypres. As can be seen in this photograph, it is a popular place for visitors to leave poppies.** (HMP)

By the end of November 1914 the "race to the sea" had resulted in the elimination of open flanks and all opportunities to out-manoeuvre the enemy were lost. Both sides dug in. From the North Sea coast of Belgium southward through France to the Swiss border, hundreds of miles of trenches eventually marked the opposing front lines.

After the German Army had been halted on the Marne, its last chance to turn the Allied positions and move upon Paris lay in sweeping round the Channel coast. To counter this, the Allies would also need to extend their front to the north-west. These moves would become known as "The Race to the Sea".

It was decided that it would be expedient to transfer the British Expeditionary Force to block this latest German move. So, on 3 October 1914, the BEF began marching. Its objective was the lovely old city of Ypres which was soon to become a devastated ruin.

The early fighting had demonstrated the terrifyingly lethal power of modern weapons. The accuracy of rifles, the weight of heavy field artillery and the volume of fire produced by machine-guns meant that troops could no longer operate in the open without suffering crippling losses. "Our rapid fire was appalling even to us," recalled Corporal John Lucy of the 2nd Battalion, Royal Irish Rifles, who was watching the Germans attacking across the open fields at Mons. "Such tactics amazed us, and after the first shock of seeing men slowly and helplessly falling down as they were hit, gave us a great sense of power and pleasure. It was all so easy."

The great offensive plans of the opposing armies, in which speed and manoeuvrability were paramount, had proven to be completely impractical as entire brigades could be held up by a few well-sited machine-guns. The only way to preserve the troops was to place them in strong defensive positions which would minimize the effectiveness of machine-guns and artillery. As soon as troops arrived in an area they would dig in. "Lord, how we appreciated those entrenching tools," wrote a now chastened Lucy.

The consequence was that all along the respective front lines, trench systems began to be formed. Though primitive in comparison with the complex networks of later years, already they were considered essential.

Nevertheless, the BEF was still moving on Ypres when, on 19 October 1914, the Germans launched their series of assaults that they believed would see them achieve the breakthrough they sought. Some accounts state that the First Battle of Ypres started on the 18th, others the 20th.

It was the men of I Corps who were the first to reach Ypres, in the very nick of time. The German attack was held but one battalion in particular, the 2nd Battalion Royal Irish Regiment, found itself surrounded and cut off from the rest of the 3rd Division. Altogether 257 men out of 578 were killed, including its commanding officer, almost all of the rest being taken prisoner.

In the days that followed the Germans continued their assaults, with the British and Belgian armies barely able to hold their ground. By 24 October 1914, Sir John French had come to the conclusion that "the utmost we could do to ward off any attempts of the enemy to turn our flank to the North, or to break in from the eastward, was to maintain our present very extended front, and to hold fast our positions until French reinforcements could arrive from the South."

Around Ypres the British occupied a salient which bulged forward with a sixteen-mile long front. The heart of the salient was the city itself – English-speaking soldiers often referred to Ypres (Ieper today) by the deliberate mispronunciation Wipers. The German attacks were centered along the axis of the Menen Road,

"We stood to in the wet shell holes and crumbling trenches under the thunder and blasting flashes of German high explosives..."

which enters Ypres from the east.

Somehow French needed to shorten his front and the idea was put forward to flood the low ground to the west. On the night of 29/30 October 1914, eight weir gates on the River Yser were opened. Over the course of the next few days, a vast area was inundated, blocking any attempts by the Germans to advance past the Allied left flank. Consequently, the Germans' last chance of winning the war in 1914 was to smash their way through the British at Ypres itself before the trenches there could be made impenetrable.

On 31 October, the hamlet of Gheluvelt, just eight miles from the imposing Cloth Hall in the centre of Ypres, fell to the enemy. The Germans were on the brink of breaking through the British lines and making a dash for the Channel ports. The entire BEF was in grave peril.

Despite their state – the previous ten days of battle had left all ranks haggard, unshaven and unwashed, their uniforms soaked in the mud of the Langemarck trenches and torn by the brambles of Polygon Wood – the men of the 2nd Battalion Worcestershire Regiment, effectively the last available reserve of the British defence, were ordered forward. Following a stand by the 1st Battalion South Wales Borderers, during the afternoon of 31 October, in one of the most remarkable actions of the entire war, the Worcesters charged the Germans at Gheluvelt.

Less than 600 men, under the command of Major E.B. Hankey, advanced with fixed bayonets >>

ABOVE: **Preserved shell craters in the grounds of the Sanctuary Wood (Hill 62) Museum. Views such as this help explain why the museum is one of the most popular destinations in the Salient for the battlefield visitor.** (HMP)

BELOW: **The original caption on the rear of this image states that it is a view of part of Sanctuary Wood after the fighting of 1914 and 1915.**

RIGHT: **When the First Battle of Ypres was at its height in November 1914, the area under shell-fire was so large and the casualties so heavy that medical work could only be carried out with the greatest difficulty. It was during this period that Corporal J. Hart, Royal Army Medical Corps, established a dressing station at Wulverghem, where for two days – 4 and 5 November – he treated the numerous French and British wounded who streamed in from the firing line. For his actions, Hart was subsequently awarded the Distinguished Conduct Medal.** (HMP)

RIGHT: **Some of the trenches that can be seen at the museum in Sanctuary Wood.** (HMP)

FAR RIGHT: **Stalemate has set in. This photograph was taken looking out into No Man's Land, and the German trenches beyond, in the area of the Ypres Salient known as Farm 14 – an image taken, no doubt at great risk, during early 1915.** (Courtesy of Jon Cooksey)

> **"A calloused knuckle on a forefinger is the hallmark of the 1914 men."**
>
> *Corporal John Lucy of the 2nd Battalion, Royal Irish Rifles*

in the opposite direction to a stream of retreating British units. Having crossed the fields between Polygon Wood and Gheluvelt village under fire, Hankey and his men stormed into the grounds of Gheluvelt Château were they fell upon the leading German unit.

In the grounds of the château the Worcesters combined surprise and aggression to achieve an unlikely victory that temporarily halted the advance of an entire German Army Group. Their actions saved the BEF from a humiliating capture or almost certain catastrophic defeat. If the Worcesters had not saved the day, the outcome of the war on the Western Front could have been very different for Britain.

Indeed, it is easy to understand why the name of Gheluvelt was once famous across the entire English speaking world. Indeed, a contemporary saying went: "When the time shall come when the British heart no longer thrills at the name of Gheluvelt its pride will indeed be lost for the last hour of the British Empire will have struck."

Still the Germans threw themselves against the British front. Their last attempt to achieve a breakthrough began on 11 November 1914, when twelve-and-a-half divisions attacked across a nine-mile front. Facing the 18,000 German soldiers, were just 8,000 troops from the BEF.

Unable to have been relieved, the battered remnants of Corporal Lucy's battalion were amongst those that stood directly in the path of the Germans at a place known as Sanctuary Wood. "We stood to in the wet shell holes and crumbling trenches under the thunder and blasting flashes of German high explosives," he subsequently wrote. "There is no need to describe this bombardment, except to say that it was the worst in my experience."

Situated just two miles from Ypres town centre on ground that rose to sixty-two metres above sea level, allowing observation across the low, flat Flanders terrain, Sanctuary Wood was viewed as a key point in the British line. John Lucy continued his description of the furious bombardment that had descended upon the Irish that morning: "A few of our fellows broke under it, and one

poor chap entirely lost his head and ran back out of his trench. He had not a chance in the open. The earth was vomiting all round us and he tumbled over in a few yards."

As Lucy and those around him observed all too painfully, the man would have stood a far better chance if he had just held his nerve and stayed where he was.

Those who did stay in the trenches were far from safe, however, because of the intensity of the German bombardment. "The trenches were filled with the acrid smell of shell smoke," continued Lucy. "Heavy shrapnel burst right down on us, its pall of smoke roofing the trench and blotting out the sky. I was flung about by the concussion, and thrown flat against the trench bottom. My whole body sang and trembled. One ear was perforated by the concussion, and I could hardly hear". A runner came by and saw Lucy so badly knocked about that he stopped to help the corporal. Lucy was unable to communicate to the runner's anxious enquiry, other than to nod that he was "all right".

The runner then delivered his message. The order he carried was to 'Stand to' because the Germans were massing in front ready to attack. With the observation that where Lucy's section was positioned was "a nasty spot, this," he ran off with two close shell bursts to hurry him on his way.

When the German attack came, the Royal Irish Rifles manned the broken parapet of their shallow trench. "Stand to, stand to, everyone," was the order and their rifles lined the parapet. Facing the enemy were eleven British battalions which, after three months of fighting, had been reduced to around 4,000 men.

Confident as always, the Germans advanced as if on parade. "The magnificent Prussian Guards made a review of it," marvelled Lucy. "They executed their famous goose-step in the sight of their foe, and the field-grey waves came on. The Kaiser was close behind in some neighbouring town, ready to receive reports of the great breakthrough."

The Royal Irish Rifles were in the path of the left wing of the Prussian Guards. Farther along the British line the 1st Prussian Guards Brigade pushed back the British 1st (Guards) Brigade, under Brigadier General Charles FitzClarence. This brigade contained battalions from the Scots Guards, Camerons and Black Watch regiments, and had around 800 men. They were outnumbered three to one by the Germans but they offered enough resistance to blunt the attack which then stalled.

"We stopped the Germans on our front, and they were the finest troops of Germany, led by the flower of her noblest houses. That was all," Lucy commented laconically on what was an historic battle, the one that finally ended Germany's hopes of an early victory.

The First Battle of Ypres still had a few more days to run before the Germans accepted that they had failed to break the British line. By the end of November 1914 both the Allied and the German forces on the Western Front were exhausted. They had been fighting almost continuously since early August and their human and material resources were spent. Men dug all along the line and the winter of 1914/15 gave the soldiers time to consolidate their trench networks and reinforce them with concrete and steel. The war of speed and movement had ground to a halt. Stalemate had been reached on the Western Front.

ABOVE: **The reality of the stalemate that developed on the Western Front as 1914 drew to a close. Peering out from the depths of their dugout, two young officers – Captain George Hewitt and Lieutenant Henry Colver – grin mischievously at the camera. It is July 1915, and these officers' battalion, the 1/5th Battalion York and Lancaster Regiment, has just entered the line on the banks of the Yser Canal at the northern extremity of the British Army's presence on the Western Front. Lieutenant Colver would not survive the war, being killed in action on 19 December 1915. He was just 23 years old.** (Courtesy of Jon Cooksey)

A German prisoner being brought in during the Battle of Gheluvelt.

Britain Und

BOTTOM LEFT: **St Barnabas in Hart Road, Hartlepool, after having been hit by one of the 1,000 or so shells fired at the town by the German warships during the bombardment on 16 December 1914.** (HMP)

BOTTOM RIGHT: **The damage caused to Abbey Lodge, Whitby, following the German bombardment of 16 December 1914.** (HMP)

Within weeks of the outbreak of war, the British population suddenly found itself on the front line when the German Navy launched a series of attacks on the East Coast.

On Tuesday, 3 November 1914, a German battlecruiser squadron shelled the port of Great Yarmouth. "It began soon after 7 o'clock and went on furiously for 20 minutes," noted one reporter in *The Times*. "The many who were asleep in the town were rudely awakened by the reverberation of the guns and the clattering of windows and shaking of homes. The few that were awake quickly made their way to the beach. All they could see was flash after flash on the horizon followed by the dropping of shells in the sea and the leaping of great cascades of water."

Despite the barrage, little damage was done to the town, though the residents were badly shaken by the unexpected attack. As soon as news of the attack reached the Admiralty a British battlecruiser squadron set off to engage the enemy warships but was too late to prevent the Germans returning to Wilhelmshaven.

Having seen how the Royal Navy responded to the attack on Great Yarmouth, Admiral Reinhard Scheer, Commander-in-Chief of the Imperial German Navy's High Seas Fleet, believed that if he conducted further attacks upon Britain's East Coast he could lure the Royal Navy into a trap.

With the Kaiser's agreement, Admiral Scheer opted to put his plan into action with a raid upon the Hartlepools and Scarborough. As part of Scheer's strategy a strong force would shell the coastal towns whilst, 130 miles further east, flotillas of torpedo-boats and the rest of the High Seas Fleet would be waiting to ambush the Royal Navy. The final part of the plan was for the English coast to be mined six miles off shore and for U-boats to be patrolling off Harwich and the Humber to attack British warships as they put to sea.

Originally scheduled for 29 November 1914, the operation was postponed until the night of 14/15 December. The Admiralty, however, was in fact expecting just such an attack. Codebooks retrieved from the light cruiser *Magdeburg* which had run aground in the Baltic had been handed over by the Russians and these helped Naval Intelligence gain some inkling of what the Germans had in mind. As a consequence, on

r Fire

the evening of 14 December, Winston Churchill, then the First Lord of the Admiralty, was warned that an attack upon the east coast was imminent.

Early on the morning of Wednesday, 16 December 1914, three workmen, repairing a cliff-top cottage to the north of Scarborough, caught sight of three naval vessels steaming close inshore. Unaware of the intention of these ships, they continued with their work. They were not, however, the only ones to notice the activity out to sea. At his post in the coastguard station on Castle Hill an alert lookout reported by telephone that "some strange ships are approaching from the north. I cannot make out what they are. They do not answer my signals."

The three vessels were in fact the German battlecruisers *Derfflinger* and *Von der Tann*, and the light cruiser *Kolberg*. Possibly aware that they were being watched, the captain of *Von der Tann* gave the order to open fire. The crew of *Derfflinger* immediately followed suit, whilst *Kolberg* detached itself from the small fleet, steaming on ahead to commence laying mines.

Back on Castle Hill the lookout saw, rather than heard, the first signs of the thunderous broadside. His next message had, understandably, a more urgent tone: "They are Germans – they are firing on us." Within a matter of seconds the 11-inch and 5.9-inch shells from this initial barrage fell upon Scarborough. The damp, cold, morning air in the streets of the slumbering town was rent asunder by exploding shells, falling masonry, and whistling shell splinters.

Produced in 1915, this poster is seen by some as one of the most successful of such images to emanate from the First World War. The damage depicted on this poster, embellished by the emotive addition of a little girl and her doll, was at No.2 Wykeham Street, Scarborough. This house was the scene of the worst casualties from the shelling. A total of four persons were killed there – Mrs. Johanna Bennett, her son, Albert, and two other children. (US Library of Congress)

MAIN PICTURE: **The attackers on 3 November and 16 December 1914 - warships of the Imperial German Navy's High Seas Fleet in Kiel.** (NARA)

No.1 Gun Emplacement

The original First World War-era No.1 gun emplacement at Hartlepool's Heugh Battery as it is today, forming part of the Heugh Battery Museum. For display purposes, the emplacement has been equipped with a QF 5.25-inch Mk.II gun which was used for land service. When the Heugh Battery, and the nearby Lighthouse Battery, opened fire on the German warships, they gained the distinction of being the only coastal batteries in England to fire their guns in anger during the First World War. (Courtesy of the Heugh Battery Museum)

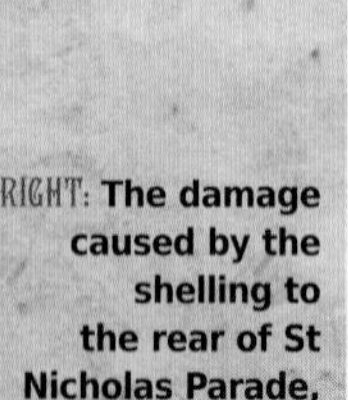

RIGHT: The damage caused by the shelling to the rear of St Nicholas Parade, Scarborough. (HMP)

FAR RIGHT: A relic of the shelling of Scarborough – the nose cap of a German shell that was recovered in the aftermath of the attack. (HMP)

The first shells of the fusillade had been targeted at the signal station located prominently on the high point of Castle Hill. As a direct result Scarborough Castle, its days of shot and shell thought to have been long past, once again found itself on the front line. The Keep was hit twice and some damage inflicted upon the twelve-foot thick castle walls. By virtue of its location against the castle walls, the barracks, thankfully unoccupied at the time, were also badly damaged. And so the shells continued to fall on the town. The Grand Hotel was another early victim, as well as the private residence of a local MP. Then the Spa itself was struck, shells and shrapnel fragments gouging large chunks from the surrounding sea wall.

The first fatality followed soon after. A Chemist shop, at 2 South Street, was demolished as a single shell struck the roadway outside. The blast dug a large crater, and the shell splinters it unleashed killed the shop's porter, 49-year-old Leonard Ellis, as he opened the door to the shop. Sadly, Ellis therefore gained the mantle of being the first civilian to die on the British mainland as a result of enemy action in the First World War.

Thirty or so minutes after the first shots, the German ships ceased fire and set course northwards at speed. Behind them lay a battered Scarborough. Eighteen civilians were dead or dying. Of this total eight were women and four were children. A further eighty or more were reported to be injured.

As can be imagined, as well as the human cost of the shelling, the fabric of the town itself had taken a heavy beating. One list suggests that no less than 632 buildings were damaged, included in which were hotels, boarding houses, churches, chapels, private homes, schools, warehouses, workshops, and mansions.

At Hartlepool the men of the 18th Battalion Durham Light Infantry were already at their posts. Shortly before midnight on the 15th the Fortress Commander at the Heugh (pronounced "Yuff") Battery, situated on the Headland in Hartlepool, had received a telegram: "A special sharp look-out to be kept all along east coast

ABOVE: The youngest victim of the bombardment of Scarborough, one John Shields Ryalls, aged just 14 months, is pictured in the arms of Miss Bertha MacEntyre. Both were killed at 22 Westbourne Road when a shell smashed through the rear part of the building's roof. (IWM Q53464)

ABOVE LEFT: The plaque which marks the spot where the first shell fell, near Heugh Battery, during the attack on Hartlepool. (Courtesy of Andrew Curtis, www.geograph.org.uk)

at dawn tomorrow, December 16th." The Fortress Commander told his men to take post from 07.00 hours to 08.30 hours after which, if everything was quiet, they could return to their billets.

All seemed quiet until, at about 08.00 hours, a message was received from the South Gare Battery a few miles away at the mouth of the Tees. It stated that dreadnoughts had been seen steaming north. This was followed almost immediately by a message from the Port War Signal Station in the Lighthouse stating that three warships *Seydlitz*, *Moltke* and *Blücher* were approaching at great speed.

The first shell from the leading ship fell beside the low wall which formed the boundary between the Heugh Battery and the pathway leading to the nearby promenade. The blast killed Private Theophilis Jones and three other members of the battery. Jones was declared to have been the first soldier killed by enemy action on British soil in the First World War and the first since the Battle of Culloden in 1746.

All around this scene of carnage, the German shells continued to fall on Hartlepool. People were literally running into the street by this time and the hot metal fragments cut down the people in the streets. "The work of destruction now began upon the two boroughs," recalled one witness. "A group of enormous gasholders were the first to go, 'picked off as clean as a whistle'. Each became a roaring column of flame. No area seemed to have been untouched. It was as if a gigantic rake had been drawn across each spot, a gigantic 'search and sweep'. Shipyards, marine engineering works, railway stations, churches, schools and streets, even the private houses of heads of businesses on the low ridge above West Hartlepool, received shells of various calibre."

Despite the odds, Captain Oscar Trenchman, the Battery Commander at Heugh Battery, and Captain Jack Farmer, his counterpart at the nearby Lighthouse Battery, ordered their men into action. The two guns in Heugh Battery engaged *Seydlitz*, whilst the single gun at the Lighthouse Battery fired on *Blücher*.

The gunners' aim was good, for the third round from the Lighthouse Battery scored a direct hit. An immense sheet of flame shot up from the *Blücher*'s after-deck. The deck supply for one of the 5.9-inch guns had been detonated by the battery's shell, and the effect was transmitted to the next gun, whose ammunition also ignited. Half of the after-bridge was brought down, and eleven seamen were killed.

The artillery duel continued until the battlecruisers disengaged; they had caused the deaths of 112 (also given as 119) men and women with a further 200 wounded. Of those that were killed only twenty-three died in their homes, the rest were struck down in the streets. The war had come to the British population with lethal consequences.

Further south, *Von der Tann* and *Derfflinger*, having bombarded Scarborough, had moved on to Whitby which they shelled for ten minutes. They then disengaged and withdrew to rendezvous with the *Seydlitz* detachment which had sailed to meet them. Admiral Hipper now had to steam back across the North Sea, hoping to draw a proportion of the Royal Navy's Grand Fleet into the range of the guns of the High Seas Fleet.

As soon as Admiral Jellicoe was made aware of the German attack he ordered his squadrons of the Grand Fleet to give chase. The scene was set for the great naval battle that both sides expected.

However, as Hipper raced across the North Sea he learnt that the High Seas Fleet, fearful of becoming embroiled with the battleships of the Grand Fleet, had put back into port. Hipper followed suit, reaching the safety of German waters before Jellicoe could intervene.

In the days that followed, the Germans tried to portray the attack on Britain's East Coast as a great success but in reality the killing of civilians created a huge public outcry which prompted many thousands of men to join up and fight the enemy. Over the following days recruiting offices across the country were besieged by would-be servicemen.

Perhaps *The Daily Mirror*, in passing its judgement on the German bombardment, summed up the situation perfectly. With barely disguised derision of the German Navy's actions, it declared: "Many thanks von Tirpitz: you bagged some eighty-odd civilians, a church and two ruins – we get two new army Corps."

Carols, Plum Pudding, Beer and Bullets

The Christmas Truce 1914

DURING THURSDAY, 24 December 1914, the weather across the Western Front turned cold but dry. A hard frost fell across the trenches. As the day wore on, in some areas of the front British soldiers were astonished to see Christmas trees with candles and paper lanterns appearing on enemy parapets. Later that evening, and through the night, the singing of carols, hymns and popular songs added to the atmosphere.

By the following day, the first Christmas of the Great War, a war that would become famous for its horror and brutality, a number of British and German soldiers found themselves in No Man's Land in an act of fraternisation that has given rise to the legend that is the Christmas Truce.

Feldwebel Lange, from Leipzig, told how, as his unit was putting up decorations – fir trees – over their trenches, English-speaking voices asked what they were up to. After initial explanations, junior officers on both sides agreed to a private truce on Christmas Eve and Christmas Day.

In Fleurbaix, a village three miles south of Armentières, British soldiers soon realised that the flickering lights on the German side of the line were not the muzzle flashes of Mauser rifles, but Christmas tree lights. The Saxon soldiers came out into No Man's Land with their Christmas trees, lit by candles, and started a slow walk towards the British. The latter did likewise. Gradually, hesitatingly, both sides met, and exchanged cigarettes or even, to the surprise of the British, cigars. Some on each side had photos of their loved ones with them, and showed them to one another, a simple act which was to be repeated many times the next day.

"It sounds hardly credible what I now report, but it is pure truth," wrote Josef Wenzl, of the Bavarian Reserve Infantry Regiment 16, to his parents on 28 December 1914. "The British waved to us. Gradually, they came completely out of the trenches, our people ignited a Christmas tree they had brought, put it on the wall [parapet] and with bells ringing ... Between the trenches, the hated and bitter opponents meet around the Christmas tree and sing Christmas carols. This once in a lifetime vision I will not forget."

What began on Christmas Eve, increased on Christmas Day itself. At daybreak, soldiers on both sides left their trenches. They shook hands, wished each other "Merry Christmas", and exchanged experiences, such as how to cope with the plague of lice.

In places, the Germans and British agreed to bury the dead who lay in No Man's Land. In some cases, not only did they help each other prepare the graves, they also organised joint ceremonies. "This is something we will probably never see again," wrote a 19-year-old Scot to a schoolmate.

Private Frank Richards, a reservist called up in 1914, was serving in the 2nd Battalion Royal Welch Fusiliers. In the trenches at Houplines (roughly two miles south of Ploegsteert on the banks of the River Lys), he would later recall how he turned down a day of rest out of the line so that he could "see what would happen". He noted that the first tangible signs of the Truce came on the morning of Christmas Day when a couple of Fusiliers stuck up a board with the message "A Merry Christmas" on it. The Germans opposite did likewise.

"Two of our men then threw »

BELOW: A contemporary artist's depiction of the Christmas Truce, 25 December 1914. (HMP)

their equipment off and jumped on the parapet with their hands above their heads. Two of the Germans done the same and commenced to walk up the river bank, our two men going to meet them. They met and shook hands and then we all got out of the trench.

"They were Saxons and some of them could speak English. By the look of them their trenches were in as bad a state as our own. One of their men, speaking in English, mentioned that he had worked in Brighton for some years and that he was fed up to the neck with this damned war and would be glad when it was all over."

Private Frank Sumpter was serving in the London Rifle Brigade: "We heard the Germans singing

Lieutenant Bruce Bairnsfather...

One of those who those who found himself embroiled in the Christmas Truce near Ploegsteert was Lieutenant Bruce Bairnsfather - the creator of the famous First World War cartoon character "Old Bill". Bairnsfather later recalled: "A complete Boche figure suddenly appeared on the parapet, and looked about itself. This complaint became infectious. It didn't take 'Our Bert' ... long to be up on the skyline. This was the signal for more Boche anatomy to be disclosed, and this was replied to by our men, until in less time than it takes to tell, half a dozen or so of each of the belligerents were outside their trenches and were advancing towards each other in No Man's Land. I clambered up and over our parapet, and moved out across the field to look. Clad in a muddy suit of khaki and wearing a sheepskin coat and Balaclava helmet, I joined the throng about half-way across to the German trenches". This is Bairnsfather's own depiction of his meeting in No Man's Land. (HMP)

RIGHT: **This wooden cross, erected by the Khaki Chums in 1999, commemorates the Christmas Truce of December 1914. It can be found not far from Ploegsteert Wood.** (HMP)

"We heard the Germans singing 'Silent Night, Holy Night', and they put up a notice saying 'Merry Christmas', so we put one up too."

RIGHT: **A snapshot taken by a British officer showing German and British troops fraternising on the Western Front during the Christmas truce of 1914.** (IMPERIAL WAR MUSEUM; Q11718)

'Silent Night, Holy Night', and they put up a notice saying 'Merry Christmas, so we put one up too. While they were singing our boys said, 'Let's join in', so we joined in and when we started singing, they stopped. And when we stopped, they started again. So we were easing the way. Then one German took a chance and jumped up on top of the trench and shouted out, 'Happy Christmas, Tommy'. So, of course, our boys said, 'If he can do it, we can do it', and we all jumped up."

For 29-year-old Private Ernest Holden, not that far from Private Frank Richards in trenches in the Frelinghein-Houplines sector, the Truce was a thought-provoking event: "It seemed very strange to go out and clasp your enemy by the hand and wish him a Merry Christmas. It made one wonder why we were at war at all."

For some, there was very little sign of any Christmas Truce. Eventually reaching the rank of Brigadier General, Alexander Johnston had arrived in France in August 1914 as the signals officer for 7 Infantry Brigade. Christmas Day found his unit in the trenches near

German soldiers of the 134th Saxon Regiment photographed by Second Lieutenant Cyril A.F. Drummond, Royal Field Artillery, with men of the Royal Warwickshire Regiment in No Man's Land during the Christmas Truce. At least one account states that this was a picture taken on Boxing Day. Drummond later wrote: "They were very nice fellows to look at ... and one of them said, 'we don't want to kill you and you don't want to kill us. So why shoot?' ... I lined them all up and took a photograph". (IWM HU35801)

Kemmel: "Considering that we are in the front line, we could not have had a better one. It had frozen hard in the night and the country was white with hoar frost, with a blue sky and a pink sunrise made the effect very pretty. We did not get shelled all day, but there was a little sniping and we bagged six of their snipers who I think were drunk."

In 1921 His Majesty's Stationery Office published lists of those who died or were killed during the First World War. Statistics taken from these would seem to suggest that for the whole of the month of December 1914, Christmas Day was one of the worst in France and Flanders. Indeed, on that day forty-one British soldiers were killed in action. Only eight days throughout the whole month saw worse losses.

If you then also take into account those men who died of wounds, illness or other causes, the total for 25 December 1914, was sixty-nine men; only nine other days that month were worse.

The unofficial Truce often ended just as it had begun: by mutual agreement. Captain C.I. Stockwell, of the Royal Welsh Fusiliers, in trenches near Ploegsteert Wood, recalled how, after a truly "Silent Night", he fired three shots into the air at 08.30 hours on Boxing Day. He then climbed on to the parapet. A German officer who had given him some beer the previous day also appeared on the German side of No Man's Land. Both men bowed, saluted, and climbed back into their trenches.

A few moments afterwards, Stockwell heard the German fire two shots into the air. Then, in his words, "the war was on again".

FAR LEFT: This depiction of the Christmas Truce, entitled "The Light of Peace in the Trenches on Christmas Eve", was first published in the British press on 9 January 1915. (HMP)

British and German troops photographed in No Man's Land in the Bridoux-Rouge Banc Sector, 25 December 1914. The British troops are from the Northumberland Hussars, 7th Division. (HMP)

THE EMPIRE ST

BELOW: Canadian soldiers pictured on the march at Canadian Forces Base Valcartier in 1914. Due to its proximity to the Port of Quebec, Valcartier became the largest military camp on Canadian soil, being the temporary home to some 32,000 men and 8,000 horses. (US Library of Congress)

When the Central Powers found themselves at war with Britain, they were not pitting themselves against a country; they were taking on an empire. From as far afield as Canada, Australia, India and Nigeria, scores of countries contributed to the war effort and to the defeat of the Central Powers.

The Germans were well aware of the might of the British Empire which covered 11,400,000 square miles of land, encompassed scores of countries and could count 400 million people living under its sway. They believed, though, that many of those people under British rule wanted independence and they would take advantage of the war to rebel against their British masters. Nothing could be farther from the truth. "From end to end of the Empire," wrote one historian, "controversies were forgotten, differences passed out of sight, and men united in one plea – What can we do?"[1]

Canada, Australia and New Zealand began immediately to raise armies to send to Europe. South Africa followed suit and Indian princes mustered their subjects. From the warrior nations of the Zulu and the Basuto young men stepped forward to join the war and even those from tiny Pacific islands whose names were scarcely known in Britain were prepared to fight for the flag of an empire.

Over 2,500,000 men served in the armies of the Dominions as well as thousands of volunteers from the Crown colonies. Their efforts at Gallipoli, the Middle East and on the Western Front helped tip the tide of victory in favour of the Allies.

Canada set the early pace, with streams of men pouring in from every province to the various military headquarters to offer their services. Farmers drove twenty and thirty miles or more, cowboys rode from the prairies and mechanics left their workshops. An expeditionary force of 22,000 men was the Canadian Government's initial target for deployment in Europe, and private organisations provided gifts of every kind for the Motherland.

Less than eight weeks after the declaration of war a list was drawn up of what had already been offered to Britain. This included half a million bushels of oats from Alberta, with that province's civil servants giving five per cent of the salaries of those earning up to £300 a year and ten per cent of those that earned more. British Columbia gave 25,000 cases of tinned salmon, Manitoba 50,000 bags of flour, New Brunswick 100,000 bushels of potatoes and Nova Scotia 100,000 tons of coal, to name just some of the contributions. Individual cities made cash donations, with French-speaking Montreal leading the way with £30,000. Quebec gave 4,000,000lbs of cheese whilst Saskatchewan provided 1,500 horses.

Australia had been planning for war for some considerable time and had around 50,000 men under arms before the outbreak of hostilities. To this cadre, or framework, new recruits were added and by November 1914 Australia could boast more than 100,000 men within the ranks of its army. The first batch of men to sail for the Middle East was 20,338 strong and was followed by additional regular, monthly, batches of 2,000 or 3,000 men. Every man was a volunteer for none were liable to serve outside Australia unless they wished. Australians, both individually and corporately, also gave freely to various funds created to help the war

> "Over 2,500,000 men served in the armies of the Dominions as well as thousands of volunteers from the Crown colonies."

KES BACK

ABOVE: **A recruitment poster published in Newfoundland during August 1914. "If England falls you fall! Every man of you must go, as we, too, must go!" was the message from Sir Rider Haggard. On the evening of 4 August 1914, Walter Davidson, the Governor of Newfoundland, received a cable informing him that Britain was at war. As a colony, Newfoundland and Labrador officially entered the war when Britain did. One of Davidson's first steps, on 8 August, was to send a message to London to say that Newfoundland and Labrador would raise 500 men for land service and 1,000 for naval service.** (US Library of Congress)

effort which, apart from money, provided scores of thousands of carcasses of mutton, and large quantities of such items as wine, butter, bacon, cheese and condensed milk.

The population of New Zealander likewise sent money and goods to the UK, and when the Maoris learnt that Britain was employing Indian troops it was impossible to stop them joining in the Empire's effort, which many thousands did.

New Zealand was also well-prepared and rapidly assembled an expeditionary force of 8,000 men, the first of who were ready to sail for Europe on 24 September 1914. "Time was, not very long ago," noted Lord Liverpool, the Governor, "when the sight of a troopship in the New Zealand harbour denoted the arrival of troops from the Old Country. To-day the position is reversed. England has need of all her sons to-day, and the young Dominion is sending home to the Motherland of her best."

However, the departure of these men was postponed at the last minute – possibly due to the activity of German warships and raiders in the Pacific. In time they did sail, but only as far as Egypt. Here they joined forces with Australian contingents prior to the landing at Gallipoli in April 1915, and the term ANZAC was born, this being the acronym formed from the initial letters of the Australian and New Zealand Army Corps. Whilst the term ANZAC was initially used to describe a man who was at the landings and who fought at Gallipoli, it later came to mean any Australian or New Zealand soldier of the First World War.

The various peoples and lands of the Indian sub-continent, so often divided by culture and religion, came together almost as one. Regiments were raised at the personal expense of the wealthy princes, and the regular India Army, 160,000 strong with 40,000 more reservists, was made available for operations. The Indian Expeditionary Force, which was despatched to Europe in September 1914, amounted to 70,000 men. Other troops were sent to Mesopotamia and elsewhere.

Such was the scale of India's support, by the spring of 1915 it ➤➤

ABOVE: **An Australian recruitment poster from 1917.** (US Library of Congress)

RIGHT: **"The Empire needs men! The overseas states all answer the call. Helped by the young lions the old lion defies his foes. Enlist now!" This recruitment poster, sparked by the manner in which the nations of the British Empire reacted after the outbreak of war and issued by the Parliamentary Recruiting Committee in 1915, was intended to send a clear message to the men at home in the United Kingdom.** (US Library of Congress)

ABOVE: **Australian troops marching along Eddy Avenue next to Sydney's Central Railway Station whilst en route to embark for overseas service.** (Courtesy of the Australian National Maritime Museum)

ABOVE RIGHT: **Australian troops on the quayside at Wharf 2, Garden Island, whilst waiting to embark.** (Courtesy of the Australian National Maritime Museum)

had put into the field in the several theatres of war, including those British troops sent from India at the same time, a force equivalent to nine complete infantry divisions with artillery, and eight cavalry brigades. She had placed at the disposal of the empire twenty-eight regiments of cavalry and 174 regiments of infantry. The British Prime Minister, Herbert Asquith, once stated the following in a speech in London: "When we look at the achievements of the force so spontaneously dispatched, so liberally provided for, so magnificently equipped, the battlefields of France and Flanders bear an undying tribute to their bravery."

If the Germans had placed much confidence in the Indians using the distraction of the war to make a bid for freedom, they had even higher hopes of the South Africans. The Boer War, which had seen much suffering due to Kitchener's uncompromising tactics, had ended just twelve years earlier. Nevertheless, Jan Smuts raised the South African Defence Force which, led by Louis Botha, successfully invaded German South West Africa and German East Africa. In addition to this, 136,000 South African troops fought in the Middle East and on the Western Front.

Even the smallest of Britain's colonies or dominions, whether geographically or in terms of population size, played their part. Bermudians, for example, enlisted for service overseas in considerable numbers. The local forces at that time were divided largely on the basis of colour, with black Bermudians serving in the Bermuda Militia Artillery which was attached to the Royal Garrison Artillery, whilst white Bermudians were to be found in the Bermuda Volunteer Rifle Corps, mostly associated with the Lincolnshire Regiment.

Newfoundland, then a separate country from Canada,

The global nature of the First World War meant that a large proportion of the British territories were involved in, or were close to, the various theatres of war. So it was that Australia and New Zealand conquered German Pacific territories such as German Samoa, Papua New Guinea, and the Bismarck Archipelago. A British Indian army attempted to capture Baghdad, and a combined Indian and Japanese force seized the German enclave of Tsingtau on the Chinese coast. Trinidadians and Guianans in the British West Indies Regiment fought in Jordan, Mesopotamia, and Palestine. Ghanaians invaded German Togoland and West Indians crossed the border from Sierra Leone into German Cameroons. The Ceylon Planters Rifle Corps went to Egypt in October 1914, where they helped guard the Suez Canal.

In East Africa, a 300,000-strong British Imperial force was engaged with the German guerrilla forces under Colonel Paul Emil von Lettow-Vorbeck in a campaign that spanned Kenya, Tanganyika, Nyasaland, and Northern Rhodesia, before the Germans surrendered three days after the Armistice had passed in

BELOW LEFT: **A photograph of soldiers standing in front of a window which displays a recruitment poster for the 5th Regiment Royal Highlanders of Canada, during the First World War.** (US Library of Congress)

G. R.

"We are fighting for a worthy purpose, and we shall not lay down our arms until that purpose has been fully achieved."

THE KING

MEN OF THE EMPIRE

To ARMS!

GOD SAVE THE KING!

FAR RIGHT: **An early recruitment poster published by the British Government's Parliamentary Recruiting Committee in 1914 – in fact it was only the organisation's fourth of the war.** (US Library of Congress)

1918. The Falkland Islands was home to the shore base HMS *Pursuivant* and was used by Admiral Sturdee's battlecruisers whilst hunting for von Spee's force following the Battle of Coronel.

Other overseas shore bases included HMS *Cormorant* at Gibraltar, headquarters of the East Atlantic Station, HMS *St Angelo* on Malta, and HMS *Alert* in the Persian Gulf. HMS *Tamar* in Hong Kong was headquarters of the navy's China Station, and the North America and West Indies Station was served by HMS *Terror* on Bermuda, helping to police a region in which British warships and patrol boats protected shipping from German submarines.[2]

Equally the Australian and Canadian navies played key roles throughout the war. The Canadians mounted anti-submarine patrols and helped escort convoys along the North American West and East coasts. At the outbreak of war the Royal Australian Navy numbered sixteen ships, including the battlecruiser HMAS *Australia*, the light cruisers HMAS *Sydney* and HMAS *Melbourne*, the destroyers *Parramatta*, *Yarra*, and *Warrego*, and two submarines. The RAN's most notable encounter of the war was when HMAS *Sydney* sank the German raider SMS *Emden*. The Canadians also helped by assembling 550 US-built motor launches for the Royal Navy.

Logistics are of vital importance in military operations and the war saw the employment of manual workers from across the Empire to support British battle fronts. Egyptians were recruited in their hundreds of thousands to serve in the Sinai campaign, as were Africans employed as porters in the East African campaign. Over 150,000 Chinese were taken to the Western Front. Smaller contingents came from all over the Empire – 30,000 men from South Africa, Basutoland, Bechuanaland and Swaziland formed the South African Native Labour Contingent for service in France, and Fiji also sent a labour battalion to Europe. Four hundred men of the Zion Mule Corps formed the only support available when the British 29th Division landed at Gallipoli, and 1,700 Mauritians formed a labour battalion to help work the inland waterways of Mesopotamia.[3]

A few after the outbreak of war, the King wrote the following:

"During the past few weeks the peoples of my whole Empire at home and overseas have moved with one mind and purpose to confront and overthrow an unparalleled assault upon the continuity of civilization and the peace of mankind … I rejoice that every part of the Empire is with me."

Germany might have thought that the British Empire would strike against the Motherland when it became embroiled in a European war, but in the event it was the Empire, on land and at sea, which struck back at Germany and in doing so ensured victory for the Allies.

LEFT: **Indian soldiers pictured on the Western Front during the winter of 1914-1915. One million Indian troops would serve overseas, of whom 62,000 died and another 67,000 were wounded.** (US Library of Congress)

"The various peoples and lands of the Indian sub-continent, so often divided by culture and religion, came together almost as one."

NOTES:

1. J.A. Hammerton, *A Popular History of the Great War*, vol.1, 87-104.
2. Taken from Ashley Jackson, "The British Empire and the First World War", *BBC History Magazine*, 9, 11 (2008).
3. Ashley Jackson, *ibid.*

BELOW: **The first Bermudian to be killed in the First World War was 22-year-old Officer's Cook 1st Class William Edmund Smith, who, of Afro-Caribbean extraction, had joined the Royal Navy. He was drowned when the Cressy-class cruiser HMS *Aboukir*, seen here, was torpedoed in the North Sea by a German U-boat on 22 September 1914. Ninety Bermudians would make the ultimate sacrifice during the First World War.** (US Library of Congress)

Timeline 1915 - Events that Shaped The First World War

January
15 The War Council authorised a naval attack on the Dardanelles
19 The first Zeppelin raid on Great Britain took place at Great Yarmouth
24 Battle of Dogger Bank between Royal Navy and the German Navy
26 Defence of Suez Canal began

February
4 Germany declared the waters around Great Britain to be a "war zone"

March
10 Battle of Neuve Chapelle began
13 Battle of Neuve Chapelle ended
14 Light cruiser *Dresden*, the last German cruiser left at sea, sunk by Royal Navy
15 First merchant ship, SS *Blonde*, attacked by aircraft
18 Anglo-French naval attack on Dardanelles repulsed
28 The first passenger ship, SS *Falaba*, is sunk by a German submarine

April
17 Capture of Hill 60 near Ypres
22 Second Battle of Ypres began
First use of chlorine gas at Ypres
24 Battle of St Julien began
25 Allied landings undertaken at Gallipoli
26 A secret treaty with the Triple Entente brought Italy into the war on the side of the Allies

May
4 Battle of St Julien ended
7 RMS *Lusitania* sunk by a German U-boat
9 The leading division of the British New Armies sailed for France
25 Second Battle of Ypres ended
31 First Zeppelin raid on London area

June
5 First Conference of British and French Ministers to co-ordinate war policy and strategy held at Calais
7 First German airship (L37) successfully attacked by RFC fighter

July
2 Ministry of Munitions formed in Great Britain
9 German forces in South-West Africa surrendered
11 SMS *Königsberg* is scuttled
15 National Registration Act became law in Great Britain
19 Action at Hooge

August
6 Attempted breakout from Anzac Cove to capture nearby heights
Operations of the landing at Suvla began
12 First enemy ship is sunk by torpedo dropped by a British seaplane
16 Lowca and Harrington, near Whitehaven (Cumberland), shelled by German submarine

September
25 Battle of Loos began
British Army used poison gas for the first time
30 Lord Derby assumed control of recruiting in Great Britain

October
3 Allied troops landed at Salonika
8 The Battle of Loos ended
12 Edith Cavell executed in Brussels by order of a German court martial

November
11 Advance on Baghdad began

December
6 Advance on Baghdad ended
7 Ottoman forces begin their siege of the town of Kut, 100 miles south of Baghdad, which was held by a British-Indian garrison
19 Douglas Haig succeeded Sir John French as commander of the BEF
20 Allied evacuation of Anzac and Suvla completed
23 British naval operations on Lake Tanganyika began
25 The second Christmas Truce
28 Evacuation of remainder of Gallipoli Peninsula ordered

YPRES: Murder in the Mud

The Hooge Crater

This is the so-called Hooge Crater looking towards the Menin Road to Ypres which is some fifty yards away. On the morning of 30 July 1915, this area formed part of the British front line. The German *Flammenwerfer* attack was made here and eventually succeeded in pushing the 8th Battalion, The Rifle Brigade back beyond the Menin Road. The crater is now in the grounds of a hotel; visitors can enter the site and walk part way around it for a nominal fee. (HMP)

The "Race to the Sea" had ended in stalemate and the opposing forces had hurriedly sought to hold the territory upon which they stood by digging in and fortifying their positions. The Germans, though, still saw the salient which the British and Commonwealth forces had formed to defend the city of Ypres as vital in their bid to break through the Allied lines on the Western Front.**

The city of Ypres stands in the Belgian province of Flanders. The word Flanders means "flooded land" and habitation and cultivation of this area was only made possible through the construction, and maintenance, of a complicated network of drainage ditches. The winter of 1914 and 1915 saw the trenches and fields in the salient around Ypres turn into a quagmire through the passage of heavy equipment and vehicles and the incessant shelling of the German artillery which destroyed the drainage ditches.

"The countryside [was] bare and open," wrote Private Donald Fraser. "Shell holes were everywhere and most contained slimy, muddy water. The terrain was a wilderness of mud ... We watched the shells send up fountains of mud and water as they exploded. For quite some distance you could see eruptions taking place at various points resembling geysers or mud volcanoes."

Life in the trenches in the Ypres Salient was one of mud, dirt and terror. Because of the high level of the water table, the parapets of the trenches were above ground and in many places were composed only of sandbags and were not always bullet-proof. "We had to be most careful not to expose ourselves anywhere near the front line," explained a member of the 1/5th Battalion, Leicestershire Regiment, "for to do so meant immediate death at the hands of his [the enemy's] snipers."

Private H.S. Clapham of the Honourable Artillery Company described just how bad the area around the salient had quickly become: "The ground all around was in a horrible condition, churned and flung in small hillocks, overlooking evil-smelling water-holes. It was strewn with bones, broken tools, burst sandbags, and pieces of clothing."

No serious activity could be attempted in such conditions, but with the approach of spring and the prospect of drier weather, the Germans planned to launch a massive assault upon the British and Allied lines.

The reason why Ypres was so important to both sides was that control of the town gave control of the surrounding countryside, in addition to which all the major roads converged there. As a consequence, Ypres became the focus of some of the most intense and savage >>

LEFT: **A sentry from the 1/4th Battalion, Royal Berkshire Regiment using a trench periscope to observe German positions near Ploegsteert Wood, south of Ypres, in the spring of 1915.** (Imperial War Museum; Q50687)

A picture showing the devastation wrought in the area surrounding Hooge, in the Ypres Salient, during the First World War. Hooge Château and its stables was the scene of extremely fierce fighting throughout the war, being lost and regained a number of times. (HMP)

RIGHT CENTRE: **The Menin Gate is one of four memorials to the missing in Belgian Flanders which cover the area known as the Ypres Salient. It bears the names of more than 54,000 officers and men whose graves are not known, and its location was chosen because of the hundreds of thousands of men who passed through it on their way to the battlefields of the Salient.** (Courtesy of the Commonwealth War Graves Commission)

Honourable Artillery Company Attack!

An image that shows an attack underway in the Ypres Salient as men of the 1/10th King's (Liverpool) Regiment (Liverpool Scottish) and the Honourable Artillery Company attack the area known as Y Wood on 16 June 1915. The First Attack on Bellewaarde, sometimes referred to as The Battle of Hooge or Menin Road, was fought in an area between the Menin Road and the Ypres-Roulers railway line. At the time of attack, part of the German front line on the Ypres Salient ran along the edge of Y Wood. The action began with a highly accurate artillery bombardment which commenced at 02.50 hours on 16 June. When it stopped at 04.15 hours, 7th Brigade advanced on the German line. This image was taken by Private F.A. Fyfe, a bomber with 'Z' Company, Liverpool Scottish, at 06.00 hours on the 16th. It shows a detachment of the 1st Battalion H.A.C. taking cover under the parapet of the German front line trench. The flag in the centre is one of those put up to show that the enemy trench had been captured and that the troops were going on. (HMP)

fighting of the First World War.

The valiant defence of Ypres in October and November of 1914 had been termed the First Battle of Ypres. The attack unleashed by the Germans in April 1915 was the Second Battle of Ypres and it would see a new kind of horror on the battlefield – gas.

At around 17.00 hours on 22 April 1915, the Germans released more than 168 tons of chlorine gas against the part of the line held by French Territorial and Colonial troops. Some 6,000 French troops died in the space of just ten minutes and a wide gap was opened in the Allied line. In a bid to fill that gap, the 1st Canadian Division was rushed forward from its safe billets behind the front.

Two days later the Germans released more gas and this time the Canadians were directly in its path. On this occasion just fifteen tons of gas was released. As the grey-green cloud ebbed towards the Canadian troops occupying the village of St Julien, word spread through their ranks instructing them to urinate on their handkerchiefs and place these over their noses and mouths.

Despite this being sound advice, as the urea in urine would react with chlorine, forming dichloro-urea and effectively neutralizing it, these precautions proved ineffective in the confused circumstances of the attack, and German assault was ultimately a success. The Canadians were pushed back and the village of St. Julien was taken.

Curiously, it was noted that those Canadians that had stood and fought through the gas attack had generally suffered less than those who had run away. The reason for this was explained in the Official History: "It early became evident that the men who stayed in their places suffered less than those who ran away, any movement making worse the effects of the gas, and those who stood up on the fire step suffered less – indeed they often escaped any serious effects – than those who lay down or sat at the bottom of the trench. Men who stood on the parapet suffered least, as the gas was denser nearer the ground. The worst sufferers were the wounded lying on the ground, or on stretchers, and the men who moved back with the cloud." Fortune, on this occasion at least, favoured the brave.

Private W. Hay of the Royal Scots arrived in Ypres just after the gas attack. "We knew there was something wrong," he recalled. "We started to march towards Ypres but we couldn't get past on the road with refugees coming down the road. We went along the railway line to Ypres and there were people, civilians and soldiers, lying along the roadside in a terrible state. We heard them say it was gas. We didn't know what the Hell gas was. When we got to Ypres we found a lot of Canadians lying there dead from gas the day before, poor devils, and it was quite a horrible sight for us young men."

The Germans used gas on a large scale on only two more occasions during the Second Battle of Ypres, both times in the first week of May 1915. Located four miles outside Ypres to the south-east of the town, Hill 60 was a low rise on the southern flank of the Salient which was named after the 60-metre contour which marked its bounds. Despite the fact that it was man-made, arising from the spoil removed during the construction of the railway line nearby, Hill 60 was seen as a strategically significant area of high ground by both sides, and was, consequently, heavily fought over. It was also the scene of some of the earliest, and intense, underground warfare seen on the Western Front.

Hill 60 was the scene of an attack on 1 May 1915, which was witnessed by Company Sergeant Major Ernest Shephard of the 1st Battalion

Dorsetshire Regiment: "First we saw a thick smoke curling over in waves from the enemy trenches on the left. The cry went up that this was gas fumes. The scene that followed was heart-breaking. Men were caught by fumes and in dreadful agony, coughing and vomiting, rolling on [the] ground in agony. Very shortly after gas was pumped over to us, the enemy were seen running from their own trenches as a part of the fumes blew back to them ... Men caught by fumes badly were at this stage dying, and we fully realized our desperate position ... When we found our men were dying from the fumes we wanted to charge, but were not allowed to do so ... Hell could find no worse the groans of scores of dying and badly hurt men."

On the morning of 30 July 1915, a new and terrible weapon was unleashed upon the unsuspecting British troops defending positions at Hooge in the Ypres Salient – the flamethrower or *Flammenwerfer*. The Germans had only six of these weapons at the time of their attack at Hooge, but the effect they had upon the British troops was profund, as Private A.P. Hatton observed:

"We first heard sounds as of a splashing to our front, then there was a peculiar smoky smell just like coal tar; next, a corporal of 'C' Company cried out that he had been hit by a shell; yet when we went to look at him we found that a huge blister as from a burn was on his forehead, while the back of his cap was smouldering.

"We had no time to notice anything else, for after that preliminary trial the Boches loosened their liquid fire upon us with a vengeance. It came in streams all over the earthworks, while shells containing starlights ignited the black fluid. Sandbags, blankets, top-coats, and anything of the sort that was handy smouldered and then flared. We were choked by the smoke and half scorched by the heat. Our first instinct had been to fly to our dug-outs under the parapet where the liquid fire could not touch us."

The fighting in the Salient eventually saw British and Allied troops being driven back almost to the walls of Ypres itself, but somehow the salient held, though much reduced in depth. It meant that the Germans could shell Ypres with even greater effectiveness. The Germans also held the low ridge which runs in a wide sweep from Passchendaele in the north-east, via Messines in the south, to beyond Kemmel in the south-west. From that ridge observers could watch every movement around Ypres in the salient below.

Gradually, Ypres was shelled almost to destruction, as Huntley Gordon described: "For sheer concentrated shelling the Menin Gate stands alone. There is of course no gate there, merely a gap in the stone ramparts of the town, and a causeway crossing the wide moat beyond. Most of the traffic supplying the line in front of Ypres must pass through here, and the Boche takes heavy toll of it – night and day. The bridge, whether originally arched or not, is now a solid mass of stonework, supplemented, indeed cemented, by the remains of smashed vehicles and the fragmented bodies of horses and men."

From the high ground the Germans were able to direct their artillery with devastating precision. Sir John Glubb wrote the following of the village of Zillebeke, some one-and-a-half miles south-east of Ypres, in December 1915: "Every shattered fragment of a house is full of filth, old clothes, rags and bedding, left behind by the original inhabitants when they fled, and since used for sleeping on or torn up to dress wounds. Everything is soaked with rain, blood and dirt. Strewn around are thousands of half-empty jam or bully-beef tins, the contents putrefying, together with the remains of rations, scraps of bone and meat."

The British and Commonwealth troops could never hope to escape the continual bombardment unless they seized the ridge. This became the objective of the Allied forces over the course of the following two years. It would culminate in the Third Battle of Ypres and would concentrate on the ridge to the north and east of Ypres, in the area around a village they called Passchendaele.

BELOW: **A group of officers of the 1/5th Battalion York and Lancaster Regiment try on their newly issued respirators in a stretch of the Western Front north of the Ypres Salient. It is worth noting that this image was taken just days after the Germans had unleashed the spectre of chemical warfare on the world with the first use of poison gas near Ypres on 22 April 1915.** (Courtesy of Jon Cooksey)

The War at Sea

RIGHT: **Taken from HMS *Invincible*, this photograph shows HMS *Inflexible* standing by to pick up survivors from SMS *Gneisenau* on 8 December 1914, during the Battle of the Falklands Islands. Such was the decisive nature of this British victory, German commerce raiding on the high seas by regular warships of the Imperial German Navy was brought to an end.** (HMP)

Traditionally, the projection of Britain's military might had often been through the Royal Navy. For the first months of the war, however, Britannia struggled to assert her rule of the waves.

The sea lanes of the oceans were the commercial highways of the world, and those routes were policed by the Royal Navy, the mightiest armed force the world had ever known. Britain's naval dominance had enabled it to create the largest over-seas empire in history which, by the end of the nineteenth century, encompassed a quarter of the globe.

The might of the Royal Navy had been emphatically displayed at the famous Spithead Review of 1897. The ships reviewed by Queen Victoria had stretched for five miles and included twenty-one battleships, forty-two cruisers, thirty destroyers and seventy-two other craft. Staggering though these numbers were, they represented only half of Britain's navy, the absent craft, 165 in total, were guarding the Empire.

Germany, the new major European power, looked on jealously. If Germany was ever to rival Britain in world affairs it needed a comparable naval force. The result was a ship-building programme on a scale never seen before, but when war broke out in 1914 Germany still lagged behind the United Kingdom.

It was, therefore, perhaps predictable that Britain's first action of the war was at sea. This occurred when, just hours after the declaration of war, the German minelayer *Königin Luise* was sunk by the First and Third Destroyer Flotillas based at Harwich.

Though *Königin Luise* could carry 200 mines, she was no match for the two destroyers that located her – HMS *Lance* and HMS *Landrail*. As soon as *Königin Luise*'s crew spotted them approaching she turned and ran, moving into a rain squall where she proceeded to lay more mines. HMS *Lance* opened fire on the fleeing

"The sea lanes of the oceans were the commercial highways of the world, and those routes were policed by the Royal Navy, the mightiest armed force the world had ever known."

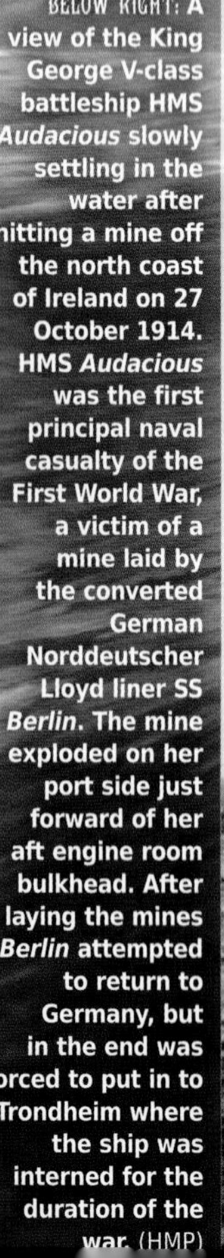

BELOW RIGHT: **A view of the King George V-class battleship HMS *Audacious* slowly settling in the water after hitting a mine off the north coast of Ireland on 27 October 1914. HMS *Audacious* was the first principal naval casualty of the First World War, a victim of a mine laid by the converted German Norddeutscher Lloyd liner SS *Berlin*. The mine exploded on her port side just forward of her aft engine room bulkhead. After laying the mines *Berlin* attempted to return to Germany, but in the end was forced to put in to Trondheim where the ship was interned for the duration of the war.** (HMP)

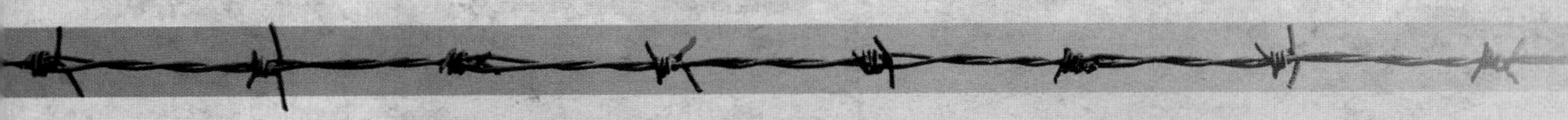

minelayer with her forward 4-inch gun. It was the first shot of the war at sea.

Königin Luise tried to escape into neutral waters to the south-east through the minefield she had just laid. *Lance* and *Landrail* continued to pursue, being joined by HMS *Amphion*. By noon on 5 August the minelayer had been scuttled. The Royal Navy had drawn first blood.

That, though, was not quite the end of the story as on the next day, 6 August, *Amphion* struck one of *Königin Luise*'s mines and sank. Amongst those that went down with *Amphion* were most of the survivors from the minelayer.

It was in the North Sea that the next significant naval encounter took place. It had been seen that the Germans were using destroyers to conduct patrols along their coast, watching for the approach of the Grand Fleet. Having observed that the Germans maintained a predictable frequency in their operations, the Admiralty decided to try and ambush one of these patrols. A force of thirty-one destroyers and two cruisers commanded by Commodore Tyrwhitt, supported by a flotilla of submarines under Commodore Roger Keyes, crept up towards Heligoland Bight on the night of 27 August 1914. The submarines took up positions to watch for the appearance of the German patrol.

At 06.35 hours a German destroyer was spotted and the light cruiser HMS *Arethusa* gave chase. The German ship immediately turned towards the German base at Heligoland. Admiral Hipper, in charge of the German defence of the area, ordered his force of destroyers to intercept the British warship.

HMS *Arethusa* soon found itself facing a host of German destroyers and torpedo boats as the main body of the patrol joined in the action. More and more ships steamed into the fight as both forces were drawn into a confusing battle in the early morning mist which hung over the water. At one point the destroyers of the Third Flotilla found themselves steaming directly into the path of the German cruiser *Mainz*. "The enemy opened a very hot fire, and as the range was only a little over 3,000 yards the little craft soon found themselves in the midst of flying shells," ran the words of one account. "They altered course ten points to port, returning the German fire with interest, but receiving many wounds themselves, for the *Mainz* gunners got the range at once and took full advantage of it.

"*Laurel* [an L-class destroyer] steamed away, a mass of smoke, her foremast funnel shattered, and the midship gun platform knocked to pieces. The gun itself remained mounted but was a poor and solitary-looking object. *Liberty*'s commander was killed, her bridge damaged, and her mast shot away. *Laertes*, which stopped and fired a torpedo, was put out of action, her port boat being shattered and a hole knocked in her second funnel. The torpedo, however, hit *Mainz*, which >>

Historic Shell

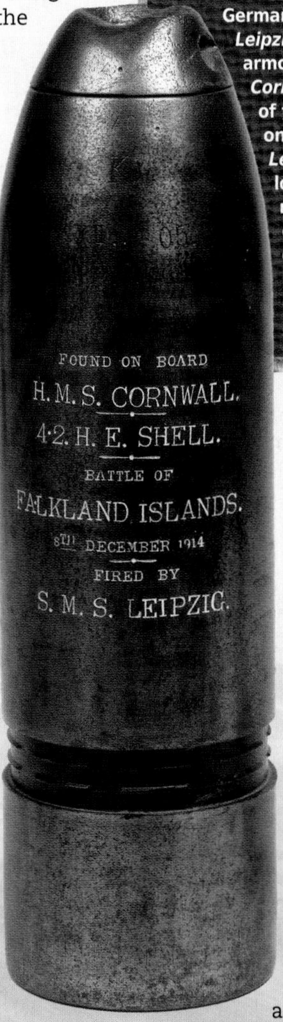

A 10.5cm shell fired from the German light cruiser SMS *Leipzig* at the British armoured cruiser HMS *Cornwall* during the Battle of the Falkland Islands on 8 December 1914. *Leipzig* was sunk with a loss of 267 officers and men, after a prolonged engagement with HMS *Cornwall* and the light cruiser HMS *Glasgow*. (Imperial War Museum; MUN3274)

BELOW: **An artist's depiction of either *Scharnhorst* or *Gneisenau* sinking during the Battle of the Falkland Islands. Casualties and damage during the engagement were extremely disproportionate; the British suffered only very lightly. German survivors, on the other hand, amounted to just 215 men; most were from *Gneisenau*, nine were from *Nürnberg* and eighteen were from *Leipzig*. There were no survivors from *Scharnhorst*. Admiral Spee and his two sons were among the German dead. One of *Gneisenau*'s officers who lived had been the sole survivor on three different guns but was pulled from the water saying he was a first cousin of the British commander (Stoddard).** (HMP)

ABOVE: HMS *Pegasus* encountered the German heavy cruiser SMS *Königsberg* on 20 September 1914, off the east coast of Africa. The original captain states: "During the action the flag of the *Pegasus* was shot away from its staff. A Marine at once ran forward, picked it up, and waved it aloft. He was struck down while standing on the deck exposed to the enemy's fire, but another came forward to take his place. Until the end the flag was kept flying." This illustration was one of a number produced during the First World War in an attempt to obscure the fact that *Pegasus* had actually struck her colours. (HMP)

HMS Hermes is sunk

An early loss of the war for the Royal Navy. On 30 October 1914, the seaplane carrier HMS *Hermes* docked at Dunkirk with a cargo of seaplanes having sailed from Portsmouth earlier the same day. Early the next morning she set out on the return journey. However, *Hermes* had barely left harbour when it was sighted by *U-29*, which then fired two torpedoes. Both struck the former cruiser with devastating effect. Despite remaining afloat for nearly two hours, HMS *Hermes* eventually slipped beneath the waves. Twenty-two of the ship's crew (including four members of the Royal Marine Light Infantry) were lost; all but two have no known grave. (HMP)

soon began to show signs of the mauling she was receiving."[1]

At this stage of the battle the German cruisers were undoubtedly getting the better of the smaller British vessels. Even Tyrwhitt's lead ship, *Arethusa*, had been badly damaged, though was still fighting. The German cruisers *Köln*, *Strassburg* and *Ariadne* had also arrived from Wilhelmshaven to join *Mainz*.

It seemed that the British squadron was in serious trouble but then the trap was sprung. What the Germans did not know was that hiding over the horizon was Vice Admiral Beatty with the battlecruisers HMS *Lion*, HMS *Queen Mary*, HMS *Princess Royal* and Rear Admiral Moore with HMS *New Zealand* and HMS *Invincible*. "There straight ahead of us in lovely procession, like elephants walking through a pack of ... dogs came *Lion*, *Queen Mary*, *Princess Royal*, *Invincible* and *New Zealand*," one British officer commented as he watched the arrival of the battlecruisers. "How solid they looked, how utterly earthquaking. We pointed out our latest aggressor to them ... and we went west while they went east ... and just a little later we heard the thunder of their guns."[2]

The Germans had been tricked into committing some of their important cruisers against much heavier British battlecruisers. At the end of the fighting the Germans had lost three cruisers, one destroyer and two torpedo boats, with a further three cruisers and three destroyers damaged.

The defeat at the Battle of Heligoland had a profound effect upon the Germans. This was subsequently noted by the First Lord of the Admiralty, Winston Churchill, who wrote with his usual rhetoric: "Henceforward, the weight of British Naval prestige lay heavy across all German sea enterprise ... The German Navy was indeed 'muzzled'. Except for furtive movements by individual submarines and minelayers, not a dog stirred from August till November."[3]

At the outbreak of war a German naval squadron under Admiral Maximilian Reichsgraf von Spee was stationed in the Caroline Islands in the western Pacific. It was joined by other warships until von Spee's force consisted of two armoured cruisers and three light cruisers. This presented a serious threat to Allied and neutral shipping and the South Atlantic Squadron was sent to deal with von Spee.

This squadron, composed of old and under-gunned ships commanded by Rear-Admiral Christopher Craddock, located the German squadron off Coronel on the coast of Chile on 1 November 1914. Though he was hopelessly outgunned Craddock (who was considered by some who knew him to be "constitutionally incapable of refusing action") charged the German ships.

At first von Spee turned away from Craddock's ships, but, as night fell, he reduced the distance between the two squadrons and battle was joined. The outcome was all too predictable.

Three of Craddock's cruisers were sunk, including HMS *Good Hope*, the end of which was described by one of the German officers: "We opened fire at short range. It was terrible for me to have to fire on the poor fellow who was not able to defend himself. But the colours were still flying and when we ceased fire for several minutes, he yet did not haul them down. So we ran up for a fresh attack and caused him to capsize by our

The wreck of SMS *Königsberg* photographed having sunk into the bottom of the Rufiji delta. Having surprised and sunk the Royal Navy cruiser HMS *Pegasus*, *Königsberg* retreated into the Rufiji River to repair her engines. Before the repairs could be completed, British cruisers located *Königsberg*, and, unable to steam into the river to destroy her, set up a blockade. After several attempts to sink the enemy ship, the British sent the monitors HMS *Mersey* and HMS *Severn* to destroy the German cruiser. On 11 July 1915, the two monitors got close enough to severely damage *Königsberg*, forcing her crew to scuttle the ship. The surviving crew salvaged all ten of her main guns and joined the fighting on land. (Deutsches Bundesarchiv)

gun-fire. The ship sank with flying colours, and we were unable to save a single man."

This devastating engagement was Britain's first naval defeat in over 100 years and the first for a Royal Navy squadron since 1810. The Admiralty was stung into action, despatching a large and powerful force to intercept the victorious German cruiser squadron. The forces met in the waters of the South Atlantic near the Falkland Islands, where Von Spee had planned to raid Port Stanley

This time the weight of metal was decidedly in the Royal Navy's favour, particularly in respect of the two battlecruisers HMS *Invincible* and HMS *Inflexible*.

The German ships were soon in trouble, coming under fire from the battlecruisers. SMS *Scharnhorst* was the first to be sunk, her propeller still lashing the foam as she went down head first. SMS *Gneisenau* was reduced to a complete wreck, riddled through, the dead and dying lying in heaps, her guns falling silent one by one. She settled by the head and then slid out of sight leaving a mass of struggling men in the water.

SMS *Leipzig* caught fire, forcing her to be abandoned. A final salvo from HMS *Cornwall* was followed by an explosion on the German cruiser. The main mast tottered and fell slowly. She was glowing along her length like a furnace and the end came as she rolled right over and sank.

The defeat of von Sheer's squadron, and the death of the admiral himself, marked the end of Germany's attempts to attack Allied shipping with warships of its navy. From now on it would rely instead on submarines and armed merchant cruisers.

It was also the last large-scale naval engagement until the two main fleets met at Jutland in 1916 in the greatest naval battle of the First World War.

NOTES:

1. W.L. Wyllie RA and M.F. Wren, *Sea Fights of The Great War* (Cassell, London, 1918), p.21.
2. Robert Massie, *Castles of Steel: Britain, Germany and the Winning of the Great War at Sea* (Johnathan Cape, London, 2004), p.146.
3. W.S. Churchill, *The World Crisis*, Volume I (Thornton Butterworth, London, 1932), p.309.

Passengers on the RMS *Olympic*, on the far right, watch the attempts to recover the sinking HMS *Audacious*. Despite the presence of these witnesses, the decision was taken by the Admiralty to maintain a veil of secrecy around the loss of the battleship. This situation was maintained until 14 November 1918, when the following notice was published in *The Times*: "The Secretary of the Admiralty makes the following announcement: HMS *Audacious* sank after striking a mine off the North Irish coast on October 27, 1914. This was kept secret at the urgent request of the Commander-in-Chief, Grand Fleet, and the Press loyally refrained from giving it any publicity." (HMP)

GAS! GAS! GAS!

Today the use of chemical and biological weapons is seen as morally indefensible but no such issues troubled the minds of the generals when gas was used on a large scale for the first time in warfare in 1915.

Located about three miles south-east of Ypres, Hill 60 is not a natural feature, but was made from the spoil removed during the construction of a nearby railway line. Because it was a small area of elevated land in a flat landscape, it attracted a strategic importance in the battles that raged in the Ypres Salient.

Hill 60 had been captured by men of the British 13th Brigade on 17 April 1915, and, despite repeated counter-attacks to try and regain this vital position, the British held on. The Germans, though, were determined to capture Ypres and they had at their disposal a secret weapon, and from their vantage point on the hill, the British troops had a grandstand view of the first time this terrifying new weapon was deployed.

As the sun was beginning to sink on the afternoon of 22 April, the crash of heavy artillery shattered the relatively peaceful scene. The volume of fire to the north-east increased with every discharge, and one 42cm shell landed in the heart of the stricken city of Ypres, barely a mile away from where the men of the Queen's Victoria Rifles had been resting. Anthony R. Hossack, who had joined the QVR in 1914, witnessed the dramatic events that were about to unfold:

"As we gazed in the direction of the bombardment, where our line joined the French, six miles away, we could see in the failing light the flash of shrapnel, with here and there the light of a rocket. But more curious than anything was a low cloud of yellow-grey smoke or vapour, and, underlying everything, a dull confused murmuring.

"Suddenly, down the road from the Yser Canal came a galloping team of horses, the riders goading on their mounts in a frenzied way; then another and another, till the road became a seething mass with a huge pall of dust over all. Plainly something terrible was happening. What was it?"

The men, officers and riflemen alike, stood and gazed in amazement at the apparently terror-stricken horsemen and the strange cloud that was drifting towards them on the northerly breeze. They watched, "awestruck and dumfounded", as gradually a pungent, nauseating smell overcame them. It tickled the throat and began to make their eyes smart.

"The horses and men were still pouring down the road, two or three men on a horse," continued Hossack, "while over the fields streamed mobs of infantry, the dusky warriors of French Africa; away went their rifles, equipment, even their tunics that they might run faster. One man came stumbling through our lines. An officer of ours held him up with leveled revolver. 'What's the matter, you bloody lot of cowards?' says he. The Zouave was frothing at the mouth, his eyes started from their sockets, and he fell writhing at the officer's feet."

The Queen Victoria Rifles fell in and moved up to the front line in anticipation of a German attack. But the enemy failed to follow up the

BELOW: **Completed in March 1919 by the American artist John Singer Sargent, *Gassed* is an evocative oil painting that serves as a powerful testimony of the effects of chemical weapons. On 21 August 1918, Sargent witnessed what he described as "a harrowing sight, a field full of gassed and blindfolded men". This was the aftermath of a German mustard gas attack which had been launched on 21 August 1918, at Le Bac-du-Sud, between Arras and Doullens, against advancing British troops during the Second Battle of Arras.**

LEFT: **German troops occupy an Allied trench after launching the first poison gas attack of the First World War, April 1915.** (With the kind permission of Brett Butterworth)

"More curious than anything was a low cloud of yellow-grey smoke or vapour, and, underlying everything, a dull confused murmuring."

Men of the Argyll and Sutherland Highlanders pictured in a trench during May 1915, wearing early issue pad respirators and goggles. These early British anti-gas respirators consisted of a pad of cotton waste enclosed in a pad of muslin that was tied over the nose and mouth of the wearer. The pad was soaked in a solution of sodium hyposulphite, washing soda, glycerine and water (in theory buckets of 'hypo' solution were to be provided in front line trenches). Eyes were protected by a separate pair of anti-gas goggles. The 'pad respirator' was issued to British troops in early May 1915, following the first mass use of cloud gas (chlorine) by the Germans at Ypres in April 1915. (HMP)

advantage that they had gained in this sector. The Rifles maintained their position unchallenged until midnight when they fell back once again.

Unsettled and uncertain, the men of the QVR would soon learn that they had witnessed the aftermath of the first use of gas by the Germans on the Western Front.

The next morning the Rifles were moved to the area where the French Colonial Corps had been the previous evening. Hossack recalled the scene:

"Ambulances were everywhere, and the village of Brielen, through which we passed, was chocked with wounded and gassed men. We were very mystified about this gas, and had no protection whatever against it."[1]

It was this feeling of helplessness that created such fear in hardened troops – men that had faced all manner of conventional weapons and had endured the shells and the machine-guns with equanimity. Against such weapons one could fight back in kind; but how can you fight a cloud of gas? Bullets can miss, deep trenches can be dug to mitigate the effects of even the largest shells, but the heavy gas permeates the very air that the men had to breathe.

Though this first use of gas >>

RIGHT: **Men of 'B' Company, 1st Battalion Queen's Own Cameron Highlanders, pictured preparing to meet a gas attack in the Bois Grenier Sector near Armentières on 20 May 1915. The men are wearing the early issue pad respirators and goggles. Initially worn from May 1915 with the veil, or pad respirator, the goggles were designed to protect the eyes from irritant agents.** (HMP)

OPPOSITE PAGE, TOP LEFT: **A contemporary drawing from May 1915, showing British troops during a gas alarm. Metal shell cases, steel triangles, watchmen's rattles, klaxon horns and similar objects were all adopted as methods of giving the alarm.** (HMP)

British Gas Casualties

For the British Expeditionary Force in the First World War, around 1 per cent of all deaths are attributable to gas as were 3.3 per cent of all non-fatal injuries and sickness – in round numbers about 7,000 and 180,000 respectively.

had come as a shock to the front line troops, both the German and the Allied high commands had been contemplating the use of chemical weapons for some weeks, despite the naïve belief amongst some that "civilized" men would never resort to such tactics. In the attack of 22 April, the Germans had released 168 tons of chlorine gas on a four-mile front. It took just five minutes to empty the 5,700 or so gas cylinders.

Those watching had seen "two curious greenish-yellow clouds on the ground either side of Langemarck in front of the German line. These clouds spread laterally, joined up, and, moving before a light wind, became a bluish-white mist, such as is seen over water meadows on a frosty night."[2]

The grey-green cloud that resulted drifted over the French lines, held by French Colonial troops, and caused mayhem. The French soldiers – the blow had fallen upon the French 45th (Algerian) and 87th (Territorial) divisions – abandoned their trenches, creating an 8,000-yard long gap in the Allied line. Though just as uncertain about the gas that preceded them, the German infantry, wearing gas masks, had followed the gas cloud and had taken the French position. Losses amongst the French troops were upwards of 6,000 killed, wounded or gassed.

Predictably, the Germans were keen to follow up this success. Equally predictable was that the Allies would soon retaliate with their own chemical weapons. The next gas attack was delivered on 24 April 1915, against the Belgians and Canadians holding the line of the Ypres Canal. The Germans released fifteen tons of chlorine gas along a 1,000-yard front. The men only had wet towels, handkerchiefs or soft caps to help protect them from the gas.

It was at this point, as the grey-green cloud ebbed towards the Canadian troops, that word spread through their ranks instructing them to urinate on their handkerchiefs and place these over their noses and mouths. Some accounts state that the order came from Captain Francis Alexander Carron Scrimger RCAMC who was serving with the 2nd Canadian Field Ambulance; whoever was responsible for the instruction, the chemistry was valid. The urea in urine would react with chlorine, forming dichloro-urea and effectively neutralize it.

However, these precautions proved ineffective and the German attack was ultimately a success. The Canadians were pushed back and the village of St. Julien was taken. Curiously, it was noted that those Canadians that had stood and fought through the gas attack had generally suffered less than those who had run away! The reason for this was explained in the *Official History*: "It early became evident that the men who stayed in their places suffered less than those who ran away, any movement making worse the effects of the gas, and those who stood up on the fire step suffered less – indeed they often escaped any serious effects – than those who lay down or sat at the bottom of the trench". Fortune, on this occasion at least, favoured the brave.

A further gas attack on 5 May resulted in the Germans finally taking Hill 60. It is generally accepted that the Germans' use of gas around Ypres in April and May 1915 had tactical benefits – almost all the ground that was captured as a result was held without interruption by the German Army until August-September 1917.

The actual statistics of that attack perhaps reveal a somewhat different picture than that experienced by the men in the front line. Just ninety men died from gas poisoning in the trenches or before they could be got to a dressing station. Of the 207 taken to the nearest dressing stations, forty-six died almost immediately and twelve after a period of prolonged suffering.

The British were not slow to follow the German example and in September

British soldiers wearing their PH (Phenate Hexamine) helmets, an early design of gasmask introduced in October 1915. Note how one of the men has his incorrectly adjusted – an action which could have deadly consequences in the field. The 'P' (or Phenate) Helmet, officially called the Tube Helmet, appeared in July 1915, replacing the simpler Hypo Helmet. It featured two mica eyepieces instead of the single visor of its predecessor, and added an exhaust valve fed from a metal tube which the wearer held in his mouth. In October 1915 it was, in turn, replaced by the 'PH' Helmet (Phenate Hexamine) – seen here. Around fourteen million were manufactured and it remained in service until the end of the war by which time it was relegated to second line use. (HMP)

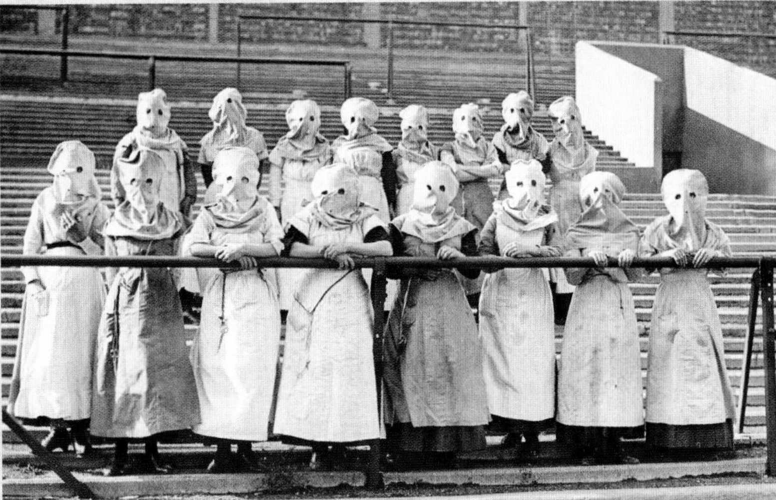

LEFT: Such was the demand for protective equipment, by July 1916, part of Tottenham Hotspur's football ground had been turned into a workshop manufacturing gas mask helmets and other anti-gas equipment - work which was predominantly undertaken by women.

First-hand Experience

"I experienced gas twice and it's still with me now. The first time it was mustard gas, and the second lot, I only got a whiff of it, goodness knows what it was ... This particular gas made my eyes water. You couldn't stop crying - water was running from your eyes ... The gas is still with me today. It makes me itch every morning, and at six every night .. It feels like a needle pricking you. And that's from ninety years ago."
Albert Elliot "Smiler" Marshall (1897 - 2005) First World War Veteran

1915 launched their first gas attack at the Battle of Loos. Despite the fact that Germany, France and Britain had been signatories to the Hague Convention of 1911, in which they agreed never to use chemical weapons, both sides continued to use chemical weapons, with shells becoming the favoured method of delivery.

In terms of the effects of gas, it has been estimated that of the 2,900,000 British casualties in the war, only around 3% died due to the effects of gas, though, of course, gas was not used in the first year of the war. In 1917, 7.2% of British casualties were caused by gas, this figure rising to 15% in 1918.

Further statistics show that there were about 1,286,863 gas casualties in all the armies of the First World War, with about 75% being caused by gas shell and the rest by gas cloud. Of this total, 93% survived the experience, although 12% would have some form of permanent disability.

In total forty-six types of gas, thirteen smoke agents and nine incendiary agents were used in the war. The most extensively produced gasses were chlorine, phosgene, diphosgene, mustard gas, chloropicrin and cyanide. Germany manufactured 68,100 tons of what were described as "battle gasses"' during the war, with France producing 36,955 tons and Britain 25,735 tons. The United States, Austria, Italy and Russia all manufactured these chemical weapons, amounting to 19,210 tons.[3]

The above figures indicate that gas was not the most efficient way to kill and maim the enemy, though it did have its advantages, as one observer pointed out: "The gas cloud is inescapable. It sweeps over and into everything in its path. No trench is too deep for it, no dugout, unless hermetically sealed is safe from it. Night and darkness only heighten its effect. It is the only weapon that is effective in a fog or the inky blackness of a moonlit night as in the most brilliant sunshine." It was for those reasons that the combatants continued to use gas throughout the war.

Some indication of the effects gas can have on an individual come from a German soldier at the Battle of Courtrai in 1918: "We were subjected for several hours to a heavy bombardment with gas bombs, which continued throughout the night with more or less intensity ... About midnight a number of us were put out of action, some for ever. Towards morning I also began to feel pain. It increased with every quarter of an hour; and about seven o'clock my eyes were scorching as I staggered back and delivered the last despatch I was destined to carry in this war. A few hours later my eyes were like glowing coals and all was darkness around me."

That soldier was a runner for the 16th Bavarian Reserve Infantry Regiment. His name was Adolf Hitler.

BELOW LEFT: A group of British soldiers, all wearing their early issue pad respirators and goggles. (HMP)

NOTES:

1. Sir John Hammerton (Editor), *The Great War … I was There!* Part Nine, p.369.
2. John Terraine, *The Great War 1914-18*, (Arrow Books, London, 1965), p.85.
3. Michael Freemantle, *Gas!Gas! Quick Boys*, (Spellmount, Stroud, 2012), pp.120-1.

The War in Words

The First World War Poets

RIGHT: **Soon after McCrae's death, his poem was published in Canada. This version was illustrated with red poppies and white crosses.** (HMP)

FAR RIGHT: **A portrait of John McCrae circa 1914.** (Courtesy of Guelph Museums, McCrae House)

Many of those that experienced the horrors of the First World War could not find words to describe what they had witnessed or endured. A few, though, were able to express themselves in rhyme, and in doing do produced some of the most poignant poetry in the English language.

The war inspired an outpouring of emotion on an unprecedented scale, and for many putting those sentiments into verse was a method of dealing with the helplessness and despair that they so acutely felt. Alan Seeger witnessed the first day of the Somme and was convinced that he too would soon die as thousands had before him. "I have a rendezvous with Death," he wrote, "at some disputed barricade ... I have a rendezvous with Death on some scarred slope of battered hill ... I have a rendezvous with Death at midnight in some flaming town ... I shall not fail that rendezvous." Seeger did indeed keep his rendezvous. An American serving in the French Foreign Legion, Seeger was killed at Belloy-en-Santerre on the fourth day of the Battle of the Somme in July 1916.

Bristol-born Issac Rosenberg was actually a poet by profession but, being unable to find work, he volunteered for the Army. The war proved fertile ground for his talent, as this excerpt from his poem *Dead Man's Dump* shows. The incident this poem describes is one where artillery limbers are being pulled along over ground where unburied bodies lay: "The wheels lurched over sprawled dead but pained them not, though their bones crunched; their shut mouths made no moan. They lie there huddled, friend and foeman ... and shells go crying over them from night till night and now."

One of the most famous of the First World War poets was Siegfried Sassoon. He volunteered for the Army just before the outbreak of war, joining the Sussex Yeomanry. He was commissioned into 3rd Battalion (Special Reserve), Royal Welch Fusiliers

IN FLANDERS FIELDS.

In Flanders fields the poppies blow
Between the crosses, row on row,
That mark our place; and in the sky
The larks, still bravely singing, fly
Scarce heard amid the guns below.

We are the Dead. Short days ago
We lived, felt dawn, saw sunset glow,
Loved and were loved, and now we lie
In Flanders fields.

Take up our quarrel with the foe:
To you from failing hands we throw
The torch; be yours to hold it high.
If ye break faith with us who die
We shall not sleep, though poppies grow
In Flanders fields.

RIGHT: **A cutting showing how *In Flanders Fields* first appeared in *Punch* during December 1915.** (HMP)

The poem *In Flanders Fields* was written by McCrae as he sat upon the back of a medical field ambulance near an advance dressing post at Essex Farm, just north of Ypres, on May 3, 1915, the day after he had presided over the funeral and burial of his friend Lieutenant Alex Helmer. It is because of its links with John McCrae that the area known as Essex Farm, which includes the bunker seen here, is one of the most visited locations within the Ypres Salient. (HMP)

> "Poetry ranged from doggerel to dramatic and from parody to profundity. When we think of First World War poets we should consider not simply the great and the good, but the thousands of men who found in verse the only way of expressing the inexpressible."
>
> The late Professor Richard Holmes

LEFT: By January 1918, McCrae had been appointed as the first Canadian consulting surgeon to the British Army, becoming an acting Colonel. But it was an appointment he was never to take up. Worn out by continuous service, he died of pneumonia and meningitis on 28 January 1918. Lieutenant Colonel John McCrae's grave can be found at plot IV.H.3. in Wimereux Communal Cemetery. (Courtesy of Roger Davies)

as a Second Lieutenant on 29 May 1915. In November he was posted to the 1st Battalion in France. Sassoon was a brave and daring soldier, nicknamed "Mad Jack" by his men, who was awarded the Military Cross for "conspicuous gallantry during a raid on the enemy's trenches. He remained for 1½ hours under rifle and bomb fire collecting and bringing in our wounded. Owing to his courage and determination all the killed and wounded were brought in." He was also later recommended for, though not awarded, the Victoria Cross.

His poetry exemplifies the changing mood of many soldiers as the war dragged on for year after year. His early verses were reflective and thoughtful but following the death of his friend Second Lieutenant David Thomas he turned against the war (Thomas was leading a working party to repair wire emplacements in No Man's Land near Fricourt on 18 March 1916 when he was shot in the throat, dying whilst en route to a First Aid Post). After a period of convalescent leave, Sassoon refused to return to the front. He had already become a well-known figure, having had his first book published to critical acclaim before the war. That such a clever and demonstrably patriotic and courageous individual should refuse to take part in the war was a major embarrassment to the authorities. A less distinguished figure might well have suffered imprisonment or even execution for refusing to fight but this could not be contemplated with Sassoon.

He brazenly sent the following letter to his commanding officer in July, 1917: "I am making this statement as an act of wilful defiance of military authority because I believe that the war is being deliberately prolonged by those who have the power to end »

RIGHT: **The poet Siegfried Sassoon pictured in 1915.**

BELOW RIGHT: **Though only five of his poems were published before his death, one in fragmentary form, Wilfred Owen (seen here) is regarded by some historians as the leading poet of the First World War. He is remembered for his war poetry on the horrors of trench and gas warfare, including *Anthem for Doomed Youth, Futility,* and *Dulce Et Decorum Est.* An acquaintance of Siegfried Sassoon, Owen was killed in action on 4 November 1918 during the crossing of the Sambre-Oise Canal, exactly one week (almost to the hour) before the signing of the Armistice; he was promoted to the rank of Lieutenant the day after his death. His mother received the telegram informing her of his death on Armistice Day itself, the message reputedly arriving as the church bells were ringing out in celebration.**

it. I am a soldier, convinced that I am acting on behalf of soldiers. I believe that the war upon which I entered as a war of defence and liberation has now become a war of aggression and conquest. I believe that the purposes for which I and my fellow soldiers entered upon this war should have been so clearly stated as to have made it impossible to change them and that had this been done the objects which actuated us would now be attainable by negotiation.

"I have seen and endured the sufferings of the troops and I can no longer be a party to prolonging these sufferings for ends which I believe to be evil and unjust. I am not protesting against the conduct of the war, but against the political errors and insincerities for which the fighting men are being sacrificed. On behalf of those who are suffering now, I make this protest against the deception which is being practised upon them; also I believe it may help to destroy the callous complacency with which the majority of those at home regard the continuance of agonies which they do not share and which they have not enough imagination to realise." He reportedly threw the ribbon of his Military Cross into the River Mersey.

Rather than putting Sassoon before a court-martial, it was decided that it would be wise to declare, instead, that Sassoon was medically unfit. He was sent to Craiglockhart War Hospital in Scotland where he was officially treated for shell-shock.

He did eventually return to the front and was promoted to Lieutenant, and later Captain. Almost immediately upon his return to France he was wounded again, being shot in the head at Arras by a fellow soldier who mistook him for a German. Sassoon was returned to the UK where he saw out the remainder of the war.

One of his most moving poems was written after the war, in March 1919, which warned people never to forget the awful suffering and dreadful loss of life caused by the war. It is called *Aftermath*: "Do you remember the dark months you held the sector at Mametz – the nights you watched and wires and dug and piled sandbags on the parapets? Do you remember the rats; the stench of corpses rotting in front of the front-line trench – and dawn coming, dirty-white, and chill with a hopeless rain? Do you ever stop and ask, 'Is it all going to happen again?' Do you remember that hour of din before the attack – and the anger, the blind compassion that seized and shook you then as you peered at the doomed and haggard faces of your men? Do you remember the stretcher-cases lurching back with dying eyes and lolling heads – those ashen-grey masks of the lads who once were keen and gay? *"Have you forgotten yet?... Look up, swear by the green of spring that you'll never forget."*

This theme of remembrance is one that was taken up by subsequent generations and has become identified with many of the words of the war poets. In particular one written following the death on 2 May 1915, of a young Lieutenant in the Canadian Field Artillery who was killed by a German shell. His death led to his friend and comrade, Lieutenant Colonel John McCrae, writing what is commonly regarded as the most famous poem of the First World War, *In Flanders Fields*. Its simple lines are still repeated every year across many nations in the hope that we will, indeed, never forget.

YOUR COUNTRY NEEDS YOU!

LEFT: **Volunteers for Kitchener's New Army waiting in the churchyard of St. Martin-in-the-Fields, off Trafalgar Square, London, during August 1914.**

One of the most moving aspects of the First World War was the formation of the so-called Pals Battalions in which thousands of men volunteered to fight together with their friends and workmates.

On 5 August 1914, two days after the declaration of war, Lord Kitchener was made Secretary of State for War. This experienced general could see that an enormous effort would be required to defeat the mighty German Army. So he made a personal appeal to the men of the nation – and the response to join Kitchener's 'New Army' was greater than anyone could have imagined.

This overwhelming display of patriotism prompted Edward Stanley, the 17th Earl of Derby, to believe that men who met socially as 'pals' might respond well to a call for them to serve and fight together, rather than with men they did not know. Derby's idea was put forward in the Liverpool newspapers and he wrote personally to the larger business institutions suggesting that they encourage their workforce to enlist immediately!

Following the newspaper announcement, at 07.30 hours on 28 August, the headquarters of the 5th Battalion The King's (Liverpool) Regiment, on St Anne Street, opened its doors to a mass of young men that had gathered outside. Soon the drill hall was packed to capacity with men standing in the aisles, the doorways and even on the stairs. So many had turned up to volunteer another room below also had to be opened.

Lord Derby arrived in person to address the volunteers. He was welcomed with cheers and the waving of hats, which was repeated when he told the crowd that his brother Ferdinand was to command the new battalion. Such had been the response it was evident that there was more than enough men to form one battalion. "I am not going to make you a speech of heroics. You have given me your answer, and I can telegraph Lord Kitchener tonight to say that our second battalion is formed," Derby said to the eager volunteers. "We have got to see this through to the bitter end and dictate our terms of peace in Berlin if it takes every man and every penny in the country. This should be a Battalion of Pals, a battalion in which friends from the same office will fight shoulder to shoulder for the honour of Britain and the credit of Liverpool."[1] The first Pals battalion had been raised.

Strictly speaking the first group of colleagues forming a battalion together was the so-called "Stockbrokers Battalion", the »

BELOW: **A postcard depicting recruits to Kitchener's New Army training in civilian attire. Posted on 15 October 1914, the sender has made a note on the back explaining that he "expects they will have their uniforms next week".** (HMP)

G. R.

THE NEW ARMIES

More Men are Needed at once

COMPLETE THE SECOND HALF-MILLION

and ensure

SUCCESS ABROAD AND SAFETY AT HOM

ENLIST FOR THE PERIOD OF THE WA

Arrangements are now complete to receiv and train all who enlist.

STANDARDS HAVE BEEN LOWERED

Apply at any Military Barrack or Recruiting Office; the addresses the latter can be obtained from Post Offices or Labour Exchanges.

GOD SAVE THE KING.

War Office, 19th October, 1914.

ABOVE: **Issued by the War Office on 19 October 1914, this poster was part of the continuing drive to enlist more volunteers. The first New Army divisions were used at the Battle of Loos in the autumn of 1915, and they were sorely tested in the Battle of the Somme the following year. The initial British Expeditionary Force - a single army of five regular divisions in August 1914 - had expanded to two armies comprising sixteen divisions by the end of 1914 when the Territorials had been deployed. By the summer of 1916, however, it had grown to five armies totalling around sixty divisions and approximately two million men, of whom around half were infantry.** (US Library of Congress)

10th (Service) Battalion, The Royal Fusiliers, which was raised on 19 August 1914, though not granted battalion status until 21 August. It was composed of men who worked in the offices of the City of London who wanted to serve together. However, it was what became embodied as the 17th Battalion, The King's (Liverpool) Regiment, that was the first true 'Pals' Battalion.

The actual recruiting for the Liverpool Pals began the following Monday morning at St George's Hall on Lime Street. Even more men turned up than had the previous Thursday. In anticipation of the volunteers coming from all the various aspects of the local business community, desks had been set up in the hall representing such organisations as The Cotton Association, The Law Society and Chartered Accountants, General Brokers and The Stock Exchange, and the shipping companies, amongst many others. At Wallasey, across the Mersey, the all-male office staff of the Liverpool Gas Company was asked to go to the boardroom, where the Chairman told the men that anyone who volunteered for the Army would be granted leave of absence with half-pay.

One young man, S. Harris, has left us this description of the scene in St Georges Hall: "Hundreds of city-garbed young men [were] directed to rooms in which were clerks ready to take down recruits' personal details, name, address, age, religion and so on; and bibles on which each man swore allegiance to the King, his heirs and successors. These formalities over, the next ordeal was in other nearby rooms, where doctors were medically examining each recruit."

Such scenes were to be witnessed in recruiting

ABOVE RIGHT and RIGHT: **These two recruitment posters illustrate the fact that a number of sportsmen's battalions were formed, including three battalions of footballers - the 17th and 23rd (Service) Battalions, Middlesex Regiment and the 16th (Service) Battalion (2nd Edinburgh) Royal Scots (Lothian Regiment). The latter battalion contained the entire first and reserve team players, several boardroom and staff members and a sizeable contingent of supporters from the Scottish professional club Heart of Midlothian FC.** (US Library of Congress)

RIGHT: **A tramcar used during the recruiting campaign for the Leeds Pals, the 15th (service) Battalion (1st Leeds), The Prince of Wales's Own (West Yorkshire Regiment), which was formed in September 1914. Note how the destination on the front of the tram is given as "Berlin"!** (HMP)

time to play Games" (Lord Roberts)

RUGBY·UNION·FOOTBALLERS are DOING·THEIR·DUTY

over 90% have enlisted

"Every player who represented England in Rugby international matches last year has joined the colours."—Extract from *The Times*, November 30, 1914.

BRITISH ATHLETES! Will you follow this GLORIOUS EXAMPLE ?

> "Hundreds of city-garbed young men [were] directed to rooms in which were clerks ready to take down recruits' personal details, name, address, age, religion and so on…"

offices throughout the land. On the other side of Lancashire, in Accrington, an industrial dispute, where one of the largest employers in the town had been closed for many weeks, plus a severe recession which had resulted in as many as 7,000 cotton workers becoming unemployed or on short working, added impetus to the call for recruits. The prospect of food, a uniform, pay and an overseas adventure proved irresistible to many who had little to lose by joining up and potentially much to gain.

Across the Pennines in the coal mining village of Little Houghton near Barnsley, men completing the day shift flocked to the recreation ground to hear their local branch representative of the Yorkshire Miners' Association: "I put my weight behind Lord Kitchener's recruiting drive and I hope that miners will respond to the call. Colonel Hewitt [a local solicitor] has told me that if at Houghton we get a company's strength, or two companies, that our men will be kept together. He assures me that just as you have worked together in the pit, you will be able to work together as soldiers." After singing the National Anthem the men surged to the colliery offices and upwards of 200 men handed in their names.

Encouraged by Lord Derby's success, Kitchener promoted the idea of organising similar recruitment campaigns throughout the entire country. By the end of September 1914, over fifty towns had formed Pals battalions, whilst the larger towns and cities were able to form several battalions.

Such was the speed and spontaneity of the rush to arms that in Newcastle recruitment of a battalion of Scottish soldiers started without any form of official sanction. The result was a refusal by the War Office to allow the battalion to be authorised. "With reference to your application to raise a battalion in Newcastle upon Tyne," ran the wording of a letter dated 18 September 1914, "I am commanded by the Army Council to inform you that owing to the number of local battalions already authorised they have decided that no more such battalions can be authorised. I am to express to you the sincerest thanks of the Army Council and to say that whilst they appreciate the patriotic spirit which has prompted your proposal they much regret that they are unable to accept it."

The folly of this rejection was soon realised by an Army that needed every man it could get, especially tough »

LEFT: **Located just west of Serre on the Somme battlefield, and in the area where part of the British front line was located on 1 July 1916, is the Sheffield Memorial Park. Opened as a memorial park in 1936, the site still exhibits the scars of the fighting and shelling that occurred here. It was in the area of the park that the men of the 12th (Service) Battalion, York and Lancaster Regiment - the Sheffield Pals - went into action on 1 July 1916. That day the battalion lost over 500 men.** (HMP)

BELOW: **A recruitment parade in Bournemouth, Dorset, on 14 April 1915. Out of nearly 1,000 battalions raised during the first two years of the war, over two thirds were locally-raised Pals battalions.** (HMP)

Scots, and to make amends, the Lord Chancellor, Lord Haldane, visited Newcastle on 10 October 1914, and, in addressing a crowd of around 8,000, announced that two more battalions could be raised in Newcastle. The result was two of the most famous of the Pals battalions, the Tyneside Scottish and the Tyneside Irish.

ABOVE: **The original caption to this picture states that it shows "men of the New Army resting whilst en route to the front". Also referred to as "Kitchener's Army", this was the (initially) all-volunteer army formed in the United Kingdom following the outbreak of hostilities in the First World War and in which the Pals Battalions served. It was created on the recommendation of Lord Kitchener, the then Secretary of State for War.** (HMP)

The Accrington Pals

At the front of the Sheffield Memorial Park, near the main entrance, is a shallow depression that marks the course of a front line trench from 1 July 1916. It was actually the Accrington Pals who attacked from the trenches here on the opening day of the Battle of the Somme. It had taken just ten days to raise a complete battalion from the men who volunteered from the Lancashire towns of Burnley, Blackburn, Chorley and Accrington after Lord Kitchener had told Britons that their country needed them. The 11th (Service) Battalion (Accrington) East Lancashire Regiment became known as the Accrington Pals. Approximately 700 men from the Accrington Pals went in to action on 1 July 1916. Of that number 585 men became casualties, of whom 235 were killed and 350 were wounded in about thirty minutes. (HMP)

The men that had grown up side by side, in the same towns, even the same streets... also went over the top together, and together they died.

As well as appeals to specific nationalities, actual classes of persons were also targeted as an inducement to enlist. The idea behind this being that even if an individual was not able to join up with his workmates or neighbourhood friends, he might be induced to join if he was going to serve with people from the same social class.

Such a suggestion was made in the *Hull Daily Mail*, no doubt following complaints from potential recruits that they did not like the idea of having to live alongside men from lower classes. "Instead of some of the larger employers of labour in Hull giving big donations of money they should use their influence to organise Corps of the middle class young men – clerks, tailors, drapers' assistants, grocers' assistants, warehousemen and artisans. Then we should see men living, sleeping and training in company of others of their own class." The author of this letter to the *Hull Daily Mail* submitted it under the pseudonym "Middle Class".

In August 1914 several young men who had attended Winteringham Secondary School in Grimsby suggested to the former headmaster that he should form a battalion from his former pupils. He agreed and by the end of October he had recruited over 1,000 members into what they called the "Grimsby Chums" – officially the 10th (Service) Battalion, the Lincolnshire Regiment. Other schools, including five of Britain's leading public schools, also formed battalions.

In total there were ninety-six Pals or City battalions raised across the United Kingdom, the definition of a Pals/City battalion being a unit raised by a local authority or private body which undertook to organise, clothe, billet and feed the recruits – the provision of weapons remained the responsibility of the Army. In addition to these there were battalions raised by Public Schools, sporting organisations, commercial organisations, ethnic groups, artists and even the Boys Brigade and Church Lads Brigade. A staggering 144 privately-raised battalions were formed for the New Army.[2] They began to strengthen the British Expeditionary Force in France towards the end of 1915, with others being sent to Gallipoli.

The enthusiasm and the patriotic fever of those autumnal months of 1914 gradually softened as the routine of Army life took over. Nevertheless, when the 'Big Push' was to be made, the Pals were ready and still keen to get to grips with the enemy.

The policy of drawing recruits from amongst a local population ensured that, when the Pals battalions suffered casualties, individual towns, villages, neighbourhoods, and communities back in Britain were to suffer disproportionate losses. With the introduction of conscription in January 1916, further Pals battalions were not sought. Most pal battalions had been all but decimated by the end of 1917 and beginning of 1918 and most were amalgamated into other battalions to regularise battalion strength.

It is with the first day of the Battle of the Somme that the Pals battalions are most closely associated. On the morning of 1 July 1916, many of the Pals lined up in the forward trenches and, to the shrill blast of whistles, went over the top of the parapets. The men that had grown up side by side, in the same towns, even the same streets, had joined the Army in their patriotic rush, and had lived and trained together. They also went over the top together, and together they died.

"They did not go over after a strong ration of rum as some people imagine these affairs are carried out. No, they went over feeling themselves. The colonel watched them mount the steps and his last words were, 'Isn't it wonderful?'"

NOTES:

1. Cited in Graham Maddocks, *Liverpool Pals, 17th, 18th, 19th & 20th Battalions The King's (Liverpool Regiment) 1914-1919* (Leo Cooper, Barnsley, 1996), p.24.
2. Roni Wilkinson. *Pals on the Somme 1916* (Pen & Sword, Barnsley, 2008), p.213.

Gallipoli

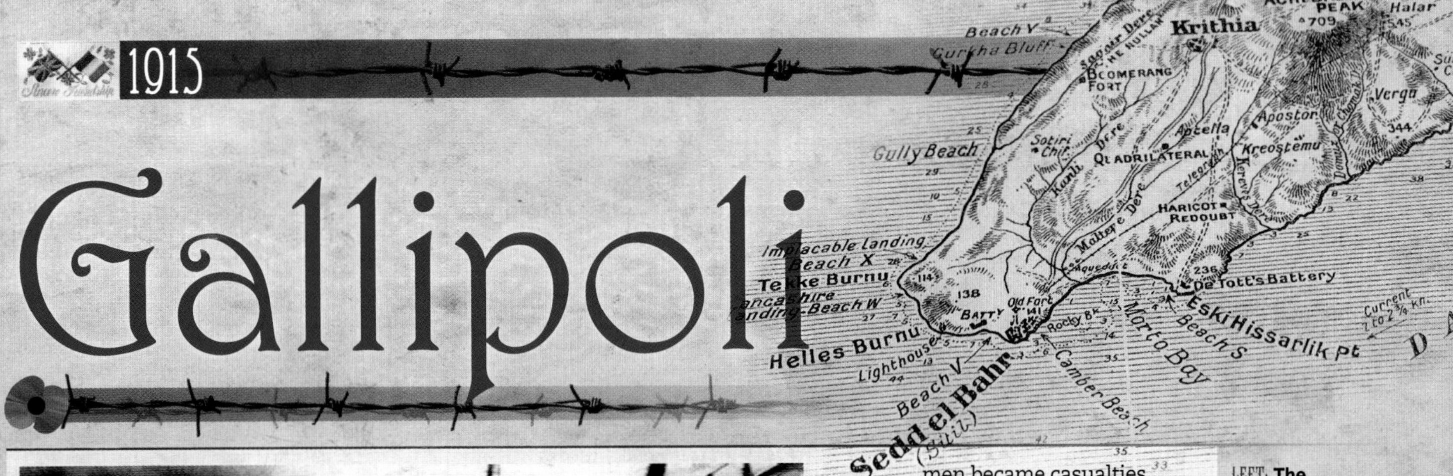

LEFT: **The Allied naval bombardment of Turkish positions underway as a battleship fires its 12-inch guns in the Dardanelles Strait in 1915. The naval operations in the Dardanelles Campaign were predominantly carried out by the Royal Navy with substantial support from the French and minor contributions from Russia and Australia.** (HMP)

BELOW: **A contemporary artist's impression of the men of the 1st Battalion, Lancashire Fusiliers landing on 'W' Beach on 25 April 1915. Note the presence of the barbed wire defences which caused the Allied troops such difficulties.** (HMP)

Like so many battles and operations in the First World War the Gallipoli campaign began with unrestrained enthusiasm and unrealistic objectives. What was supposed to be a quick victory over the Turks, with the mighty ships of the Royal Navy bombarding Constantinople into surrender, degenerated into a protracted bloodbath and a humiliating defeat.

The operation against the Turkish Ottoman Empire which began in 1915 was originally intended to be nothing more than a demonstration to help relieve pressure on Britain and France's ally, Russia. Tsar Nicholas II's forces were fighting on two fronts and barely able to hold back the Germans and Austrians, leaving them severely weakened in the Caucasus. Britain's military and political leaders, Churchill, Kitchener, Fisher, Carden and Lloyd George, turned that limited objective into a major offensive which absorbed almost half-a-million men and vast amounts of military and naval resources. Almost half of those men became casualties.

At first the campaign against Turkey was purely naval. It was led by Vice-Admiral Sir Sackville Hamilton Carden who at the time was in command of the Royal Navy's Mediterranean Squadron. As early as November 1914, as soon as hostilities between Russia and Turkey had started, Carden, with a combined Anglo-French squadron, had tried to force the Dardanelles Strait, a thirty-mile long strait in north-western Turkey which, linking the Sea of Marmara to the Aegean, is only between 0.75 to 3.7 miles wide.

Carden reported back that the Turkish batteries opened fire as soon as the Allied ships made their run. The Allied warships' counter-fire was highly effective and it was believed that some 600 casualties had been inflicted on the Turkish gunners. When, on 19 February 1915, Carden conducted a second run past the Turkish batteries and deliberately bombarded the Turkish positions from the outset, the Turkish gunners remained under cover and did not venture out to man their guns until the afternoon.

Operations continued in February and March in which landing parties captured some of the Turkish forts. Yet it was not the land defences »

RIGHT: **Soldiers of the Australian 1st Brigade row to the beach, whilst empty boats return from the shore to the destroyers, at about 09.45 hours on the morning of the Australians' landing at Anzac Cove, 25 April 1915. Those men who were landed in the morning first attacked the small plateau nearby, afterwards called Plugge's Plateau, and then went over the skyline into Shrapnel Valley.** (Courtesy of the Australian War Memorial)

RIGHT: **The Formidable-class pre-dreadnought battleship HMS *Irresistible* listing and sinking in the Dardanelles, 18 March 1915 - an image taken from the battleship HMS *Lord Nelson*. Having struck a mine at 16.16 hours, the badly-damaged *Irresistible* was left without power, causing her to drift within range of Turkish guns which laid down a heavy barrage on her. HMS *Irresistible* finally sank at about 19.30 hours, her crew suffering about 150 casualties.** (HMP)

that ultimately proved decisive but the mine fields which had been sown across the Strait.

The main Anglo-French naval attack was launched on 18 March 1915, when the fleet, comprising sixteen capital ships as well as an array of cruisers and destroyers, sought to pass the narrowest point of the Dardanelles where the strait is just a mile wide. Once through the Strait, the warships could steam on to Constantinople (now Istanbul). However, running into a minefield, three battleships were lost, three more seriously damaged and the attempt to break through to Constantinople was abandoned.

At this point, Britain and France could have scaled down their operations in this theatre. They had made the demonstration that Russia had pleaded for and if they kept a number of warships in the area, the Turks would have been compelled to maintain substantial forces on the Gallipoli Peninsula to ensure its safety. However, General Sir Ian Hamilton, who had been given command of the Allied Mediterranean Expeditionary Force, had been present with the Royal Navy on 18 March. He was not inclined to give in, though he made it clear to London that "nothing but a thorough and systematic scheme for flinging the whole of the troops under my command very rapidly ashore could be expected to meet with

"Nothing but a thorough and systematic scheme for flinging the whole of the troops under my command very rapidly ashore could be expected to meet with success..."

RIGHT: **Allied troops disembarking on one of the landing beaches on the Gallipoli Peninsula, 25 April 1915.** (HMP)

success; whereas, on the other hand, a tentative or piecemeal programme was bound to lead to disaster." That, though, is exactly what happened.

Hamilton was allowed to go ahead with the landing of British and Commonwealth troops and these operations began on 25 April 1915. In the intervening weeks the Turks had worked hard on their defences and reinforced their troops. A German officer, *Generalleutnant* Otto Liman von Sanders, who served as an adviser and military commander for the Ottoman Empire during the First World War, later noted: "The British allowed us four good weeks of respite for all this work before their great disembarkation ... This respite just sufficed for the most indispensable measures to be taken."

Lance Corporal John Elisha Grimshaw, a 22-year-old signaller of 'C' Company, 1st Battalion Lancashire Fusiliers, who would win a Victoria Cross for his actions on 25 April, later recalled what happened after the troops had left the ships: "In boats we got within 200 or 300 yards from the shore when the Turks opened a terrible fire. Sailors were shot dead at their oars. With rifles held over our heads we struggled through the barbed wire in the water to the beach and fought a way to the foot of the cliffs leaving the biggest part of our men dead and wounded."

As Grimshaw noted, many of the Allied soldiers were hit in the water as they struggled to reach the beach. They were still unable to return fire on the enemy who were secure in their trenches well above their heads.

As the men neared the sandy beach they discovered other obstacles awaiting them. The Turks had concealed a trip wire just below the surface of the shallow water. On the beach itself they had laid a field of land mines, and a wide fence of rusty wire which extended across the beach. Machine-guns, hidden in caves at each end of the semi-circular line of cliffs, able to enfilade the beach, opened fire and added to the developing scene of carnage.

Amongst the troops that landed on 25 April were men of the Australian and New Zealand Army Corps – the Anzacs. This was the first major military operation the antipodeans had been involved in and is still regarded as a defining moment in their histories, both countries only having achieved autonomy eight years earlier.

Despite the obvious fact that a very large force indeed would be required to seize Gallipoli and achieve the new final objective of capturing Constantinople, only around 80,000 men were available to Hamilton. A month after the initial landings, little progress had been made by the Allied troops. Repeated attempts to break out of the beachheads had failed, and the expeditionary force was still trapped with its back to the sea, with the Turks holding the high ground that prevented the British and Commonwealth troops from breaking inland. Casualties on both sides were shocking, and conditions for the troops, continuously exposed in the heat of spring and early summer, scarcely bearable.

This was vividly described by Hamilton himself: "The country is broken, mountainous, arid and void of supplies; the water found in the areas occupied by our forces is quite inadequate for their needs; the only practicable beaches are small, cramped breaks in impracticable lines of cliffs; with the wind in certain quarters no sort of landing is possible; the wastage, by bombardment and wreckage, of lighters and small craft has led to crisis after crisis in our carrying capacity, whilst over every single beach plays fitfully »

ABOVE: **An Australian sniper using a periscope rifle at Gallipoli, 1915 – he is aided by a spotter who is also using a trench periscope. The men are believed to belong to the Australian 2nd Light Horse Regiment and the location is probably Quinn's Post.** (HMP)

Military supplies piled up at Anzac Cove in May 1915. The cove is a mere 600 yards long and is bounded by the headlands of Ari Burnu to the north and Little Ari Burnu, known as "Hell Spit", to the south. Following the landing at Anzac Cove, the beach became the main base for the Australian and New Zealand troops for the eight months of the campaign on the Gallipoli Peninsula. (HMP)

FAR RIGHT: **'W' Beach at Cape Helles, Gallipoli, on 7 January 1916, just prior to the final evacuation of British forces. The explosion of a Turkish shell in the water, fired from the Asian side of the Dardanelles, can be seen.** (HMP)

RIGHT: **Allied troops in a captured Turkish trench at Lone Pine on 6 August 1915. Made famous by the fighting here in August 1915, Plateau 400, or Lone Pine as it is more usually known, drew its name from the fact that the Turkish defenders had cut down all but one of the trees that clothed the ridge to cover their trenches. In so doing, the view of the ridge became dominated by the single pine tree.** (HMP)

MIDDLE RIGHT: **The Gallipoli peninsula is a spectacular place with steep valleys, deep ravines and high cliffs towering above long, narrow beaches. It can be searingly hot in summer and bone chillingly cold in winter. For most of 1915, this impressive and unforgiving landscape was home to many thousands of Allied troops, all of whom had to make the most of the space available to them - as this typical view of the dug-outs they occupied reveals.** (HMP)

throughout each day a devastating shell fire at medium ranges."

Hamilton made "urgent" calls for reinforcements and in August he conducted a major assault upon the Turkish positions. This included a landing at Suvla Bay on the evening of 6 August 1915. Chaplain Kenneth Best was there. "I remember the tremendous crash of rifle and machine gun fire close to and the 'thump' 'thump' of bullets and sparks flying from the stones while an officer and six of us pushed

through the scrub towards the curve of a hill which showed darkly against the night sky. Between the bursts of fire the silence was broken by agonising cries which will always haunt me. From all around that hill there were voices crying 'Ambulance', 'Stretcher-bearers', 'Oh damn you my leg's broken' and then again 'Stretcher-bearers'. It was horrible, we would start for a voice and it would cease and another far away would begin. That hillside was a shambles."

The Suvla Bay operation was indeed a shambles and has been regarded as the most egregious display of generalship in the entire war. The man in charge, Lieutenant General Sir Frederick William Stopford, was removed from his post after just a week. Many though consider Stopford to have been made a scapegoat for failures elsewhere as the August offensive ground to a standstill.

The failure of the offensive and the evident lack of progress led to Hamilton himself being replaced in October by General Charles Munro. Munro had been instructed to report on the military situation on the

Gallipoli Peninsula and to give his opinion on whether or not, on purely military grounds, the Expeditionary Force should be evacuated or, that if further operations were continued, how many troops would be required to take Constantinople.

In his despatch Munro explained what he found: "The positions occupied by our troops presented a military situation unique in history. The mere fringe of the coast line had been secured. The beaches and piers upon which they depended for all requirements in personnel and material were exposed to registered and observed Artillery fire. Our entrenchments were dominated almost throughout by the Turks. The possible Artillery positions were insufficient and defective.

"The Force, in short, held a line possessing every possible military defect. The position was without depth, the communications were insecure and dependent on the weather. No means existed for the concealment and deployment of fresh troops destined for the offensive – whilst the Turks enjoyed full powers of observation, abundant Artillery positions, and they had been given the time to supplement the natural advantages which the position presented by all the devices at the disposal of the Field Engineer." Munro ended his despatch with this blunt statement: "In my opinion the evacuation of the Peninsula should be taken in hand."

The War Cabinet agreed. Withdrawing from contact with the enemy is one of the most hazardous operations in warfare and Hamilton had declared that an evacuation under the guns of the Turks would result in 50% casualties. He would be proved wrong, for remarkably it was achieved without the loss of a single man. Ironically, the withdrawal was the most successful part of the entire Gallipoli campaign.

Some 410,000 British and Commonwealth troops took part in the campaign alongside the French. They battled against approximately similar numbers of Turks. The British suffered 141,000 casualties, the Australians 28,000, New Zealanders 7,400, and French 27,000. This made a total of 203,400 killed, wounded or missing and it was all for nothing.

Timeline 1916 - Events that Shaped The First World War

January

8 The last British troops were evacuated from the Gallipoli peninsula, more specifically Lancashire Landing, at around 04.00 hours, bringing an end to the Dardanelles Campaign

27 Having been passed in the House of Commons, the Military Service Act 1916 received Royal Assent, marking the first time in British military history that legislation which led to conscription was introduced

31 In the so-called "Great Zeppelin Raid", nine German airships carried out a mission to bomb targets across the British mainland, some of which achieved the furthest penetration westwards of the war

February

16 The War Office assumed command of the anti-aircraft defences of London, taking over from the Admiralty

21 Germany informed the United States that armed merchant ships would be treated in the same manner as cruisers

23 The British Government formed the Ministry of Blockade; Lord Robert Cecil was appointed Minister of Blockade. The purpose of the ministry was to co-ordinate, and tighten up, the whole machinery by which economic pressure was brought to bear on the Central Powers

29 The German commerce raider *Greif* was intercepted and sunk by a force of Royal Navy warships. One of the latter, the auxiliary cruiser HMS *Alcantara*, was damaged to such an extent that it also sank

March

24 The British cross-channel steamer *Sussex* was torpedoed whilst travelling from Folkestone to Dieppe. The ship was severely damaged, with the entire bow forward of the bridge blown off

28 An inter-Allied conference ended in Paris with a declaration of unity being issued by Belgium, France, Great Britain, Italy, Japan, Portugal, Russia and Serbia regarding military, economic, and diplomatic affairs

April

18 U.S. President Woodrow Wilson presented an ultimatum to the German government regarding the latter's policy of unrestricted submarine warfare

24 Some 1,200 members of the Irish Volunteers took over positions in the centre of Dublin, launching the week-long rebellion known as the Easter Rising

25 A German battle cruiser squadron bombarded Great Yarmouth and Lowestoft

29 British forces surrendered to Turkish forces at Kut in Mesopotamia

May

1 British Summer Time introduced as a "daylight saving" measure

15 In an attempt to establish effective co-ordination between the Royal Flying Corps and the Royal Naval Air Service, the Air Board was created with Lord Curzon as its chairman

25 What was in reality universal conscription was introduced in Great Britain by a second Military Service Act

31 The Battle of Jutland began in the North Sea

June

2 German forces attacked Canadian sections of the Ypres Salient at the start of the Battle of Mount Sorrel

5 HMS *Hampshire* sunk by a mine off the Scottish coast. Field Marshal Earl Kitchener and his Staff drowned

24 The Allies opened up an artillery barrage along a twenty-five-mile front against German trenches on the Somme

July

1 The Battle of the Somme began. On what is generally accepted as the worst day in the British Army's history, there were more than 60,000 casualties – a third of them fatal

7 Lloyd George succeeded Lord Kitchener as Secretary of State for War

14 The Battle of Bazentin Ridge

15 The Battle of Delville Wood

19 The Battle of Fromelles. This combined action by British and Australian troops was partly intended to divert German attention away from the Battle of the Somme just to the south

20 British troops attacked High Wood on the Somme, but it was not captured until 15 September

27 Captain Charles Fryatt, of the SS *Brussels*, was executed in Belgium by order of a German court-martial

August

24 Anglo-French conference on finance held in Calais

September

2 The largest simultaneous attack of the war is undertaken by German airships on London and other targets across Britain

10 An Allied offensive on the Salonika Front began

15 Tanks were used for the first time during the Battle of Flers-Courcelette

26 The Battle of Thiepval Ridge began

October

1 The Battle of Le Transloy began. This was the final offensive mounted by the British Fourth Army during the Battle of the Somme

26 In a successful attack, two and a half flotillas of German torpedo boats launched a raid into the Dover Strait in an attempt to disrupt the Dover Barrage and sink Allied shipping

November

13 The last large British attack of the Battle of the Somme, the Battle of the Ancre, was launched

18 The Battle of the Somme officially ended

28 A single aircraft carries out the first German daylight aeroplane raid on London

December

7 David Lloyd George became British Prime Minister

MUCK AND BULLETS

Of all the images synonymous with First World War those of the cratered landscapes and waterlogged trenches of the Western Front are amongst the most evocative. But what was life really like in the trenches for the men fighting for king and country?

"I had heard about the previous battles but I couldn't get there fast enough," wrote a young Irishman in 1915. "We had been brought up on the history of the Boer War and patriotism and heroics and everything, and we thought the war was going to be over before we could get there. However, in about half a minute all that had gone." Private Victor Packer of the Royal Irish Fusiliers had arrived at Ypres.

The British Army found itself embroiled in a kind of warfare it had never expected to experience and was entirely unprepared for. The war of brilliant manoeuvres and great set-piece battles for which it had practised, rapidly degenerated into a gruelling war of attrition. The consequence was that the men were forced to dig trenches deep into the soil of France and Belgium often in conditions that beggar belief, though this was not always the case.

It is a popular myth that the First World War was a series of battles fought by men simply going "over the top" into the face of withering enemy machine-gun fire. Whilst this did of course occur, the nature of trench warfare dictated that life was largely geared around simply "living". Troops would normally spend between four and six days in the trenches at the front line, whilst a greater proportion of their time was occupied by being held in reserve or resting away from the lines. When in the trenches, however, their lives were largely focussed on simply existing – eating, sleeping and working.

Fighting would occur as a result of taking part in offensives, trench raids or having to defend the lines against enemy activity. Bombardment or harassing fire from enemy activity was an ever-present danger. Whilst life in the trenches

BELOW: **Soldiers of 'A' Company, 11th Battalion, the Cheshire Regiment, occupy a captured German trench at Ovillers-la-Boisselle on the Somme during July 1916. In this photograph one man keeps sentry duty, looking over the parados and using an improvised fire step cut into the back slope of the trench, while his comrades rest.** (National Archives of the Netherlands)

for the British Tommy could be difficult and dangerous, much of his time was spent maintaining trenches and defences, ensuring that the rations arrived in a timely manner, coping with the extremes of weather, finding a reasonably comfortable place to sleep or performing "stand to" at first and last light. The "working day" in the trenches actually took place at night when the enemy could not see what the troops were doing; it was also normally much warmer during the day and therefore easier to sleep. Whilst serving in the trenches was undoubtedly dangerous, it was also largely exhausting, tedious and boring.

Food, the most basic of needs, was obviously one of the main concerns of the men, but all too often they were inadequately fed. The staple diet was "bully" beef, i.e. corned beef, and bread or biscuits, but by the winter of 1916 flour was in such short supply that bread was being made with dried ground turnips. The main food by that time was pea-soup with a few lumps of horsemeat. Kitchen staff became more and more dependent on local vegetables and also had to use weeds such as nettles in soups and stews. The conditions which the Army cooks had to work in made the production of decent food almost impossible. "The cookhouse was flooded, and most of the food was uneatable," remembered Robert Sherriff of the East Surrey Regiment. "There was nothing but sodden biscuits and cold stew. The cooks tried to supply bacon for breakfast, but the men complained that it smelled like dead men."

Even finding enough water to drink at times became a problem: "To get water we used to gouge out a hole at the side of the trench ➤➤

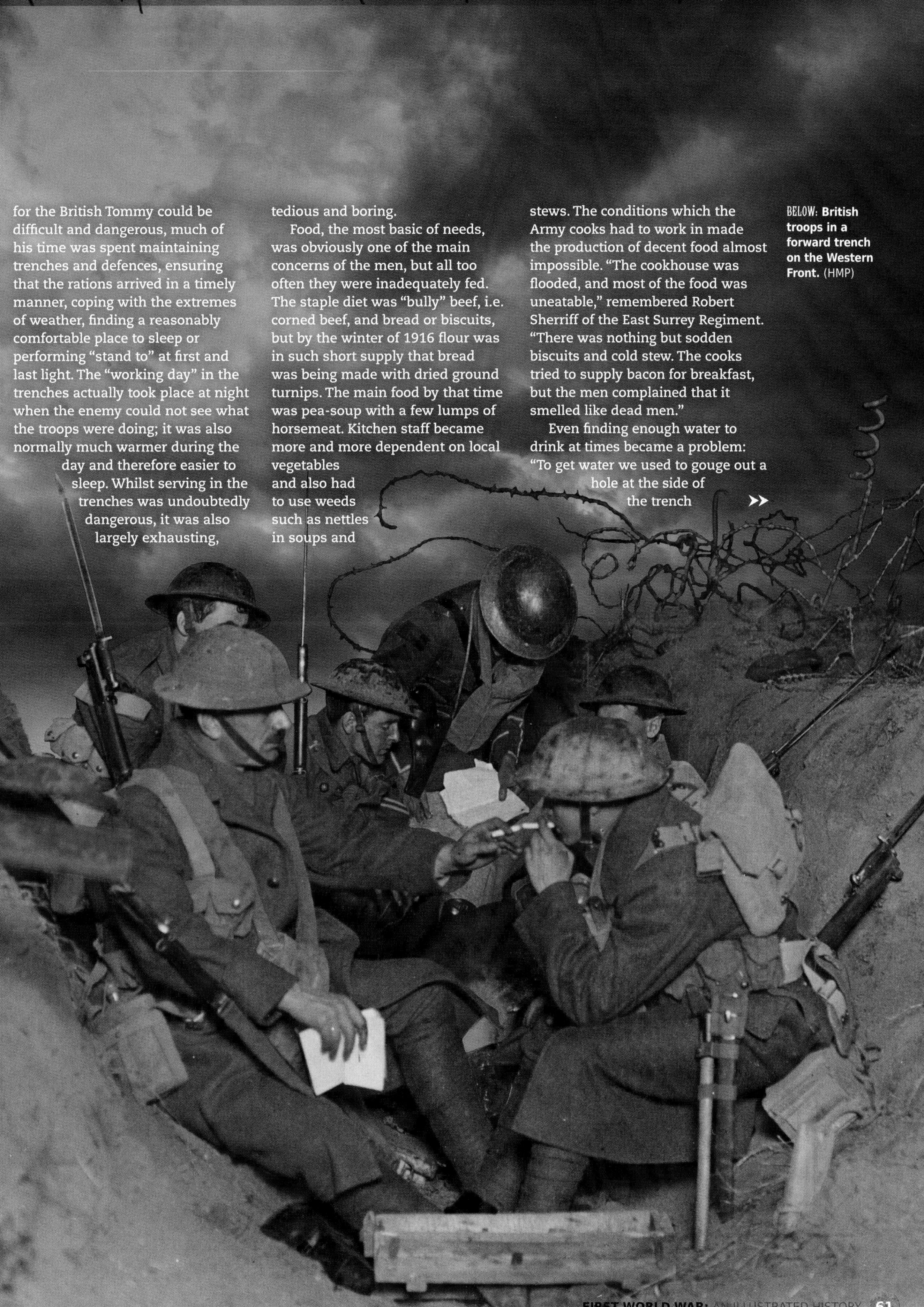

BELOW: **British troops in a forward trench on the Western Front.** (HMP)

BELOW: A shell explodes close to the parapet of a British trench. (HMP)

in the bottom of the wall of sandbags and put everything we could over it, a piece of cardboard or something or other, and in the morning that would be full of water," continued Private Packer, "but it would be teeming with all little black things floating around, but we found that if we boiled it we killed all this stuff and could drink it quite well."

Thousands of men living together in unhygienic conditions may have been unhealthy for humans but proved ideal for lice and fleas. "The lice were the size of grains of rice, each with its own bite, each with its own itch," recalled Harry Patch, who became famous before his death as the last survivor of the trenches. "When we could, we would run hot wax from a candle down the seams of our trousers, our vests – whatever you had – to burn the buggers out. It was the only thing to do. Eventually, when we got to Rouen, coming back, they took every stitch off us and gave us a suit of sterilised blue material. And the uniforms they took off, they burned them – to get rid of the lice."

It was another pest that Private Clifford Lane of 1st Battalion, Hertfordshire Regiment recalled: "Fleas, yes. Every man in the front line had fleas after about two or three weeks." Not only did the men get little rest from these insects, they also spread dysentery, typhus, cholera and pyrexia, more commonly known as Trench Fever.

Trench Fever was a serious problem – it is stated that of all the British soldiers who reported ill between 1915 and 1918, between one-fifth and one-third were suffering from the condition. Its onset was usually sudden with the victim suffering high fever, severe headache, pain on moving the eyeballs, and soreness of the muscles of the legs and back. Trench Fever affected men in Flanders, France, Italy, Salonika, Macedonia, Mesopotamia, and Egypt – three noted sufferers being the authors J.R.R. Tolkien, A.A. Milne and C.S. Lewis.

If the lice and the fleas were often the bane of the soldiers' existence in the trenches, it was another creature that they encountered which repelled them the most: "Then there were rats, of course, rats. You would not kill rats because you had no means of getting rid of them, as they would putrefy and it would be worse than if you left them alive. I think they lived in corpses, because they were huge, they were as big as cats, I am not exaggerating, some of them were as big as ordinary cats, horrible great things."

Corpses were another fact of life in the trenches. "The dead are lying all around you," one soldier explained after the war. "You could be talking to the fellow next to you when suddenly he'd be hit by a sniper and fall dead beside you. And there he'd stay for days."

Another soldier described finding a group of dead bodies while on patrol: "I saw some rats running from under the dead men's greatcoats, enormous rats, fat with human flesh. My heart pounded as we edged towards one of the bodies. His helmet had rolled off. The man displayed a grimacing face, stripped of flesh; the skull bare, the eyes devoured and from the yawning mouth leapt a rat."

Much of the land where the trenches were dug around Ypres was either clay or sand. The water could not pass through the clay and because the sand was on top, the trenches became waterlogged when it rained. The trenches were hard to dig and kept on collapsing in the waterlogged sand. As well as trenches, the artillery shells created a cratered landscape – larger craters were usually formed by the explosion of underground mines. The rain filled up the craters and then poured into the trenches.

With the men constantly wading in water a new condition, known as trench foot, became a major problem; some 20,000 casualties resulting from trench foot were reputed to have been suffered by the British Army alone by the close of 1914. This condition was described by Sergeant Harry Roberts, of the Lancashire Fusiliers:

"Your feet swell to two or three times their normal size and go completely dead. You could stick a bayonet into them and not feel a thing. If you are fortunate enough not to lose your feet and the swelling begins to go down. It is then that the intolerable, indescribable agony begins. I have heard men cry and even scream with the pain and many had

The Rum Ration

This cartoon, entitled "The Spirit of our Troops is Excellent", was drawn by the famous First World War humourist and cartoonist Captain (Charles) Bruce Bairnsfather. The rum ration was a vital part of the soldier's everyday life in the trenches, as Canadian infantryman Ralph Bell once noted: "When the days shorten, and the rain never ceases; when the sky is ever grey, the nights chill, and trenches thigh deep in mud and water; when the front is altogether a beastly place, in fact, we have one consolation. It comes in gallon jars, marked simply SRD." SRD stood for "Services Rum Diluted" or "Special Rum Distribution" (there are differences of opinion on what the letters really stood for), which, as the troops would often remark, really meant "Seldom Reaches Destination". (HMP)

ABOVE: Troops in the front line use a trench periscope to monitor the enemy's trenches. The nature of trench warfare led to the use of specialised equipment such as the trench periscope, which could be improvised locally, issued, or even privately purchased. (HMP)

MIDDLE LEFT: Creature comforts, such as they were, could be found by the more resourceful soldiers - objects such as the item of furniture seen here being retrieved from shell-damaged buildings near the front. (HMP)

to have their feet and legs amputated."

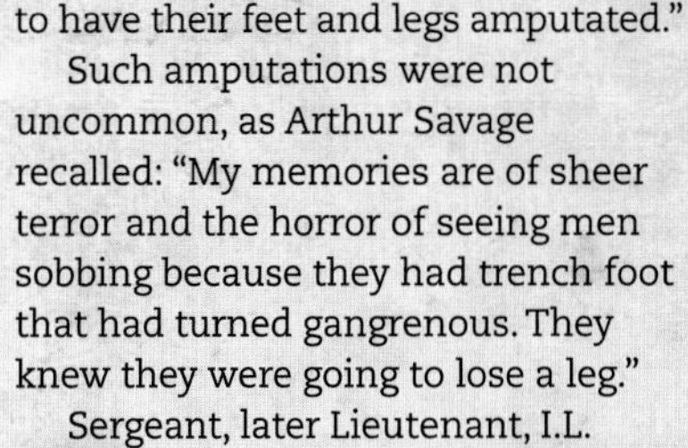

Such amputations were not uncommon, as Arthur Savage recalled: "My memories are of sheer terror and the horror of seeing men sobbing because they had trench foot that had turned gangrenous. They knew they were going to lose a leg."

Sergeant, later Lieutenant, I.L. "Dick" Read, described conditions in the winter of 1915/16: "Every now and then, huge slices of the trench sides slipped down to the bottom, loosened by the alternate frosts, rains and thaws of the previous few days. But worse was to come. The heavy rain and the thaw had flooded the trench floor, and in places the duckboard sump covers had floated off. Where earth from the sides had fallen, we unsuspecting unfortunates blundered in up to the waist ... the average depth of the morass [was] knee high, while every few minutes one of us blundered into a sump and had to be rescued by his mates."

In such circumstances, Dick Read concluded, it was simply impossible to fight. "What a war!" he remarked. "In that moment the tremendous truth dawned on us: that men find it next to impossible to hate or fight when they are cold and wet. Someone echoed our feelings with, 'what are we fighting for, anyhow?' Truth to tell, just then we had forgotten."

One phrase which has been handed down to us by veterans of the trenches, one used so many times then and since, describes life in the trenches simply and succinctly: "We were up to our necks in muck and bullets." And all too often they were.

LEFT: British troops pictured during a period of rest away from the trenches. (HMP)

The Battle of Ju

For two years the British and German navies had sought a major fleet action which would change the nature of the war at sea – one great battle to decide who would command the oceans. When that battle finally came, in the summer of 1916, it proved to be as deadly as everyone feared. Its outcome, however, was not as anyone had predicted.

It was almost by coincidence that the Royal Navy's Grand Fleet and the German High Seas Fleet encountered each other in the North Sea off Jutland on 31 May 1916. It transpired that the opposing navies had both planned major operations at the same period, with Admiral Sir John Jellicoe hoping to tempt the Germans into the open sea by sending a pair of light cruiser squadrons through the Kattegat channel between Denmark and Sweden, whilst Admiral Reingard Scheer sought the same response from the British by using his battlecruisers to bombard Britain's east coast. Both admirals hoped to lure the enemy into a trap.

What Scheer did not know, however, was that his signals were being intercepted by the Admiralty. Those signals indicated that the High Seas Fleet was preparing to put to sea. With the Grand Fleet already gearing up for action the opportunity to engage the High Seas Fleet seemed to have arrived at last. The scene was set for the greatest sea battle of the First World War and the largest fleet action since Trafalgar.

Scheer had hoped to be able to draw the Grand Fleet towards his submarines which would be lying in wait and into a newly-sown minefield. In the ensuing confusion this would cause, the battlecruisers of Admiral Hipper would engage the British who, it was expected, would give chase only to find themselves steaming onto the guns of the High Seas battleships. The Grand Fleet, though, would be out in force, a force far stronger than that of Admiral Scheer.

As the Grand Fleet left Scapa Flow, young Midshipman John Croome was watching from HMS *Indomitable*: "The grey monsters wheeled in succession round us and followed out to sea with that uncanny precision and silent majesty which marks the departure to sea of a perfectly trained fleet ... A more powerful exhibition of majestic strength and efficiency devised solely for the utter destruction of the enemy it would be hard to imagine."

Though the Admiralty had no idea of the scale or scope of the German operation, thanks to the intelligence derived from the intercepted signals the Grand Fleet was at sea before the High Seas Fleet and the German minefields and submarines proved ineffective. The Grand Fleet sailed into the open sea having been almost entirely untroubled by what was intended to be the first German battle line. Both great battle fleets were out on the highs seas and heading towards each other.

Shortly after 14.10 hours on 31 May 1916, HMS *Galatea* of the 1st Light Cruiser Squadron sighted two ships on the horizon and set off at full speed to investigate. At 14.28 *Galatea* opened fire. The Battle of Jutland had begun.

The news of the presence of the Germans was relayed to Admiral Beatty on the First Battlecruiser Squadron's flagship HMS *Lion* and he ordered his ships, along with the Second Battlecruiser Squadron, to follow. Unknown to Beatty, the signal which should have been passed onto the super-dreadnoughts of the Fifth Battle Squadron was not seen amidst the thick smoke emitted by the battlecruisers. With the passing of every minute the two parts of Beatty's

HMS *Lion* leading the battlecruisers during the Battle of Jutland. At one point in the battle, a heavy shell struck HMS *Lion's* Q-turret, entered the gun-house, burst over the left gun, and killed nearly the whole of the guns' crews. It was only the presence of mind and devotion of the officer of the turret, Major F.J.W. Harvey RMLI, that saved the flagship from sudden destruction; in spite of both his legs being shot off he was able to pass the word down to close the magazine doors and flood the magazines. Harvey thus prevented the fire which had started from reaching the ammunition, and so saved the ship, an action for which he was posthumously awarded the Victoria Cross. By the end of the battle, HMS *Lion* had been hit a total of fourteen times and suffered ninety-nine dead and fifty-one wounded during the battle. She fired 326 rounds from her main guns, but can only be credited with four hits on *Lützow* and one on *Derfflinger*. (HMP)

tland

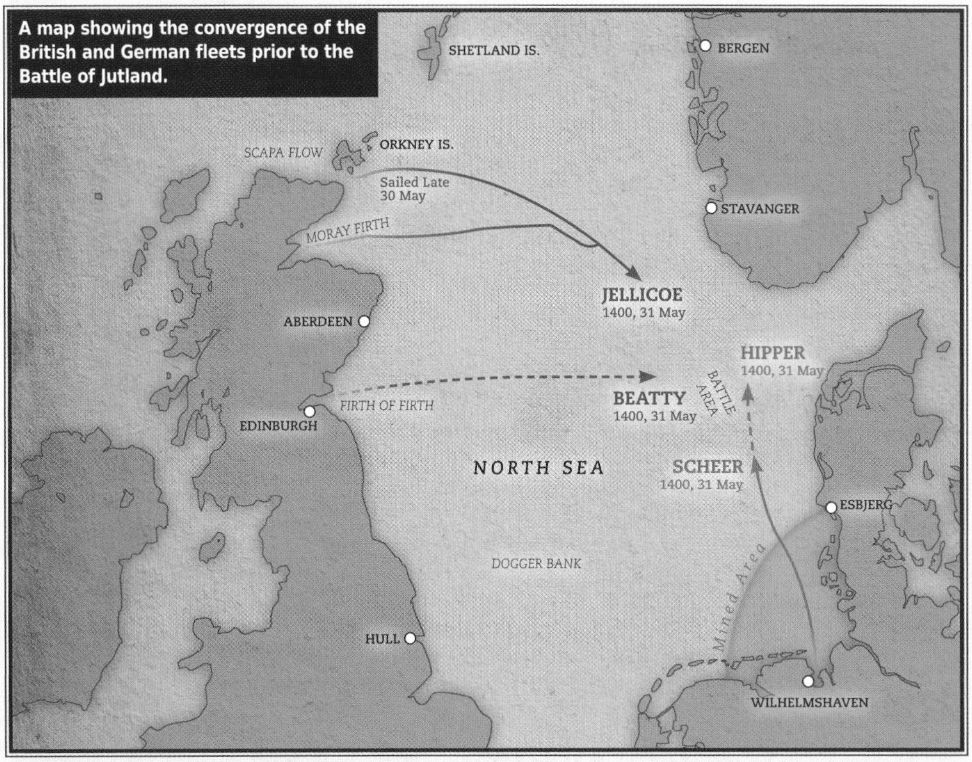

force were steaming away from each other. It was a full seven minutes before Rear Admiral Sir Hugh Evan-Thomas realised what had happened and turned the battleships to the south-west by which time he was ten miles astern of Beatty.

At 14.35 hours another signal from HMS *Galatea* indicated the sighting of a considerable number of enemy ships. The opposing squadrons, now certain to be engaged, began forming up, allowing Evan-Thomas to close the gap.

The British battlecruisers with their 13.5-inch guns could easily out-range the 11- and 12-inch guns of the German battleships. Yet the British ships did not open fire when the German ships came into range because of deficiencies in their range-finding equipment which over-estimated the distance between the opposing ships. As a result, it was the Germans that opened fire first.

"It seemed as if we were never going to open fire," reported Midshipman Gordon Eady, in the battlecruiser HMS *New Zealand*. "When our first salvo at last did go off it was speeded on its way with a huge sigh of relief."

Evan-Thomas's super-dreadnoughts *Barham*, *Valiant*, *Warspite* and *Malaya*, with their 15-inch guns, then began to join in the action. Soon, too, the destroyers of both sides added their torpedoes to the battle. Though they caused the big ships to manoeuvre to avoid the torpedoes, no harm was done to the battlecruisers and dreadnoughts. The opposing destroyers met in what was described as "a spirited little action".

Already it had been noted that whilst the shells of the British ships fell in lines, the Germans' landed in clusters. This meant that more British shells found their mark, but when a cluster of German shells did strike home, the effect was devastating. "In that case a rain of shells, falling with a steep angle of descent, practically wiped out whatever was in its course," noted one British officer. >>

A map showing the convergence of the British and German fleets prior to the Battle of Jutland.

MIDDLE RIGHT: **Admiral John Jellicoe (5 December 1859 - 20 November 1935), pictured wearing the uniform of Admiral of the Fleet, the rank he attained in 1919.** (US Library of Congress)

BELOW RIGHT: **Damage caused to a British light cruiser at Jutland. Unfortunately, it is not known which of the light cruisers damaged in the action this is. Two, *Black Prince* and *Tipperary*, were sunk, whilst HMS *Southampton* was the light cruiser hit the most times - with eighteen shells striking her.** (HMP)

BOTTOM: **HMS *Royal Oak*, HMS *Acasta*, HMS *Benbow*, HMS *Superb* and HMS *Canada* in action during the battle. The latter had originally been built for the Chilean Navy, but was purchased by the British on the outbreak of war in 1914. During the Battle of Jutland, HMS *Canada* fired forty-two rounds from her 14-inch guns and 109 6-inch shells during the battle. She suffered no hits or casualties.** (HMP)

The Death of a Queen

The funeral pyre of HMS *Queen Mary* during the Battle of Jutland. After a German salvo had hit this battlecruiser amidships, her bows plunged down and her stern rose high in the air. A few moments later witnesses reported that her propellers were still slowly turning. A few minutes later there was nothing to be seen but this pillar of smoke rising hundreds of feet into the air. All but nine of her 1,266 crew were lost - two of the survivors were picked up by German ships. Her wreck was discovered in 1991 and rests partly upside-down, on sand, sixty metres down. Much of her equipment is reported to be scattered about the wreck. (HMP)

"*Indefatigable* [battlecruiser] was the first to be struck by such an overwhelming and irresistible mass of destructive fire."

The German ships had the advantage of the circumstances in that the wind and clouds of smoke from the guns and the funnels, compounded by variable mists, frequently obscured them from the British ships which, with the sun behind them, showed up dark against the afternoon light. This meant that at times the British gunners had to pause whilst the Germans could continue to load and fire.

Beatty's position became even more precarious when the main body of Scheer's High Seas Fleet appeared – sixteen huge battleships. It must have seemed to the German commander that the long-desired opportunity to catch a significant proportion of the Grand Fleet had finally arrived.

The battlecruisers were no match for the German battleships. Everything now depended on the Fifth Battle Squadron. HMS *Barham* began to take heavy fire – as did the other dreadnoughts. But if Scheer thought that his moment had come, he was soon to realise that he had been deceived, as Beatty turned to the north towards Jellicoe's waiting battle squadrons. At 18.30 hours, to the astonishment of the Germans, the two main battle fleets came within range. "Suddenly we were practically surrounded," remarked *Obermatrose* Blessman in the German dreadnought SMS *Posen*. "The entire British fleet had suddenly appeared. We were in a tight corner."

H.E. Reid, was a Gunner on No.2 Turret of the dreadnought HMS *Agincourt*, part of the First Battle

Squadron: "A great flash and terrific crash and our two 12-inch guns recoil as their projectiles fly towards the object of interest. Everyone grins as up comes a fresh projectile for each gun. I don't know what was inscribed on the one for the right gun as I am on the left one and this was marked 'Piece be Steel'. These were immediately rammed home by the electric rammer and down again darts the cage for more.

"What with the noisy rammer, recoiling guns and tipping of these huge shells into loading trays, and other guns going off, the din was terrible. Away goes [the] fire bell again and before it finishes its single 'Ding', the guns crash back and go forward into place to the accompaniment of the shrieking air-blast which blows away all burning debris. By the time the gun regains its position, everything is ready again."

Damage to SMS *Derfflinger* pictured after the Battle of Jutland. The ship was involved in the sinking of two British battlecruisers at Jutland; *Derfflinger* and *Seydlitz* destroyed HMS *Queen Mary*, and *Lützow* assisted her elder sister in the sinking of HMS *Invincible*. During the course of the battle, *Derfflinger* was hit seventeen times by heavy calibre shells and nine times by secondary guns. She was in dock for repairs until 15 October 1916. *Derfflinger* fired 385 shells from her main battery, another 235 rounds from her secondary guns, and one torpedo. Her crew suffered 157 men killed and another twenty-six men wounded; this was the highest casualty rate on any ship not sunk during the battle. Because of her stalwart resistance at Jutland, the British nicknamed her "Iron Dog". (Bundesarchiv, Bild 134-B2100/CC-BY-SA)

Scheer responded immediately with an expertly executed 180 degree turn. Now began a desperate race, with the German ships under heavy fire from the British dreadnoughts. Scheer knew that he had to preserve his capital ships. He used his destroyers and battlecruisers to hold up the British battleships, knowing that he was sacrificing them to the enemy.

Nightfall brought a close to the battle for the day. Throughout the night there were occasional contacts but Jellicoe waited for daybreak before seeking to re-new battle. By that time, however, Scheer was too far away. The great battle which both sides had sought, believing that they could change the war, had ended inconclusively.

The Royal Navy lost fourteen ships, including three battlecruisers, and suffered 7,000 casualties compared to eleven, mostly lighter ships, lost by the Germans who suffered far fewer casualties.

Both sides claimed victory, but it was the Grand Fleet which still cruised the North Sea, never to be challenged again by Scheer's ships again.

ABOVE: **The bow and stern of HMS *Invincible* sticking out of the water as the battlecruiser sinks. The destroyer HMS *Badger* is desperately searching for survivors. *Invincible*'s remains were first located in 1919 and she was found to have been blown in half by the explosion. Pieces of the wreckage rest on a sandy bottom near each other, the stern right-side up and the bow upside-down. The roof of the aft 12-inch turret is missing, the guns still loaded.** (HMP)

THE WAR IN TH

FAR RIGHT: **The first British pilot to land in France in 1914 was Major Hubert Dunsterville Harvey-Kelly DSO, Royal Irish Regiment, attached to the Royal Flying Corps. He landed his Royal Aircraft Factory BE.2c at Amiens - he can be seen in this image, taken shortly before his departure for France, lying on the ground next to the haystack studying a map. Harvey-Kelly was killed on 29 April 1917, the 25th victim of the German Ace *Leutnant* Kurt Wolff of *Jasta* 11.** (HMP)

RIGHT: **William Rhodes-Moorhouse, Royal Flying Corps was the first airman to be awarded the Victoria Cross.** (Courtesy of Steve Snelling)

The first-ever airplane had taken to the skies, and had flown only 120 feet, just eleven years before the start of the First World War. By the end of the conflict, the first flimsy unarmed craft that took to the air in 1914 had evolved into fast fighters and heavy bombers, and an entirely new form of warfare had been born.

In August 1914 four squadrons of the Royal Flying Corps crossed the Channel to support the British Expeditionary Force. The RFC had just five squadrons in total, their purpose was to observe enemy troops movements and direct artillery fire. In addition to the Royal Flying Corps, there was a Royal Naval Air Service which started the war with ninety-three aircraft, six airships, and two balloons. As well as providing coastal defence and carrier-borne aircraft, the RNAS also sent fighter squadrons to the Western Front and the Middle East.

Reconnaissance was the primary role of aircraft in the early days of the war. The events of 22 August 1914, would show how important aerial observation would become. On this date, Captain L.E.O Charlton and Lieutenant V.H.N. Wadham (who was piloting the aircraft, a Bleriot two-seater of 3 Squadron) returned from a reconnaissance mission and provided vital information that revealed that British troops were in danger of being surrounded by the German II Corps. That this was dangerous work was evidenced by the fact that their aircraft had been repeatedly hit by fire from the ground – and which had come from both sides!

Another British pilot described the risks that the early military aviators faced: "As soon as I was in range [of the enemy positions] the Germans opened on my machine, and then during the whole reconnaissance, which consisted of circling about a small area, they didn't give me a moment's peace. I had shells bursting around my machine the whole time, simultaneously flashes of flame and loud bangs, sometimes on one side and then the other, below the machine, above it, behind it and in front, and some of them bumped the machine about unpleasantly. It was thoroughly uncomfortable."

Firing at enemy aircraft flying over your positions was one thing, but the idea of opposing aircraft shooting at each other had scarcely been considered. However, as it was obviously desirable to prevent enemy aircraft from observing the British positions, the pilots began to challenge the enemy's flying machines. As a result on 26 August 1914, three RFC 'planes forced a German aircraft to the ground by simply flying closer and closer to it until the pilot had to either land or risk collision. During the engagement one of the British pilots fired a shot from his revolver at his German counterpart, though he missed

Along with reconnaissance duties, the two other main functions of the RFC's short range reconnaissance squadrons had emerged by March 1915 – all of which gained importance following the development of trench warfare. The first was photographic reconnaissance, building up a complete mosaic map of the enemy's trench systems, whilst the second was spotting for the artillery.

Increasingly, as the weeks passed, greater endeavours were made to prevent the incursions of enemy aircraft, by throwing grenades at them, dropping bombs on them from the open cockpits and even firing rifles. It was not long before

"Despite his injuries, Rhodes-Moorhouse pressed on with his attack ... and in so doing achieved the first low-level bombing raid in history."

AIR

machine-guns were fitted to the aircraft, either for the observers or pilots to fire. Then, in April 1915, the introduction of a mechanism, known as interrupter gear, allowed forward-facing machine-guns to fire through the turning blades of a propeller. Aerial combat had become a reality.

Though it was a French pilot, Roland Garros, who had built a device that would enable forward-firing machine-guns, it was the Dutchman Anthony Fokker who perfected the interrupter gear that revolutionised aerial warfare. The aircraft Fokker produced for the German air force, known until 1916 as *Die Fliegertruppen des deutschen Kaiserreiches* (Imperial German Flying Corps), ruled the skies towards the end of 1915 and much of 1916. It was a Fokker Dr.I triplane which was flown by probably the most famous fighter pilot of all time, Manfred Albrecht Freiherr von Richthofen – the Red Baron. As the leader of *Jagdstaffel* 11 and then *Jagdgeschwader* 1, Richthofen accounted for nineteen out of his eighty victories against Allied aircraft flying his red Fokker.

Richthofen was a fighter 'Ace', a term which owes its origin to the French who, pre-war, had referred to a sportsman who excelled at his sport as an 'Ace'. This was taken up by the French Air Force, the »

Aerial Photography

The use of aircraft in a military role soon led to the development of numerous roles - one of the earliest of which was the gathering of aerial photographs - as evidenced by this image, taken at a low altitude, of French soldiers during an attack on the Somme front. On 1 April 1918 (the first day of the RAF), for example, no less than 1,047 pictures were taken, the plates brought back, images produced and then sent by despatch riders to the command HQs. (HMP)

BELOW: **An example of an Airco DH.2. Designed by Geoffrey de Havilland, the DH.2 was the first effectively armed British single-seat fighter, though because of its sensitive controls, and at a time when service training for pilots in the RFC was very poor, it initially had a high accident rate, gaining it the nickname "The Spinning Incinerator". Fourteen Aces scored five or more aerial victories using the type.** (HMP)

A contemporary, highly stylised illustration depicting Second Lieutenant William Rhodes-Moorhouse during his attack on the town of Courtrai, 26 April 1915. (HMP)

The weapons fitted to this Royal Aircraft Factory S.E.5 are far removed from those experienced by the RFC's airmen in 1914. The S.E.5 was inherently stable, making it an excellent gunnery platform – it was also quite manoeuvrable and one of the fastest aircraft of the war at 138 mph. The S.E.5 had one synchronised .303-inch Vickers machine-gun and a wing-mounted Lewis gun on a Foster mounting, which enabled the pilot to fire at an enemy aircraft from below as well as forward. (HMP)

A "Professional" Airman

Major James McCudden VC, DSO & Bar, MC & Bar, MM pictured in the cockpit of one of his aircraft. McCudden is considered to have been one of the first truly "professional" airmen, a pilot who applied a scientific approach to air combat. McCudden took great pains over his guns, aircraft, and tactics, dismissing choices of last resort such as deliberately crashing an aircraft into the enemy. A remarkable airman, McCudden received more medals for gallantry than any other airman of British nationality serving in the First World War, and became the seventh highest scoring Ace of all nationalities prior to his death in an accident in July 1918. His story is all the more remarkable as he had been promoted through the ranks, from Air Mechanic to Major. (HMP)

Armée de l'Air, and was granted to a pilot who destroyed five or more enemy aircraft. The first fighter Ace was, therefore, a French pilot called Euguene Gilbert, who amassed his score of five before being shot down himself in the summer of 1915. The Germans also adopted the term, though they raised the benchmark to ten 'kills'.

The British refused to single out individual pilots for such special attention, with Sir Hugh Trenchard, the Commander-in-Chief of the Royal Flying Corps, believing that it was inappropriate to draw comparisons between pilots. Later Trenchard would relent and eventually the Royal Flying Corps and later the Royal Air Force could count a total of 784 men who had notched up at least five victories.

"Dog-fights", as the aerial duels between the fighter pilots became known, could be bewildering affairs, as W.E. Johns, the creator of the Biggles stories, once explained: "The speed at which a dog-fight took place and the amazing manner in which machines appeared from nowhere, and could disappear, apparently into thin air, was so bewildering as to baffle description. It is beyond my ability to convey adequately the sensation of being one of ten or a dozen machines, zooming, whirling and diving among a maze of pencil-lines that marked the track of tracer bullets."

The value of aircraft, and the increased efforts at destroying enemy machines, led to a very rapid demand for pilots and observers. The Germans, who started the war with a superiority in aircraft, had, by the end of 1915, established twenty operational air training schools, leaving Britain and France to quickly try and catch up.

Though for the aircraft on the Western Front, observing the enemy's movements on the ground and directing the artillery's fall of shot remained their primary purpose (as well as preventing the enemy

BELOW: Sopwith Camels of 203 Squadron lined up at Izel le Hameau on 10 July 1918, for a review by HM King George V. The Camel was the first British fighter to mount twin forward-firing machine-guns side-by-side, a natural arrangement that soon became standard for the RAF. Alongside the SE5a, the Camel helped the Allies address the balance of the air war over the Western Front and was credited with shooting down 1,294 enemy aircraft - more than any other fighter, of any nation, between 1914 and 1918. (HMP)

from doing the same), increasingly aircraft were used to bomb positions on the ground. At first this was not an entirely imprecise science as an observer with 12 Squadron described: "The only bombing that was done usefully was against lines of communication, such as railways and bridges. You used to try and get as low as you possibly could so that you could release your bombs practically over the target. The technique was to take a sight on your target as you glided down towards it. Then, when you thought you were low enough, you used to release your bombs. That was the only technique that we followed. You just used eye-sight, that's all. We had no bombing sights. There was no accuracy at all, as a consequence."

The first air Victoria Cross of the war was awarded for a bombing operation. This took place on 26 April 1915, when Lieutenant William Rhodes-Moorhouse set out to attack the railway station at Coutrai, some thirty-five miles behind enemy lines, with a single 100lb bomb. He was subjected to heavy machine-gun fire as soon as he approached the German lines. His BE2 aircraft was hit and Rhodes-Moorhouse was seriously wounded. Despite his injuries, Rhodes-Moorhouse pressed on with his attack. Flying lower and lower as he approached his target, he reached Courtrai and dropped his bomb, and in so doing achieved the first low-level bombing raid in history.

Bombing was also another way in which the enemy could be attacked, but this had developed into a complex operation as Sergeant Sidney Attwater explained: "The bombsights were a crude affair. You set the bombsight on your own aerodrome, for height, wind, speed, on sliding graduations. You sighted your target through one sight, set a stopwatch going, and flew on until the target appeared in the next one. You stopped your watch and set the scale to the seconds, and that was it. I know I got frostbite and so did many others, setting that watch without gauntlets on."

As the important of bombing the enemy increased, specialist aircraft were built by both the British and the Germans. Instead of the solo fighters nipping across No Man's Land to dropping a couple of 20lb bombs, as the war progressed huge bombers capable of carrying 2,700lbs of bombs over 1,300 miles were flying in formation to attack towns and cities.

With the increasing sophistication of air operations, and the enormous growth in the numbers of aircraft in use, it was as early as 1916 that the first suggestions of merging the UK's two independent air arms, the Royal Flying Corps and the Royal Naval Air Service, were made. In an attempt to resolve the matter, the then British Prime Minister, Lloyd George, turned to a senior South African officer, General Jan Christiaan Smuts. Smuts had arrived in Britain early in 1917 having been invited to join the Imperial War Cabinet and the War Policy Committee. As well as undertaking these roles, Smuts soon found himself heading a government committee (whose only other member was the Prime Minister) which was charged with examining both air defence arrangements and air organization. One of the committee's most important advisers was Sir David Henderson, the first commander of the RFC in France and, since 1915, the Director-General of Military Aeronautics.

Between them, Smuts and Henderson shaped the course of British military aviation. In two reports, published on 19 July and 17 August 1917, Smuts set out his recommendations which called for the formation of an Air Ministry and Air Staff to amalgamate the RFC and the RNAS into a new Air Service that was independent of the Army and the Royal Navy. This new service was the Royal Air Force.

At the same, Smuts recognised the future of aerial warfare: "There is absolutely no limit to the scale of its future independent war use. And the day may not be far off when aerial operations with their devastation of enemy lands and destruction of industries and populous centres on a vast scale may become one of the principal operations of war, to which the older forms of military and naval operations may become secondary and subordinate."

From those early days of unarmed, slow observation machines, by the end of 1918 the RAF had 4,000 combat aircraft and 114,000 personnel. No-one doubted that in a future war whoever dominated the skies would control the battlefield. A new form of warfare had been born.

BELOW LEFT: **Pilots and personnel of a typical late-war RFC/RAF squadron, more specifically 22 Squadron, who were pictured at Vert Galant on 1 April 1918 - the first day of the RAF.** (US Library of Congress)

ABOVE: **A group of five decorated Australian Flying Corps officers in front of an Avro 504. The Avro 504 made the first organized bombing raid in history when, on 21 November 1914, three RNAS machines (Nos. 873, 874 and 875) attacked the airship sheds at Friedrichshafen.** (Courtesy of the Australian War Memorial, DAAV00160)

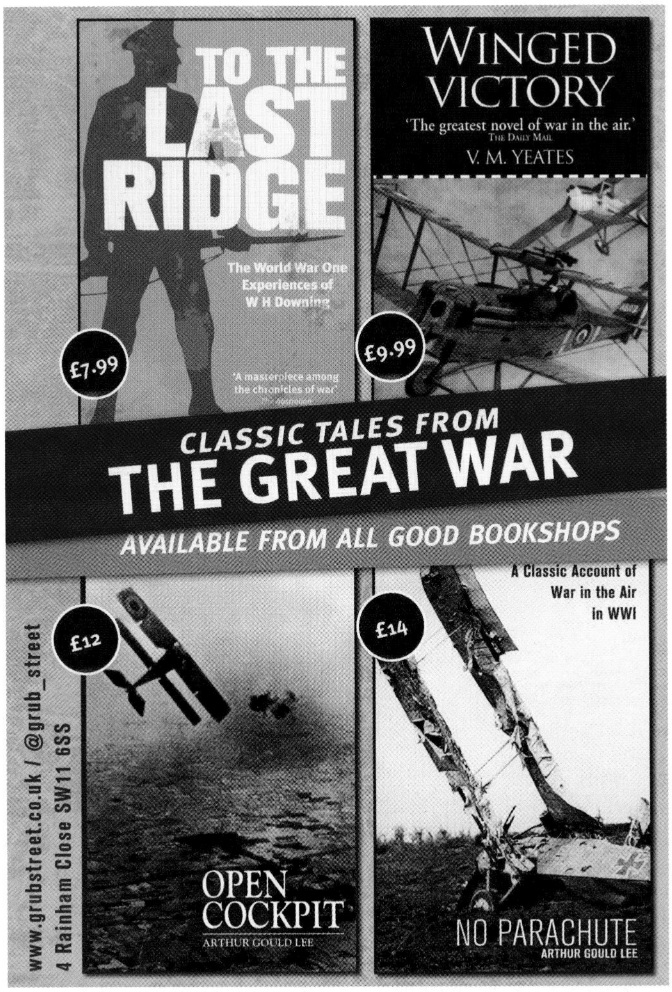

The Battle of the

In the British imagination the Battle of the Somme is seen as one of unparalleled slaughter for negligible gain. Whilst losses, particularly on the first day of the battle, were unprecedented, ultimately it helped erode the Germans' capacity, and will, to continue a war they had begun to realize they could not win.

Though the British Expeditionary Force had helped stall the German invasion of France and the Low Countries in 1914, and had stopped the attempt at outflanking the Allies at Ypres, the Germans still saw the French Army as the greater threat to its chances of victory. The people of Britain and its Empire however, had rallied to the call to arms, and a 'New' Army had been formed. Supported by the industrial might of the 'Workshop of the World', the New Army would astonish the Germans and its baptism of fire would be on the Somme.

The idea behind the Somme offensive was spelt out by Sir Douglas Haig as having three objectives. These were to relieve pressure on the French who were barely able to hold the Germans attacking Verdun; to assist the Russians by stopping any further transfer of German troops from the Western front; and finally to wear down the strength of the German forces.

The Somme was the first battle to involve substantial numbers of battalions from Lord Kitchener's New Army. Included were many of the famous Pals battalions that had formed in response to Kitchener's call for volunteers in August 1914. The only non-UK troops attacking on the British sector on 1 July 1916, were units from Bermuda and Newfoundland.

In the weeks preceding the opening of the battle, every measure that could be conceived of was undertaken to ensure success when the infantry attacked. Previous experience had demonstrated that attacks against prepared positions were unlikely to succeed. Haig, therefore, demanded that the German trenches, dugouts, strong points and barbed wire should be destroyed by artillery fire before the infantry attacked.

The preliminary bombardment by 1,437 Allied guns began on 24 June 1916 and continued on and off until the morning of Saturday, 1 July 1916.

"I watched with mixed feeling the lads mount the firestep and, when at 07.30 the barrage lifted, spring up the ladders on to the parapet – many sliding back immediately they had reached the top, killed or wounded," wrote Signaller Dudley Menaud-Lissenburg, 97th Battery, 147th Brigade, Royal Field Artillery in the 29th Division. "Coolly, it seemed, the survivors worked their way through our barbed wire in face of fierce shell and machine-gun fire, leaving many of their pals on the wire, dead. On they went up the long incline in perfect order, dropping to the ground every now and then, as though on an exercise on Salisbury Plain. The line thinned as men fell, but never faltered."

As the British and French divisions marched across No Man's Land, they found that not only had the preliminary artillery bombardment failed to cut the enemy's barbed wire entanglements in many places but also that the deep German dugouts were generally resistant to shell fire. As a result, as soon as the barrage lifted, the Germans rushed up to their positions and manned their machine-guns. Rather than the easy victory they were told to expect, the men were cut to pieces.

"There was no lingering about when zero hour came," recalled Private George Morgan, 1st Bradford Pals (16th Battalion, West Yorkshire Regiment). "Our platoon officer blew his whistle and he was the first up the scaling ladder, with his revolver in one hand and a cigarette in the other. 'Come on, boys,' he said, and up he went. We went up after him one at a time. I never saw the officer again."

"Our platoon officer blew his whistle and he was the first up the scaling ladder, with his revolver in one hand and a cigarette in the other."

Somme

One of the many memorials on the Somme is this one which commemorates the men of the 12th (Service) Battalion Gloucestershire Regiment, "Bristol's Own", who gave their lives during the fighting at Longueval and Guillemont between July and September 1916. In the background is High Wood, a small forest near Bazentin-le-Petit in the Somme département of northern France which was the scene of intense fighting for two months during the Battle of the Somme from 14 July to 15 September 1916. (HMP)

This image, purported to show British soldiers moving forward through wire at the start of the Battle of the Somme, 1 July 1916, is a still from the British film *The Battle of the Somme*. Despite now being one of the most recognizable images from the First World War, this scene is generally considered to have been staged for the camera, possibly at a Trench Mortar School well behind the lines. Nevertheless, it is regularly used to represent British troops "going over the top" at the start of an assault on the Western Front. (Imperial War Museum; Q70168)

"The enemy stood upon their parapet and waved our men to come on and picked them off with rifle fire," records the War Diary of the 16th Battalion Northumberland Fusiliers. "The enemy's fire was so intense that the advance was checked and the waves, or what was left of them, were forced to lie down."

Few of the objectives set for the first day of the battle were achieved and the cost of those few gains was utterly unprecedented. Of the 141 days that comprise the Battle of the Somme, it is the opening day of the offensive that is often seen to most represent the sacrifice of a generation of young men. Before midnight on that fateful first Saturday in July 1916 – almost the middle day of the »

BELOW: **Men of the 103rd (Tyneside Irish) Brigade, part of the 34th Division, pictured advancing from the Tara-Usna Line to attack the village of La Boisselle on the morning of 1 July 1916. The 34th Division suffered heavier losses than any other British division that day.** (HMP)

RIGHT: **An illustration showing British troops storming the Schwaben Redoubt on the Somme. First assaulted on 1 July 1916, a permanent Allied lodgment in this German defensive position was not achieved until the attacks of 26 to 28 September 1916. The Schwaben Redoubt consisted of a mass of gun emplacements, trenches and tunnels, a warren of defensive works which helped anchor the German line on the Somme until late 1916.** (HMP)

RIGHT: **In the collection of the Green Howards Museum, Richmond, this is the helmet worn by Second Lieutenant Donald Bell at the time of his death. Bell was awarded the Victoria Cross for his actions on 5 July 1916 at Horseshoe Trench on the Somme. When an attack was held up, Bell rushed across the open ground "under very heavy fire and attacked the machine-gun, shooting the firer with his revolver, and destroying gun and personnel with bombs". Five days later, whilst wearing this helmet, Bell was killed in action.**

middle year of the First World War – the British Army suffered no less than 57,470 casualties – a number that comprised 585 prisoners of war, 2,152 men missing, 35,493 wounded and a staggering 19,240 dead. Never before or since has Britain experienced loss on such a scale.

Even then, however, the chaos and confusion of that day meant that it was some time before those behind the front line appreciated the true scale of the disaster. At 19.30 hours on 1 July, General Sir Henry Rawlinson, commander of the British Fourth Army, considered his casualties to be around 16,000. The figure rose to 40,000 by 3 July and the final tally of 60,000 was not determined until 6 July (although exact figures were still not reached for some time).

Haig, though, intended to continue the battle. The French had suffered terribly at Verdun, losing on average 35,000 men for every month of that battle, which had been raging since February of 1916. With the young men of France being slaughtered Britain could not be seen to back down after one bad day.

The following morning, Haig said that "the total casualties are estimated at over 40,000 to date. This cannot be considered severe in view of the numbers engaged, and the length of front attacked." The reasons for the battle, in Haig's eyes, were still valid. He intended to wear the Germans down, regardless of how many British lives it cost. General Sir Henry Rawlinson, General Officer Commanding the British Fourth Army, was in agreement with Haig, stating that "A large part of the German reserve have now been drawn in and it is essential to keep up the pressure and wear out the defence. It is also necessary to secure, as early as possible, all important practical tactical points still in the possession of the Germans in their front line system and intermediate line, with a view to an ultimate attack on the German Second Line." So, after a brief period of consolidation, the offensive on the Somme continued.

For the next ten days the Allies kept up the pressure on the Germans. By 13 July the French had made considerable advances, pushing the Germans back as much as six miles. It was a different story on the British front, where the Fourth Army had no significant progress, but had lost a further 25,000 men.

The next major attack, on 14 July against the German positions on the Bazentin Ridge, was conducted in a different fashion to that of 1 July. Rather than announce the start of the attack with a prolonged bombardment, this time the attempt was to take the Germans by surprise with a short bombardment and a sudden assault. This time nearly all the objectives were taken.

On 22 July, Rawlinson renewed

No Longer Missing

For eighty-two years, Private George James Nugent, serving with the 22nd (Service) Battalion (3rd Tyneside Scottish) Northumberland Fusiliers, was one of the many missing on the Somme. Then, in 1998, his remains were found at this spot near the edge of Lochnagar crater. Final confirmation of his identity came when DNA tests were undertaken with his descendents. George Nugent was subsequently reburied with full military honours in Ovillers Military Cemetery on 1 July 2000. (HMP)

LEFT: **A view of the countryside at La Boisselle, looking south-east towards the Lochnagar Crater (the memorial cross at which can be seen in the trees that line the edges of this site), as it is today. The line of yellow marker flags stretching away from the camera has been laid out by the La Boisselle Study Group to mark the position of the British front line.** (HMP)

This image is another still from the British film *The Battle of the Somme*. It is part of a sequence introduced by a caption which reads "British Tommies rescuing a comrade under shell fire. (This man died 30 minutes after reaching the trenches)". The scene is generally accepted as having been filmed on the first day of the Battle of the Somme, 1 July 1916. In spite of considerable research, the identity of the rescuer remains unconfirmed. The casualty appears to be wearing a shoulder flash of the 29th Division. (Imperial War Museum; Q79501)

the offensive but the Germans had learnt not to rely upon a single, static defensive line. Instead, they turned to defence in depth, allowing them to fall back to prepared positions. The attack failed.

General Gough's Reserve Army, which included the Australian and New Zealand divisions of I ANZAC Corps, attacked the village of Pozières, a key sector of the German defences, on 23 July 1916. This offensive lasted until 26 September. The British and Commonwealth forces lost around 25,000 men in that period. This included some 8,000 New Zealanders, representing nearly one per cent of the country's population.

Clearly it would take something special to achieve a decisive breakthrough, and that something special arrived in the form of the first ever battle tanks. Though it would have been preferable if Haig could have waited until he had an overwhelming number of tanks that would punch right through the German lines, Haig needed them to be brought into action as soon as possible.

At the Battle of Flers–Courcelette on 15 September, twenty-five tanks rumbled forward, shocking the Germans who had never seen anything like them before. Ultimately, though, there were not enough of them to tip the balance in favour of the attackers. Territorial gains were certainly made, but there was no breakthrough.

Undeterred, Haig believed that the Germans were on the point of collapse and on 26 September the Reserve Army launched a major offensive against the ridge upon which sits the village of Thiepval. After two days of fighting, in which some 12,500 men were lost, Thiepval was taken. Further action saw the British extend their control of the Thiepval area.

Haig continued to drive his men forward. The final big push was at Ancre, in November, which saw the Allies taking Beaumont Hamel, St. Pierre Divion and Beaucourt. This marked the end of British operations in the region for the year. The Battle of the Somme, which had lasted for over four and a half months, had cost Britain and her Allies 623,907 men.

Awful though the battle had been for the Allies, it cost the Germans approximately 465,000 men. Ultimately, the Germans could not sustain such losses. Fighting the Russians, the French and the British meant that they were severely over-stretched. They were never able to fully recover from the effects of those terrible few months in 1916.

BELOW: **Two minutes before zero hour on 1 July 1916, the largest mine exploded on the Western Front in the First World War, the Lochnagar mine, tore through the German lines south-east of La Boisselle. This is the resulting crater pictured as it is today.** (HMP)

THE TANK

ABOVE RIGHT: A remarkable piece of First World War history - the Tank Museum's "Little Willie", which is on public display at Bovington in Dorset. (HMP)

RIGHT: Little Willie tackles a trench during a demonstration at Burton Park, Lincoln, on 3 December 1915. (Courtesy of The Tank Museum)

RIGHT: Often described as being the first official picture of a Mk.I going to action at the Battle of Flers-Courcelette, it is believed that this photograph was actually taken at Elvedon, near Thetford in Suffolk, during the preparations for the deployment of tanks to France. (US Library of Congress)

Possibly the most significant technical development of the First World War was that of the battle tank. Though its introduction was piecemeal and its reliability poor, the tank proved to be highly effective and it quickly came to dominate the battlefield.

Few knew what they really were. They were clearly British but as they moved up to their starting positions for the attack, ahead of the infantry, they ploughed through the British line crushing the sides of the trenches. The Commanding Officer of the 7th London TA Battalion was so angry at seeing his battalion's trenches crumbling under the tracks of these new contraptions he banged furiously on the armoured side of one of the tanks with his cane to try and drive it away!

"Big metal things they were, with two sets of caterpillar wheels that went right round the body," Bert Chaney remembered. "There was a bulge on each side with the door in the bulging part, and machine-guns on swivels poked out from either side ... a petrol engine of massive proportions occupied practically all the inside space". A few minutes later the tanks engaged the enemy and Bert was able to report happily that they were "frightening the Jerries out of their wits and making them scuttle like frightened rabbits".

The approach of the tanks was certainly a shock to most of the Germans but not a complete surprise: "We had heard rumours about a new Allied weapon, and our intelligence had sent us notes about a vehicle which they believed was being built in certain French factories", recalled *Leutnant* Otto Schulz. "But when we saw the first real tank it was like nothing we had ever imagined".[1] The date was 15 September 1916, and it was one of the most momentous days in the history of warfare.

Perhaps surprisingly it was the Royal Navy that could claim the credit for the first tanks. Possibly less surprising is that it was Winston Churchill who was the driving force behind the development of an armoured vehicle. This was because in the late summer of 1914 the Allies' northern flank on the Belgian coastline was still open. From a British perspective, its closure was largely a naval responsibility. Asked by Lord Kitchener if a squadron of the Royal Naval Air Service could be sent to Dunkirk, the First Lord of the Admiralty, Winston Churchill, was only too happy to oblige.

The RNAS's role at Dunkirk was to attack enemy airship bases across the frontier. Officers' own cars were shipped across the Channel and it was on these, as well as requisitioned motor lorries and London buses, that they conducted the raids. Soon the vehicles were being armed with whatever guns were available and, when in combat with the enemy, it was quickly appreciated that the vehicles would also need some kind of protection.

The result was that sixty machine-gun-armed 'fighting cars' were commissioned from three manufactures, including Rolls-Royce, which had armour protection for the engine and some for the driver. From this improvised beginning, the Royal Navy Armoured Car Division was formed and equipped with purpose-built armoured cars with a fully enclosed body and machine-gun in a revolving turret.

The fighting on the Western Front

quickly changed from mobile war to a static one with deep trenches and bomb-cratered ground in between. It was terrain over which the armoured cars could no longer operate. So, wrote Churchill, "The conclusion was forced naturally and obviously on me and no doubt upon others that if the armoured car could no longer move *round* the enemy's trenches and operate against the open flank of his army, some method would have to be devised which would enable them to traverse and pass *over* the trenches themselves."[2] And that is exactly what happened.

The Landships Committee came about when the Secretary of the War Council, Colonel Maurice Hankey, presented proposals for an armoured trench-crossing vehicle, the idea of Colonel Ernest Swinton, to Churchill after they had been discounted by senior staff in the British Army.

At the time that the Committee began its work, Caterpillar tractors were common in the USA. As a result, the Bullock creeping grip was selected. Once it had arrived from America, this pair of tracks was fitted to an armoured vehicle chassis. Tests soon revealed flaws in the Bullock tracks; every time the vehicle tried to negotiate a trench the tracks sagged and would not fit back on the wheels.

When these continued to fail, British designers came up with a new pattern – one which worked. These were subsequently fitted to the Landship that had been designed and built by the agricultural machinery company William Foster & Co. of Lincoln. This armoured vehicle, the construction of which began on 11 August 1915 and which was initially called the No.1 Lincoln Machine, would soon become known as Little Willie - said to be an uncomplimentary nickname for the German Crown Prince.

In essence, Little Willie was a rectangular box of boiler plate riveted to an angle-iron frame, the whole of which was mounted on the pair of re-worked Bullock tracks. Initially, Little Willie had a turret though this was later removed – although the turret ring can still be seen today. For the initial trials, full armament was carried. Most of the mechanical components, including the radiator, had been sourced or adapted from those employed on the Foster-Daimler heavy artillery-tractor.

The completed vehicle was running by the end of 1915. But by then a new design was already under construction; known variously as 'Big Willie', 'Mother' of 'His Majesty's Land Ship Centipede', the hull of 'Mother' was basically the same rectangular box structure that was used on Little Willie, but in place of the pivoting track frames it had two large track frames, rhomboidal in outline, fixed to the sides of the hull. It was the first of the iconic rhomboidal tanks.

This prototype, the Mk.I, was found to have a greatly improved obstacle-crossing capacity compared to its predecessor. So much so that work >>

BELOW: **A British Mk.IV tank pictured advancing through the ruins of a French village on the Western Front during the First World War.** (HMP)

RIGHT: **For all the failings in their own tank design, the Germans made extensive use of captured British tanks – such as the example seen here.** (US Library of Congress)

on the first batch of Mk.Is, numbering 100 in all, began in February 1916.

Shortly afterwards the order for 100 tanks was increased to 150. Of these, exactly half were to be Male versions (which had two 6-pounder Quick Firing guns as the primary armament) and the remaining seventy-five Females (four machine-guns as the primary armament). Internally, the hull was undivided, the crew sharing the same space as the engine. As a result, the environment inside was often extremely unpleasant. As ventilation was poor, the atmosphere was often contaminated with carbon monoxide, fuel and oil vapours from the engine, as well as cordite fumes from the weapons. It was not unknown for temperatures inside to reach as high as 50°C. Nevertheless, such faults aside, the world's first combat tank had been born.

The first tanks were available to the commander of the British Expeditionary Force, Field Marshal Haig, for his great offensive on the Somme in the summer and autumn of 1916. There had been much debate over their deployment. One school of thought was that the tanks should be used en masse to create a breakthrough which the other arms could exploit. The other view, and the one adopted by Haig, was that they should be employed in twos or threes in direct support of the advancing infantry.

Haig's views prevailed and on 15 September 1916, at the Battle of Flers-Courcelette, the tanks led the way on the first day of the engagement with somewhat mixed results. The effect upon the German troops who faced the tanks for the first time on that day are possibly exaggerated, but *Feldwebel* Weinert, serving in the 211th Prussian Infantry Regiment, clearly remembers the reaction of one of his comrades: "A man came running in ... 'There is a crocodile crawling into our lines!' The poor wretch was off his head. He ... imagined this giant of a machine, rearing up and dipping down as it came on, to be a monster."[3]

Though only thirty-two of the forty-nine tanks available to Haig reached their start positions, of which seven failed to start, the remaining twenty-five demonstrated just how effective the tanks could be if their reliability could be improved.

Haig, though, was heavily criticized for using the tanks when so few were available. If he had waited until he

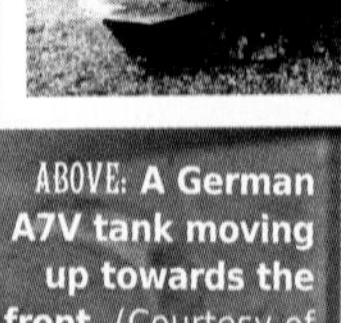

ABOVE: **A German A7V tank moving up towards the front.** (Courtesy of The Tank Museum)

A Surviving Mk. V Male Tank

Although similar in appearance to the earlier British Heavy Tanks, the Mk.V was a great improvement. As well as a new steering mechanism, the Mk.V was more reliable, more mobile, easier to control and had a powerful purpose-built engine. It was also the first heavy tank ever built that could be driven by one man! The Mk.V Male tank illustrated here (No.9199) is on display at The Tank Museum at Bovington in Dorset. It is one of just two First World War tanks worldwide that is still in running order. This tank is displayed in the markings of Tank H41 of 8th (H) Battalion Tank Corps at the time of the Battle of Amiens on 8 August 1918 (HMP)

BOTTOM RIGHT: **Christened *Dinnaken* by its Scottish commander, Lieutenant Stuart Hastie, D17 is seen lumbering along the High Street in Flers on the first day the tank was used in action – 15 September 1916. This drawing by the artist Christopher Clark was reproduced in a number of contemporary newspapers and magazines, such as *The Sphere* and the *Daily Mirror*.** (HMP)

NOTES:

1. R. Kershaw, *Tank Men* (Hodder & Stoughton, London, 2008) p.7.
2. Christy Campbell, *Band of Brigands* (Harper, London, 2007), p.44.
3. R. Kershaw, *Ibid*, p.8.
4. Holt, Major and Mrs. *Battlefields of the First World War* (Parkgate Books, London, 1998).

No sooner had the early rhomboidal Mk.I tanks entered service than the War Office started calling for the design of a lighter, faster and more agile tank. It wanted a tank that could undertake a role that was, in essence, similar to that of the traditional cavalry, capable of exploiting a breakthrough and giving chase to a retreating enemy. In effect an armoured substitute for the horse. The result, the only medium tank to see action during the First World War, was the Tank Medium, Mark A – also known as the Whippet. This picture shows wounded Australians of the 15th Brigade, and wounded German prisoners, sheltering beside a stranded Whippet tank near Harbonnières on 9 August 1918. It is one of the Whippet tanks that became unserviceable during the opening day of the Battle of Amiens on 8 August 1918. (HMP)

ABOVE: In November 1917 two tanks took part in the Lord Mayor's Show in London, generating great public interest. The National War Savings Committee then decided to despatch six Mk.IV tanks on a tour of the UK. The primary purpose of the campaign was to promote the sale of government War Bonds and War Savings Certificates. Consequently, those tanks soon earned the nickname "Tank Banks". This is one of those tanks pictured whilst on display in Trafalgar Square, London, late in 1917. (HMP)

had hundreds at his disposal he might well have achieved the breakthrough he sought. Some territory was won at Flers-Courcelette but it was of comparatively little significance, and for those few gains he had revealed Britain's great secret weapon which, had it been employed in greater numbers, might well have won the war at a single stroke.

Nevertheless, the tank had proved itself in battle and Haig ordered hundreds more to be built and their first really successful use with the British came at the Battle of Cambrai in 1917. This time Britain was able to amass 476 tanks, mostly of the new Mk.IV design (the Mk.II and Mk.III tanks were almost identical to the Mk.I with only minor changes), though less than 400 were actually engaged. The success the tanks achieved was not followed by the infantry and the overall result of the battle was unsatisfactory. The battle tank, however, had firmly established itself and henceforth would be a feature of almost every important battlefield.

The French were quick to appreciate the value of the tank and by the end of the war had produced more than any other country. The Germans, on the other hand, were far slower, producing only twenty of their ungainly A7V tanks.It was inevitable that at some point opposing tanks would meet in battle, though it was not until the last year of the war. Like British attempts at a major breakthrough, so the Germans launched their Spring Offensive in March 1918 in the hope of achieving a decisive victory. On 24 April, German artillery opened fire on British and Australian positions in and around the village of Villers-Bretonneux. Just over two hours later the German attack began, led by thirteen A7V tanks.

The German tanks performed well and three of them penetrated as far as the village of Cachy where three British tanks were stationed. Alerted by an infantryman that there were German tanks in the area, Lieutenant Frank Mitchell MC of No.1 Tank of 1st Section, 'A' Company, 1st Tank Battalion, opened a loophole to look out. "There, some three hundred yards away, a round squat-looking monster was advancing; behind it came waves of infantry, and farther away to the left and right crawled two more of these armed tortoises … so we had met our rivals at last. For the first time in history tank was encountering tank!"[4]

A shell from Mitchell's 6-pounder hit one of the German tanks, but the two other British tanks received return fire from the enemy which tore big holes in their armour. This left Mitchell facing two A7Vs alone. To his surprise the German tanks withdrew, but it was only to allow their artillery to deal with the British tank. Both sides claimed victory.

By the end of the First World War, the Germans had learnt how to deal with the Allied tanks, having devoted considerable resources into developing anti-tank weapons. At the Battle of Amiens in August 1918, for example, 72% of the 532 vehicles of Allied Tank Corps were destroyed in the first four days.

In the decades after the First Wold War tanks became more heavily armed, faster and mounted ever bigger guns and would eventually come to dominate the battlefield. A hundred years on, however, their future seems limited, for it is aircraft, manned and unmanned, and missiles that are now the arbiters of victory.

BELOW: A group of British Mk.V tanks pictured moving forward in preparation for attacks on the Hindenburg Line in September 1918. Note the heavy wooden cribs they are carrying ready for dropping into a crater, ditch or trench. (Courtesy of The Tank Museum)

Shot at Dawn

RIGHT: Overlooking the courtyard of the town hall in the Belgian town of Poperinge are a number of small cells in which the military authorities held men arrested for a variety of crimes. Whilst the majority were guilty of minor offences, such as being drunk or abusive, a small number were held in the cells whilst awaiting execution - to be "Shot at Dawn". This is the interior of a so-called "Death Cell" that is open to the public. (HMP)

ABOVE RIGHT: The Execution Post Memorial that was unveiled in the courtyard of Poperinge's town hall on 15 June 2012. (HMP)

Between August 1914 and 31 March 1920, just over 3,000 men were sentenced to death in British army courts martial. In roughly 90% of cases, the sentence was commuted to hard labour or penal servitude. Some, though, were shot at dawn.

As the British Expeditionary Force retreated from Mons, large numbers of men were lost. Many, of course, had been killed or wounded. There were also some who were missing. The Provost Marshal reported that by 30 August 1914 2,923 men had been reported as "stragglers" and there was real concern that some men had not made sufficient effort to rejoin their units after the confusion of the retreat.

On 5 September 1914, the retreat came to an end on the banks of the River Marne. That day, at 08.55 hours, a telegram was received at GHQ from the French authorities. The telegram stated that an English deserter in plain clothes had been apprehended at a farm near Tournan. To an army operating in friendly country, looting or deserting was a subject of the gravest concern. Such conduct had to be eliminated before it spread and all order and discipline was lost.

A court martial was quickly convened, on the actual day of his arrest. Private Thomas Highgate of the 1st Battalion, The Queen's Own Royal West Kent Regiment was judged to be in "sound mental and bodily health and fit to undergo punishment" and consequently passed for trial. He was charged with, "When on active service, deserting His Majesty's Service".

What virtually condemned Highgate before his case had even been heard was that his Corps Commander, Lieutenant General Smith-Dorrien, instigated Rule of Procedure 104 which stated that the proximity of the enemy rendered it inexpedient to allow a defendant the opportunity of a proper defence. Undefended, Highgate pleaded not guilty.

The evidence against him was that an Englishman who was a gamekeeper for a local aristocrat had found the accused at Tournan dressed in civilian clothes. The gamekeeper, a man named Thomas Fermor, told the military tribunal that Highgate had said to him, "I have lost my army and I mean to get out of it". Fermor then marched the soldier to the *Gendarmerie* in Tournan.

Highgate then gave his side of the story. He had been marching with his battalion and had popped into the bushes to "ease" himself. When he returned, he found his comrades had gone. "I got strolling about," Highgate explained, "went down into a farm, lay down in an empty house and have a slight remembrance of putting some civilian clothes on, but I do not remember exactly what happened until the man came down to arrest me. I was coming back to see if I could find my clothes and my Regiment, but I was taken to a police station."

Offences For Which Death Sentences Were Carried Out

Mutiny	2
Cowardice	18
Desertion	266
Murder	37
Striking or violence	6
Disobedience	5
Sleeping on post	2
Quitting post	7
Casting away arms	2

The court martial found Highgate guilty of deserting His Majesty's forces on active service. He was sentenced to death. Within four hours, the Corps Commander endorsed the verdict and the very next day, Sir John French confirmed the sentence.

At dawn on 8 September 1914, the sentence was carried out. Highgate was buried in a now anonymous grave on the outskirts of Tournan.

Thomas Highgate's case was a straightforward one. He had clearly deserted and it was important to the military authorities that deserters were robustly dealt with. If the soldiers knew that an alternative to being shot at by the enemy was a prison sentence, then many might make such a choice. If, though, desertion meant the very real possibility of death by firing squad, then facing the enemy was a better option. Such discipline, harsh though it may seem, was entirely understandable at the time.

Other cases, however, were not so clear-cut. An example of this is that of 31-year-old Second Lieutenant Eric Skeffington Poole, 11th Battalion, West Yorkshire Regiment (Prince of Wales's Own). Born in Nova Scotia, Canada, on 20 January 1885, Poole and his family had emigrated to Britain and settled in Guildford, Surrey.

In October 1914, Poole joined the Honourable Artillery Company, in which he served as a driver in 'B' Battery for some seven months. His Territorial Force form reveals that he earned a commission as a temporary second lieutenant in the 14th Battalion of the West Yorkshire Regiment in May 1915. A year later, Poole was transferred to serve in France with the 11th Battalion, shortly before it was due to go into action at the Battle of the Somme.

According to the medical history sheet compiled for Poole's general court martial in November 1916, he suffered shell shock after being struck by debris – described as clods of earth – thrown up by the nearby explosion of an enemy shell during fighting at Contalmaison on the Somme on 7 July 1916.

"I rejoined the battalion about Sept. 1st when they were in the trenches at Ploegstreet [sic]. From there I went with the battalion to the Somme. Since I have had shell shock I at times get confused and I have great difficulty in making up my mind. I was in this condition on October 5th. I did not realise the seriousness of not going up to the front line on October 5th. I went to an aid post as I had a slight touch of rheumatism. I went away about 5pm – I did not leave anyone in charge of the platoon." At the time, the battalion had been moving forward into front line trenches at Flers.

For two days Poole remained at large until he was detained near Hénencourt Wood some three miles west of Albert. In early November, it was decided to try Poole by general court martial for deserting "when on active service". At Poole's court martial, held in Poperinge on 24 November 1916, the prosecution called six witnesses. In the subsequent testimony, it was variously noted that Poole's "nerves seemed rather shaken" and that he had confessed to feeling "damned bad" on the morning of 5 October. Two men spoke in Poole's defence, one of whom was a RAMC officer who believed that the "mental condition" of the accused had precluded him from intentionally deserting his company.

Despite such statements and the pleas of Poole's defence team, he was found guilty of desertion. Poole was duly sentenced to be shot. On 6 December 1916, General Sir Douglas Haig simply endorsed the trial papers with the word "Confirmed". On the same day, Haig wrote in his diary that "it is ... highly important that all ranks should realise the law is the same for an officer as a private". >>

The emotive Shot at Dawn Memorial at the National Memorial Arboretum near Alrewas, Staffordshire. The memorial portrays a young British soldier blindfolded and tied to a post ready to be executed by a firing squad. Created by the artist Andy de Comyn and unveiled in June 2001, the memorial was modelled on a likeness of 17-year-old Private Herbert Burden, who lied about his age to enlist in the armed forces and was later executed for desertion. The memorial is surrounded by a semicircle of stakes on which are listed the names of the 346 British and Commonwealth soldiers executed for cowardice and desertion in the First World War. (Photo by Alan Tunnicliffe)

"Legislation passed on 8 November 2006 ... pardoned those men in the British and Commonwealth armies who were executed."

BELOW: The grave in Poperinghe New Military Cemetery of a soldier shot at dawn – Private William Henry Simmonds, 23rd (Service) Battalion (2nd Football) Middlesex Regiment. (HMP)

Just before dawn on 10 December 1916, Poole was taken from his cell at Poperinge and placed before the firing squad. The rifles rang out at 07.25 hours. Eric Poole was the first British army officer to be sentenced to death and executed during the First World War.

Private William Henry Simmonds, the son of William and Emily Simmonds, of 18 Sidney Terrace, Bedfont Lane, Feltham, Middlesex, was another soldier who had deserted on the Somme only to find himself in a cell at Poperinge.

Serving in the 23rd (Service) Battalion (2nd Football) Middlesex Regiment, on 30 September 1916, Simmonds' platoon was entering the front line near Longueval when a shell exploded nearby. Simmonds fled from the scene; two weeks passed before he was arrested.

When he was tried with desertion at a Field General Court Martial, held on 19 November 1916, at Poperinge (to where his battalion had moved), Simmonds entered a plea of "not guilty". Found guilty of desertion once more (he had previously received a sentence of five years' penal servitude which was subsequently commuted to ninety days' Field Punishment for the same offence), Simmonds was executed at 07.00 hours on 1 December 1916.

Britain was not alone in executing its own soldiers (though none suffered death by sentence of Court Martial in the UK itself). The French are thought to have killed about 600. The Germans, whose troops outnumbered the British by two to one, shot forty-eight of their own men, and the Belgians thirteen. Twenty-three Canadian servicemen were executed, as were five New Zealanders. No American or Australian soldiers were executed.

There has been much debate in recent times over the execution of soldiers in the First World War. Indeed, legislation passed on 8 November 2006, and included as part of the Armed Forces Act, pardoned those men in the British and Commonwealth armies who were executed in the First World War.

Yet it is significant that in not a single one of the surviving files containing the court martial papers is there any argument that the wrong man had been convicted, or that a completely innocent man had been executed. What does come through, however, is – in a number of the cases – a failure by the court to recognise extenuating circumstances which might have mitigated punishment.

Nevertheless, the fact that the various Commanders-in-Chief refused to endorse the death sentence in almost ninety per cent of cases might suggest that such punishment was only meted out with the greatest reluctance and where considered absolutely necessary, the sentence usually being commuted to a lesser penalty. The official statistics of the First World War, for example, notes that of the "soldiers who suffered death by sentence of Courts-Martial, 91 were under suspended sentences. Of the 91 men, 40 had been previously sentenced to death, in 38 cases for desertion, in 1 case for quitting post, and in 1 case for disobedience. One soldier had been sentenced to death on two previous occasions for desertion, and in 9 cases the accused were under two suspended sentences."

It would be wrong today for us to judge the actions of those accused and of those asked to try them. The story of these executions needs to be considered in the military, social, legal and medical context of the time, in a world where psychiatry barely existed, where the death penalty was still widely applied and where young men had suddenly become exposed to the often terrible shock of the new industrial warfare. As the author L.P. Hartley famously wrote, "The past is a foreign country; they do things differently there."

Location of Executions

Between 4 August 1914 and 31 March 1920, there were 346 trials that resulted in the execution of officers and soldiers of the British Army, camp followers, native labourers and Chinese coolies, all of whom were subject to the Army Act. These 346 executions occurred in the following theatres:

France and Belgium	322
East Africa	5
Mesopotamia	4
Constantinople	4
Gallipoli	3
Salonika	3
Egypt	2
Italy	1
Palestine	1
Serbia	1

WOMEN AT WAR

FAR LEFT: **Two female ambulance drivers pictured in the ruins of a devastated village on the Western Front. Amongst those who served as VADs during the First World War were the author Vera Brittain, novelist Agatha Christie, and the aviation pioneer Amelia Earhart.** (US Library of Congress)

LEFT: **A contemporary First World War drawing depicting a female munitions worker - commonly referred to as "munitionettes" or "canaries", the latter being a reference to the yellow hue that skin exposed to sulphur acquired.** (HMP)

With such a large proportion of the male population away at the Front, women, for the first time, kept the British economy running and the home fires burning.

Soldiers alone cannot win wars. Skilled workers are also required to help to feed the guns, build the ships and forge the weapons. Yet with as much as forty per cent of the male workforce of the United Kingdom having joined up the only way the war could be sustained was by allowing women to take over many roles which had always been the preserve of the men. Despite the obvious national need, this was a highly contentious matter and negotiations had to be undertaken with the trade unions to allow this to happen. Even when it had been agreed that women could do "men's work", they were still paid much less.

Nevertheless, a total of 4,814,600 women were employed in one capacity or another by 1918. Of these nearly 200,000 women were employed in government departments and half a million became clerical workers in private offices. Women worked as conductors on trams and buses, whilst a quarter of a million worked on the land, 20,000 of whom formed part of the Land Army, which had been formed in 1915. Of the latter, the majority of the Land Girls already lived in the countryside but more than a third came from London and the industrial cities of the north of England.

Around 800,000 women were employed in all aspects of industry, with some 594,600 working under the aegis of the Ministry of Munitions. Of these, the largest proportion, almost 250,000, were engaged in the filling and manufacture of shells; the remainder helped create artillery pieces, rifles, ammunition and the chemical used in gas warfare.

In many factories women would come to outnumber ➤➤

BELOW LEFT: **A mobile YMCA canteen which, according to the legend on the side of the vehicle, was managed by a Mrs Hoares.** (US Library of Congress)

RIGHT: **Female ambulance drivers parade beside their vehicles on the Western Front. The nature of the uniforms they are wearing suggests that these women may be serving with the Voluntary Aid Detachment. During the five years of war 38,000 VADs worked in hospitals and served as ambulance drivers and cooks. VADs operated near the Western Front, as well as in Mesopotamia and Gallipoli. VAD hospitals were also opened in most large towns in Britain.** (US Library of Congress)

RIGHT: **A group of female munitions workers during the First World War. After the introduction of conscription in March 1916 the British Government encouraged women to take the place of male employees who had been released from their normal occupations to serve at the front. Whilst in July 1914, 212,000 women worked in the engineering and munitions industries, by 1918 the total had risen to nearly a million.** (HMP)

men. In the huge National Filling Factory at Gretna, for example, 11,576 women were employed, comprising almost 70 per cent of the workforce, and there they produced cordite, nitroglycerine and other explosives.

Working with such materials was, of course, dangerous work, as exemplified by an incident that occurred in a munitions factory at Silvertown in London's West Ham in January 1917. The factory was built in 1893 and turned over to munitions manufacture in 1916 due to a crippling shortage of shells which was severely restricting the offensive plans of the British Expeditionary Force in France.

The factory was used to purify TNT, a process more dangerous than manufacturing the actual product itself. On the evening of 19 January 1917, a fire broke out in the melt-pot room which ignited fifty-one tons of TNT. The entire TNT plant was destroyed instantly, as were many nearby buildings. Seventy-three people were killed (sixty-nine immediately, whilst four died later from their injuries), and more than 400 injured. Up to 70,000 properties were damaged, 900 nearby ones were destroyed or damaged irreparably.

In another incident, one woman demonstrated that it was not only men that could perform deeds of courage in the face of danger. Mabel Lethbridge had only been working at the National Filling Factory No.7 at Hayes, Middlesex, for six days when she saw a notice asking for volunteers to work in "The Danger Zone". All the girls from Mabel's work bench put themselves forward for this hazardous new job. Little could they, or Mabel, realise what the following days would bring.

The women who had volunteered for the Danger Zone were employed in the Amatol Section where they filled shells with amatol soda and TNT. The mixture was poured into shell casings and then compressed by a heavy weight dropped from a height. When the contents were sufficiently compressed the fuze was screwed on.

After performing one of the simpler tasks, on Monday, 23 October 1917, Mabel was chosen to train as an operator of the device that performed the compressing or 'stemming' function. As the girls were working away a scream echoed around the building. The girl performing the same job as Mabel on a similar machine had been hit by the weight as it dropped down onto the shell. Badly hurt, she was carried away.

The other girls told Mabel that she would be a fool to carry on and none would take the injured girl's place. Mabel told them that she was going to carry on regardless and she even persuaded another girl to operate the other machine.

Despite the dangers that women working in the armaments industries often faced, their terms and conditions were usually worse than those of their male counterparts. Leading trade-unionist Mary MacArthur, Secretary of the Women's Trade Union League since 1903, led an energetic campaign to demand they were paid as much as the men employed in the same industry – the women only got half the men's wages – but by the end of the war the proportion was roughly still the same. (HMP)

> "The women who had volunteered for the Danger Zone were employed in the Amatol Section where they filled shells with amatol soda and TNT."

They worked through the day when suddenly there was a dull flash and a deafening roar. "I felt myself being hurled through the air, falling down, down, down into darkness," recalled Mabel. She lay quietly on her side but then there was a blinding flash. "I felt my body being torn asunder. Darkness, that terrifying darkness, and the agonised cries of the workers pierced my consciousness. I struggled to rise, turning and twisting my body. 'Help! Help! ... Mother of God, have mercy'."

The cries of Mabel and the other girls turned to piercing shrieks as the dreaded word "Fire" added further fear to the already terrifying situation. There was a desperate rush for the doors as the workshop turned into a blazing furnace.

"In the glare I saw girls rise and fall shrieking with terror, their clothes alight, blood pouring from wounds. I made one last effort to get to the doors ... huge sliding doors of steel. I crawled through the pile of blazing boxes which had surrounded my machine ... the agony was indescribable. I made an almighty effort to rise, catching at some machinery with my hands. The sickening stench of burning flesh met my nostrils, cries of anguish escaped my lips. I saw my hands; they were blackened and seared. The machinery I was holding was red-hot. 'God help me,' I cried, sinking down among the flames, unable to stand the torment any longer."

Mabel Lethbridge was rescued and taken to St Mary's Hospital, Paddington, in what was described as "a dying condition". She had thirteen serious wounds, any one of which might have proven to be fatal. Her head, face and left jaw were badly crushed and her right leg and thigh were fractured. Both Mabel's arms had also been broken. The sockets of her eyes were torn by the force of the explosion and both eyes were burnt. Her left leg had been severed above the knee.

On 1 January 1918, just before she underwent further surgery, she was handed a telegram. The telegram informed her that because of her courage in continuing to work in the face of obvious danger she had been awarded the Order of the British Empire.

Though full of potential risk, such work gave women from the lower classes a level of wages ▸▸

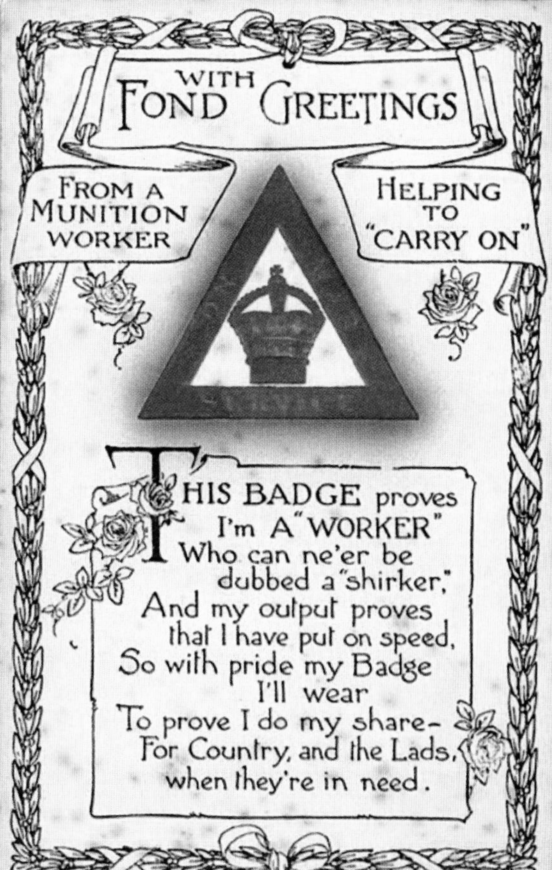

CENTRE LEFT: **A postcard introduced in the First World War supporting the issue of "On War Service" badges. The design of the triangular brass badge was introduced in May 1916 for those women involved in munitions production and was issued after the completion of two months' work.**

BELOW LEFT: **The number of women employed in the transport industry during the First World War expanded by 555% to roughly 100,000. In Britain's railway workshops the number of unskilled women labourers increased from just forty-three in 1914 to 2,547 by 1918. They tackled portering, varnishing and painting engines, sweeping, storekeeping and cleaning. Women also worked as ticket collectors, conductors and, from 1917, railway Police Constables. Until April 1915 women were paid two-thirds less than their male counterparts until the railway unions admitted women and the National Union of Railwaymen demanded that companies should pay women at least the minimum male wage for the job.** (US Library of Congress)

The King during a visit to a munitions factory in the First World War. It has been stated that "munitionettes" produced 80% of the weapons and shells used by the British Army between 1914 and 1918. (HMP)

BELOW: **A British Voluntary Aid Detachment dressing station. As early as 1909 it had been decided to form Voluntary Aid Detachments to provide medical assistance in time of war. By the summer of 1914 there were over 2,500 separate Voluntary Aid Detachments in Britain. Of the 74,000 VAD staff serving in 1914, two-thirds were female.** (US Library of Congress)

never previously attainable. For the wealthier levels of society, whilst work on the land and in factories was unacceptable, caring for the wounded soldiers was a way that they could contribute to the national effort. It was in the hospitals at home that these women could assist with the returning wounded, joining such organisations as the Red Cross and the Voluntary Aid Detachment (VAD).

Another of these organisations was the Queen Alexandra's Imperial Military Nursing Service (QAIMNS) which had 10,000 regular and reserve nurses serving in war zones in countries such as France, India, East Africa, Italy, Palestine, Egypt, Mesopotamia, Salonika and Russia. The QAIMNS was formed in 1902, replacing the Army Nursing Service which was created in the 1850s as a result of the Crimean War where there were a large number of casualties who needed expert care. One account states that the "members of the QAIMNS were all over the age of 25 (or just possibly widowed), educated, of impeccable social standing, and had completed a three year course of nurse training in a hospital approved by the War Office".

The vital contribution that women could, and indeed would, make to the war effort had been quickly recognised across society. Indeed, David Lloyd George, later the Prime Minister, said in July 1915 that "Without women, victory will tarry".

Even in the Army itself, it was seen that there were many functions women could perform. Consequently in January 1917, the government announced the establishment of a new voluntary service, the Women's Auxiliary Army Corps (WAAC). The plan was for these women to serve as clerks, telephonists, waitresses, cooks, and as instructors in the use of gas masks. It was decided that women would not be allowed to hold commissions and so that those in charge were given the ranks of controller and administrator. Between January 1917 and the Armistice over 57,000 women served in the WAAC.

There was also the Women's Royal Air Force (WRAF). Initially, members of the Women's Royal Naval Service and the Women's Army Auxiliary Corps (WAAC) worked on air stations belonging to the Royal Flying Corps and the Royal Naval Air Service. When the decision was taken to merge the RFC and RNAS to form the RAF, concerns were raised about the loss of their specialised female workforce. This need for a separate women's air service led to the formation of the WRAF on 1 April 1918. Some 30,000 women served with the WRAF between 1918 and 1920.

Prior to her death on 4 February 2012, Florence Green had been the last surviving service veteran of the First World War. Born on 19 February 1901, Florence enlisted in the WRAF, aged 17, in 1918, Mrs Green recalls working in the officers' mess at Marham and was also based at Narborough airfield. Speaking of her First World War service, Florence had once said: "I enjoyed my time in the WRAF. There were plenty of people at the airfields where I worked and they were all very good company. I would work every hour God sent but I had dozens of friends on the base and we had a great deal of fun in our spare time. In many ways I had the time of my life. It was a lovely experience and I'm very proud."

A world war the 1914-18 conflict may have been, but it was also a national war in which every strata of society and women as well as men joined together to defeat a common enemy.

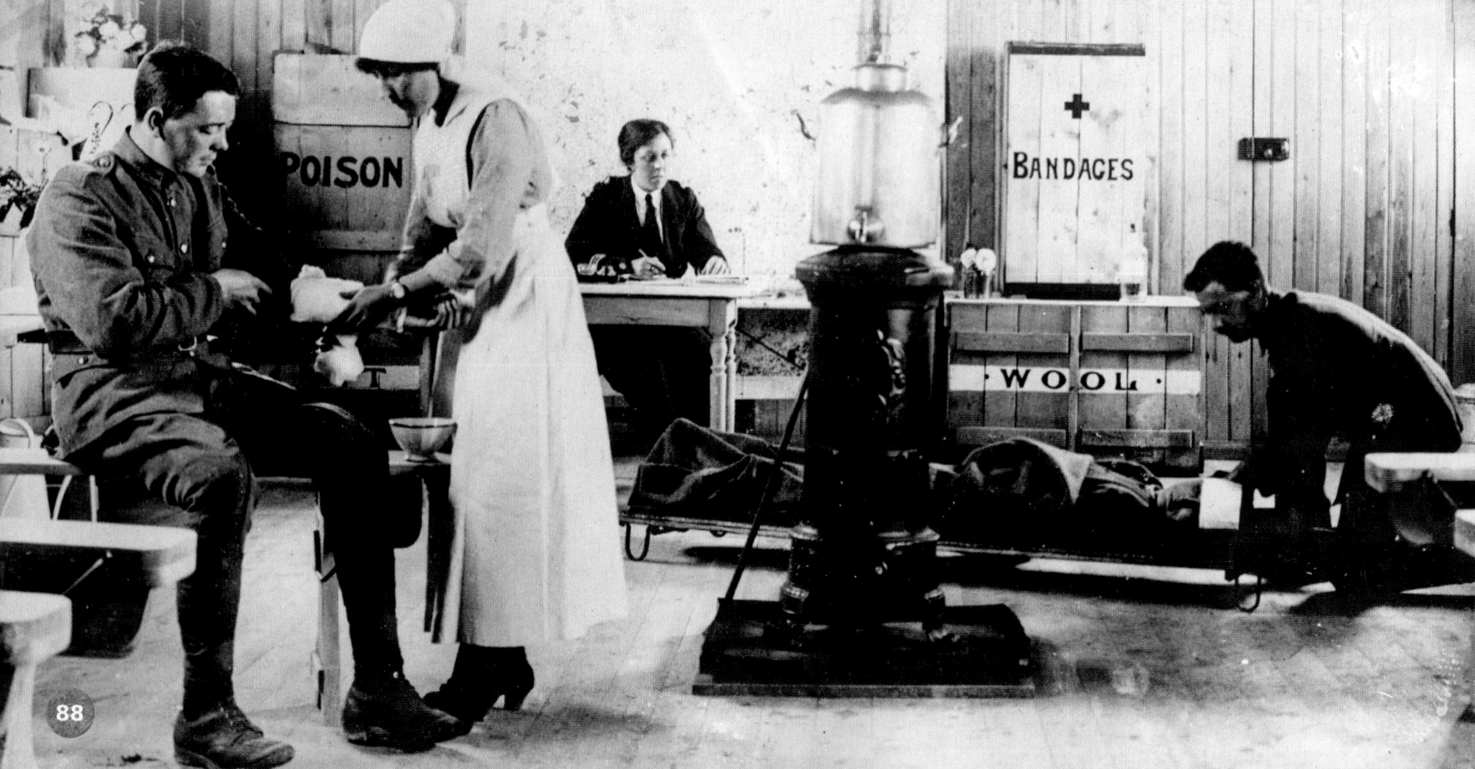

Timeline 1917 - Events that Shaped The First World War

January

8 A British offensive to clear Turkish troops out of Sinai began. Late in the evening, mounted units including the Anzac Mounted Division, the Imperial Camel Corps Brigade, the 5th Mounted Yeomanry Brigade, and No.7 Light Car Patrol and supporting artillery, rode out of El Arish and, the next day, attacked the 2,000 to 3,000-strong Ottoman Army garrison at El Magruntein (also known as Rafa or Rafah)

31 Theobald von Bethmann-Hollweg, the Chancellor of the German Empire, announced to the German Reichstag government that the policy of unrestricted submarine warfare would resume the next day, 1 February

March

11 After a two-year campaign, British troops, including large numbers of men from the British Indian Army, captured the city of Baghdad from Ottoman forces. A provincial capital, this meant that the first Ottoman province had fallen under Allied control

14 Allied troops began a cautious advance in the footsteps of the German forces as the latter continued their well-planned withdrawal to the Hindenburg Line – British patrols first reported that the enemy was pulling back in February. The German strategic withdrawal was known as Operation *Alberich*. German forces destroyed everything on the ground as they left, flattening villages, poisoning wells, cutting down trees, blowing craters on roads and crossroads, and booby-trapping ruins and dugouts. The withdrawal was to an immensely powerful and shorter line, positioned to take every tactical advantage of the ground

17 Allied troops occupied the town of Bapaume following the German withdrawal to the Hindenburg Line

26 The First Battle of Gaza was fought between Allied and Turkish troops during the initial attempt by the Egyptian Expeditionary Force to invade the southern region of the Ottoman-controlled territory of Palestine. The fighting ended in a Turkish victory

April

9 The large-scale British offensive known as the Battle of Arras began. As part of this, British, Canadian, New Zealand, Newfoundland and Australian troops attacked the German front near Arras

17 Following the disastrous First Battle of Gaza, the Ottoman defenders achieved victory during the Second Battle of Gaza

May

10 In an attempt to defeat the German U-boats, the convoy system was officially introduced

15 The Arras offensive ended. By the standards of the Western front, the gains of the first two days in particular were nothing short of spectacular. A great deal of ground had been gained for relatively few casualties

23 German Gotha bombers unsuccessfully attacked London

June

7 The Battle of Messines Ridge, south of Ypres, began. It lasted for seven days. Despite strong German counter-attacks, the offensive is generally considered to have been a British tactical and operational success. In 1919, Ludendorff noted that the British victory cost the German army dear and drained German reserves. Hindenburg wrote that the losses at Messines had been "very heavy" .

24 General Pershing landed in France with the first contingent of the American Expeditionary Force.

July

18 The opening bombardment of the Battle of Passchendaele, or Third Battle of Ypres, commenced

31 The offensive for control of the ridges south and east of Ypres, the Battle of Passchendaele, which was part of the strategy decided upon by the Allies at conferences in November 1916 and May 1917, began

August

2 The offensive around Ypres was temporarily suspended due to bad weather

17 General Smuts published a report on the air-defence of Great Britain in which he proposed the formation of a single independent air force. His recommendations were accepted, leading to the eventual formation of the Royal Air Force

September

20 The Battle of Menin Road Ridge, sometimes called the Battle of the Menin Road, the third general British attack of the Battle of Passchendaele, commenced. It lasted for five days and is described as an Allied victory

October

26 Brazil declared war on Germany

November

10 The village of Passchendaele was captured. The Canadian Corps launched a final action on this date to gain control of the remaining high ground north of the village, in the vicinity of Hill 52. It was an attack that brought an end to the offensive in Flanders

20 The Battle of Cambrai, which involved large numbers of tanks, commenced

25 German forces withdrew from Portuguese East Africa

30 German troops launched a counter offensive at Cambrai, regaining much of the ground lost in the preceding days

December

3 Haig ordered a retreat from the salient at Cambrai and by 7 December the British gains had been abandoned except for a portion of the Hindenburg line around Havrincourt, Ribécourt and Flesquières

8 The Battle of Cambrai ended with a small victory for the Allies

9 General Allenby's Egyptian Expeditionary Force captured Jerusalem. It was the first defeat of a Central power that resulted in a substantial loss of territory in the war

THE STRANGLEHOLD

RIGHT: **A number of U-boats pictured in their home port alongside a depot ship. Such vessels were the scourge of the trans-Atlantic shipping lanes, particularly those from the United States and Canada, for much of the First World War.** (US Library of Congress)

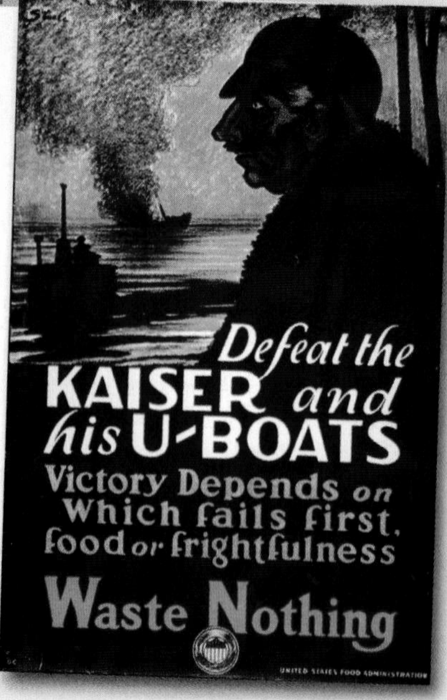

FAR RIGHT: **This poster, "Defeat the Kaiser and his U-boats", was published by the United States Food Administration and was intended to reinforce the message, on both sides of the Atlantic, regarding the need to conserve food stocks.** (US Library of Congress)

For much of its recent history Britain has been dependent on food imports to feed its population. Well aware of this the Germans attempted to starve Britain into surrender in the First World War by deploying their submarines against British and Allied merchant ships.

On 15 February 1915, the German Chancellor, Theobald von Bethmann-Hollweg, made the following announcement: "The waters around Great Britain and Ireland, including the whole of the English Channel, are herewith declared to be in the War Zone. From 18 February onward, every merchant-ship met with in this War Zone will be destroyed, nor will it always be possible to obviate the danger with which passengers and crew are thereby threatened.

"Neutral ships, too, will run a risk in the War Zone," he continued, "and owing to the hazards of naval warfare, it may not always be possible to prevent the attacks meant for hostile ships from being directed against neutral ships."

The first attacks on British merchant ships had begun as early as October 1914, but there was no systematic approach taken by the Germans, and in the five months until February 1915 only nineteen ships had been sunk. The adoption of so-called "unrestricted" warfare following Bethmann-Hollweg's announcement, however, saw a major effort by the Germans.

Their U-boat fleet was based at ports such as Ostend and Bruges, from where they could operate easily in the Channel. Though at first they only had twenty submarines, they achieved considerable results, sinking around 100,000 tons a months, at an average of 1.9 ships per day.

In those early days of submarine warfare the Royal Navy did not have the ability to detect submerged vessels nor even the methods of destroying them. This meant that the submarines could easily avoid the prowling warships, so other methods of combating the U-boats had to be found.

One of these was the re-introduction of the convoy system. This had been used effectively in the Napoleonic Wars against French surface warships but had been abandoned in the age of steam. Convoys, with strong naval escorts, were used systematically, and to great effect, from 1916 onwards and their use was, without question, instrumental in maintaining the flow of goods to Britain and France. Aircraft and airships also provided protection for ships and convoys along coastal routes.

Another method designed to combat the submarines was the use of "dazzle", or disruptive, camouflage on ships. Credited to the artist Norman Wilkinson, this technique consisted of a complex pattern of geometric shapes in contrasting colours, interrupting and intersecting each other. Dazzle did not conceal the ship but made it difficult for the enemy to estimate its type, size, speed and heading. The first attempt at this strategy was a large white wave painted on the bows of fast ships to give the appearance of speed. The idea was that the unsuspecting U-boat might, for example, suppose that its

Women and children wait in a bread line in Britain during the First World War. Though formal rationing was not introduced until 1918, food shortages had been an ever-present factor of life on the Home Front from the very start of the war. Initially caused by panic buying in the summer of 1914, such shortages continued. In April 1916, for example, Britain only had six weeks of wheat left, a desperate problem when you consider that bread was a staple part of most people's diets. The problems were greatly exacerbated by Germany's policy of unrestricted submarine warfare in 1917 and 1918. (US Library of Congress)

prey was steaming twenty-five knots when it was only going twelve and as a consequence fire their torpedoes prematurely. Over 2,000 ships were camouflaged.

The Admiralty had also offered £1,000 to the captains and crews of any merchant ship that succeeded in sinking an enemy submarine. To support this, the industrialist Alfred Yarrow placed £20,000 with Lloyd's Register so that the amount a merchant crew could receive for destroying or capturing an enemy submarine would be doubled to £2,000.

Yarrow also offered an inducement to merchant crewmen to spot submarines. He made his offer in a letter to *The Times* of 1 March and 2 April 1917: "It goes without saying that it is of the utmost importance to sight a submarine at the earliest possible moment. To encourage everyone to keep a sharp look-out, I beg to offer a reward of £20 (up to a total expenditure of £10,000) to anyone on board a commercial vessel who first draws the captain's attention to an enemy submarine in the vicinity."

This was well-received and many men benefitted. In many cases the £20 gift was presented by the captain of the ship in the presence of the crew or at the individual's home. Its success led to the Lords Commissioners of the Admiralty writing to Alfred Yarrow in June 1918 to thank him for his generosity, stating that it had "a most stimulating effect in promoting efficiency in the system of look-out on board vessels of our Mercantile Marine". In fact so diligent did merchant crews become, the £10,000 fund was soon exhausted but it was continued by the Chamber of Shipping and other bodies.

It was well known that the column of smoke from a ship's funnel was generally the first indication of the presence of a ship in the ➤➤

BELOW: **A scene more reminiscent of the Second World War – a trans-Atlantic convoy forms up, in 1916 or 1917, prior to setting out for British ports.** (US Library of Congress)

RIGHT: A photograph of a merchant ship, arrowed, with the Yarrow Anti-Submarine Smoke System performing as intended. The original caption states that the duct in the Yarrow system has been opened "on the wind side of the vessel in order to see the effect, and it will be noted that it forms an excellent smoke screen, enveloping the entire vessel when looked at from aft. This smoke screen can be produced in a few seconds by putting on fresh coal and reducing the air supply to the furnaces." (Courtesy of Ian Wolff)

TOP RIGHT: The Yarrow Anti-Submarine Smoke System in action, with water spray issuing at an angle of 45 degrees. This photograph gives some idea of the velocity with which the waste gases were ejected. (Courtesy of Ian Wolff)

BELOW: Naval escorts, some of them US Navy vessels, at anchor prior to joining a convoy crossing the Atlantic. (US Library of Congress)

distance. Clearly, if the smoke was not allowed to form a long trail in the sky, it is reasonable to assume that many ships would pass by entirely unnoticed.

Yarrow, therefore, sought a method of dispersing the smoke. In January 1918, he suggested to the Admiralty that the smoke from funnels, instead of being allowed to pass up into the sky, should be conducted over the sides of the ships. The smoke would then be sprayed with water which would cool the products of the combustion. The cooled gasses would then become heavier than air and would descend, rather than rise up into the air. Somewhat surprisingly this also had a beneficial side-effect in that the down force of air from the side funnels reduced slightly the draught of the vessel which in turn reduced drag and enabled an increase in speed. The resulting equipment was known as the Yarrow Anti-Submarine Smoke System, which was being fitted to an increasing number of merchant vessels when the war ended.

A more pro-active method of dealing with the German submarines was also introduced. It had been noted that the German submarines rarely used their valuable torpedoes to sink smaller merchant vessels. Generally, when a suitable target had been identified the U-boat would surface and sink the ship with gunfire. It was on the surface, of course, where the submarines were at their most vulnerable. So a plan was devised to arm a number of merchant ships with a number of guns but to have this armament concealed so that the U-boats would, unsuspectingly, surface to engage the merchant ship with its gun. The decoy ship would then drop its pretence and open fire on the U-boat. For this the merchant ships had to have collapsible deck structures concealing the guns that could be rapidly dropped in action.

An example of how this worked is provided with this story about HMS *Penshurst*, otherwise known as HMS *Q-7*. With her three masts, low freeboard and funnel aft, *Penshurst* resembled an oil tanker. In fact she was armed with two 4-inch guns as well as two 6-pounder and two 12-pounder guns.

HMS *Q-7* first went into action in November 1916 when she sank *UB-19* on the 30th of that month, in what has been described as a text-book Q-ship engagement. Captain Francis Grenfell described the action: "I passed the word to the guns that she [*UB-19*] was coming round to our starboard quarter, and then slithered across the deck and had another spy-hole cut in the screen in a moment. Then I saw her coming round the stern, and when she was on the quarter and the guns were all bearing on her I leapt for the signal bell and signalled 'open fire'.

"Inside ten seconds the 3-pounder got off its first shot, which carried a man clean off the conning tower; the second immediately afterwards went through her engine room. The 6-pounder and the 12-pounder took up the game almost at once, and the shells began to burst all over the sub. We hit her mostly in the conning tower and the after part. Shells burst all along her water line ….

"Most of the conning tower was blown clean away, and one shell blew a great sheet of deck plating spinning into the air. We could see the men running on her deck, and falling or diving overboard. A knot gathered at the fore and where the shells were less numerous. It was a grand sight – and I must admit I mafficked [celebrate, as in Mafeking Day] – I had to run down and shake old Naylor, at the 12-pounder, by the hand.

"All this time the sub was going ahead … and we learned afterwards that our second shot, besides preventing her submerging, also prevented them stopping engines. The submarine was now partly shrouded by the smoke of the bursting shells, and a shout went up that the men on her were waving in token of surrender. I stopped the firing, but as I was mindful of Admiral Colville's injunction to me when we commissioned not to take any chances, but to go on firing until the sub sank, I commenced firing again. A very little more, however, convinced

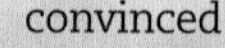

LEFT: **Dazzle camouflage on an Allied warship – in this case the USS *Nebraska* in the US Navy's yard at Norfolk, Virginia, on 20 April 1918.** (US National Archives)

Trawling for Submarines

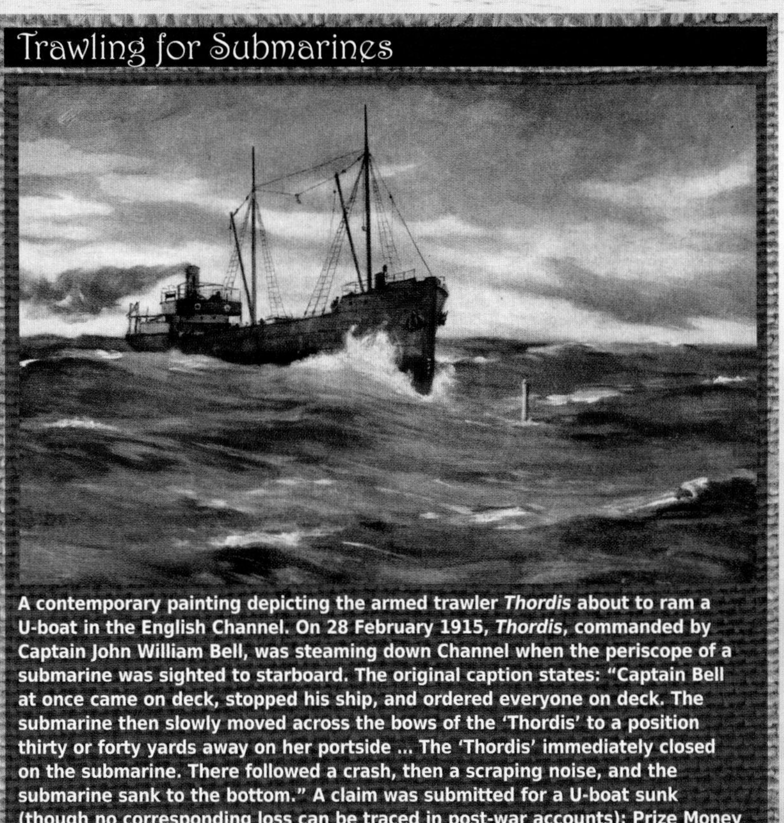

A contemporary painting depicting the armed trawler *Thordis* about to ram a U-boat in the English Channel. On 28 February 1915, *Thordis*, commanded by Captain John William Bell, was steaming down Channel when the periscope of a submarine was sighted to starboard. The original caption states: "Captain Bell at once came on deck, stopped his ship, and ordered everyone on deck. The submarine then slowly moved across the bows of the 'Thordis' to a position thirty or forty yards away on her portside ... The 'Thordis' immediately closed on the submarine. There followed a crash, then a scraping noise, and the submarine sank to the bottom." A claim was submitted for a U-boat sunk (though no corresponding loss can be traced in post-war accounts); Prize Money was distributed among the Captain and crew. Captain Bell also received the Distinguished Service Cross, and was given a commission in the Royal Naval Reserve. (HMP)

ABOVE: **The captured German minelayer submarine *UC-5* on the Thames. After a successful career, sinking twenty-nine ships in the same number of patrols, and having been the first U-boat minelayer to penetrate into the English Channel, *UC-5* ran aground while on patrol on 27 April 1916 and was scuttled. Her crew was captured by HMS *Firedrake*; the submarine itself was captured and subsequently displayed at Temple Pier on the Thames and in New York.** (US Library of Congress)

me that all was up with her."

For the destruction of *UB-19* Grenfell was awarded the Distinguished Service Order which he received at Buckingham Palace on 14 February 1917. For their part, the Q-ships sank eleven U-boats but the Germans soon realised what was happening and became more cautious. They even began to use torpedoes at long-range rather than risk a close combat with what might not be the merchant ship that appeared in their periscopes.

Much effort was also put into preventing the U-boats from putting to sea in the first place. In the summer of 1914, a force of destroyers was sent to Dover to join the warships already based there, becoming the nucleus of what became known as the Dover Patrol. The patrol's aim was simple – keep the enemy submarines penned into their bases and prevent them from using the English Channel as a route to the Atlantic.

As the war progressed, the patrol included cruisers, monitors, destroyers, armed trawlers and drifters, paddle minesweepers, armed yachts, motor launches and coastal motor boats, submarines, seaplanes, aeroplanes and even airships, mirroring the resources of the so-called Northern Patrol. A base was also established at Dunkirk.

The Dover Barrage was also constructed. Begun in February 1915, the barrage eventually consisted of a series of steel nets anchored to the sea bed at various points and used to "trap" enemy submarines. The nets were accompanied by extensive minefields, all of which were regularly patrolled. The first success came on 4 March 1915, when *U-8* was caught in the indicator nets, attacked and sunk. Shocked, the German Navy forbade its U-boat captains to use the English Channel for the best part of a year.

Such was the success of the Allied efforts that by the end of the war the U-boats were being effectively blockaded within their own harbours, dramatically reducing the effect they had on the vital trans-Atlantic shipping.

Whilst the German submarines did sink 12,850,815 tons of shipping, it was at the cost to themselves of 178 U-boats, which represented fifty per cent of the entire submarine fleet deployed during the war.

Desert Warrior

Lawrence of Arabia

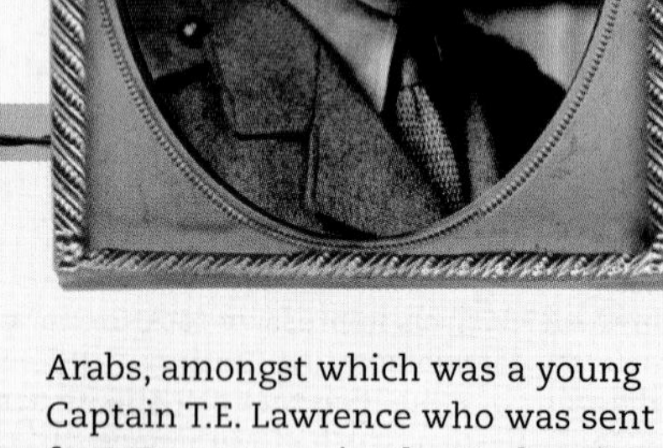

RIGHT: A portrait of T.E. Lawrence taken while he was serving as British Liaison Officer to Emir Faisal at the Versailles Peace Conference in 1919. (HMP)

BELOW RIGHT: The Arab Revolt underway. This picture, taken by T.E. Lawrence himself on 3 January 1917, from the back of a camel, shows Faisal bin Hussein bin Ali al-Hashimi, Sharif and Emir of Mecca, leading Arab fighters northwards towards the Red Sea port of Al Wajh. It was from Al Wajh that the assault on Aqaba was subsequently launched. (Courtesy of Steve and Liz James)

T.E. Lawrence, Lawrence of Arabia, was just one of a number of British officers operating with the Arabs in guerrilla actions against the Ottomans during the First World War. Yet his exploits have become legendary, almost fictional in their drama and daring.

Long before Tsar Nicholas I declared Turkey to be "the sick man of Europe", the Ottoman Turks had struggled to maintain their authority over the many nations of which their empire was composed. Not the least of these were the Arabs, who sought their own identity and a separation from Constantinople. This was prompted, ironically, by Turkish nationalism which placed the needs of the Turkish state above any other influence, including religion. Turkish nationalism led to Arab nationalism – revolt was inevitable.

With the outbreak of war in 1914, Turkey joined the Central Powers (secretly on 2 August 1914; openly on 29 October 1914). Fearing trouble from the Arabs the Turks arrested, tortured (and later executed), many of the leading figures amongst the Arab nationalist movements in the key centres of Damascus and Beirut.

These and other oppressive measures prompted Grand Sharif Hussein bin Ali, the guardian of the holy city of Mecca, to enter into an alliance with Britain and France sometime around 8 June 1916. As part of this, the British High Commissioner in Egypt, Henry McMahon, promised Hussein that after the war the Arabs would have their own nation stretching from Persia to Egypt.

The Arab Revolt began with attacks upon the Turkish garrisons at Medina and Mecca. Though Medina remained in Turkish hands, by the end of September 1916 the Arabs had seized many of the Red Sea ports, with the help of the Royal Navy, and taken 6,000 Turkish prisoners.

The Arabs had far less success in the Hejaz region of what is now Saudi Arabia, which was held by a strong Turkish force of 15,000 men. Britain sent a number of Army officers into the Hejaz to help the Arabs, amongst which was a young Captain T.E. Lawrence who was sent from Egypt to assist the Hashemite forces in the Hejaz in October 1916.

Lawrence, who had graduated from Oxford with First Class Honours, had been working as an archaeologist in the Middle East before the war and knew the area well and he understood the Arabs and their customs. He was quickly accepted by the Arabs and became a close friend of two of the principal Arab leaders, Faisal (later King Faisal) and Abdullah. Through these friendships Lawrence was able to co-ordinate the activities of the Arabs in support of British forces in the region.

With considerable aid and money from Britain and France, the Arab Revolt's momentum was maintained. Lawrence persuaded Faisal not to continue throwing his men at the walls of Medina but instead to attack the Hejaz railway. This tied down large numbers of Turkish troops in guarding and repairing the line

In the 1980s this impressive rock formation in Wadi Rum was named "The Seven Pillars of Wisdom" after Lawrence's memoir, commemorating the fact that he was based there for many of his operations during the Arab Revolt. Indeed, the ruins of a building that can still be seen by visitors in the Wadi near this spot are reputed to be those of Lawrence's accommodation. Much of the filming of David Lean's 1962 film Lawrence of Arabia was undertaken in Wadi Rum. (Courtesy of Thomas Edward Lawre)

without incurring Arab casualties.

By early 1917, some 70,000 Arabs had joined the revolt, but between them were only twenty-eight thousand rifles. The attacks on the Hejaz railway, nevertheless, did not require rifles, and throughout 1917 raids upon the railway caused immense disruption to Turkish supplies. These actions did not necessarily include Lawrence. Other British officers, such as Lieutenant-Colonel Stewart Newcombe, Lieutenant Hornby and Major H. Garland, led many of these attacks.

The operation for which Lawrence has become best known is the Aqaba campaign of 1917. Aqaba is a port on the Red Sea. It was held by the Turks and it posed a threat not only to the revolt but also to British forces in Palestine and Egypt, as it was from here that the Turks had mounted an attack upon the Suez Canal in 1915. It was also suggested by Faisal that the port could be used by the British to supply his Arab forces as they moved further north.

An attack from the land was considered impossible because it was surrounded by the Nefud Desert which was believed by many to be impassable. Lawrence would prove the doubters wrong.

With only a small force, Lawrence set off in May 1917, encountering only slight resistance from small bands of Arabs in Turkish pay. In fact Lawrence's force lost more men through snakes and scorpions than enemy action!

In order to disguise the true nature of the operation, Lawrence mounted further attacks on the Hejaz railway, hoping that the Turks would think he was marching towards Damascus or Aleppo. On one occasion he undertook one such attack entirely single-handedly.

After an astonishing journey of eight weeks, Lawrence's force, which grew as numbers of local Bedouin joined their brother Arabs, seized Aqaba on 2 July. In the battle Lawrence was nearly killed when he accidentally shot the camel he was riding in the head and he was thrown to the ground.

Aqaba became Faisal's base from which his newly-titled 'Arab Northern Army' mounted raids into Jordan and Syria, with Lawrence being able to make contact with nationalists in Damascus. However, the Arabs could not hope to defeat the Turks alone and it was the Egyptian Expeditionary Force (EEF), under the command of General Edmund Allenby, which was ultimately able to secure victory in the Middle East.

The EEF, consisting of around 40,000 British, New Zealand and ➤➤

BELOW: **A view of the kind of terrain over which T.E. Lawrence's Arab forces operated in 1917. Corporal 1489 J.W. Thomas, who, as a member of the 1/6th Battalion Manchester Regiment had been assigned to T.E. Lawrence as a signaller, made the following comment on the picture's reverse: "Not a tree or shrub to give shade. Blistering hot by day, blistering cold by night."** (Courtesy of Steve and Liz James)

RIGHT: Captioned by Corporal Thomas as having been taken during the operations against Aqaba, he also added: "Trigger happy Bedouin swarming around the area. Notice the casual way they carried their arms. Glad to get away from them without being killed accidentally!" (Courtesy of Steve and Liz James)

ABOVE: The moment when Jerusalem surrendered. Reputedly taken at 08.00 hours on the morning of 9 December 1917, this picture shows the moment that the Mayor of Jerusalem, Hussein Bey al-Husayni, in the centre with the walking stick, met Sergeant F.G. Harcomb and Sergeant J. Sedgewick of 2/19th London Regiment, under the white flag of surrender. (US Library of Congress)

Entering Jerusalem

General Allenby's party is pictured about to walk through Jerusalem's Jaffa Gate during his formal entry into the city on 11 December 1917. The leading figure is that of Borton Pacha, the British Military Governor of the city, followed by his two Aides-de-Camp. Further behind, from right to left, are Colonel de Piepape, commander of the French detachment, General Edmund Allenby, and Lieutenant Colonel D'Agostino, CO of the Italian troops. Unlike the Kaiser during his visit in 1898, out of respect for the status of Jerusalem as the Holy City, Allenby elected to dismount and enter on foot. "I entered the city officially at noon, 11 December," he later wrote, "with a few of my staff, the commanders of the French and Italian detachments, the heads of the political missions, and the Military Attaches of France, Italy, and America... The procession was all afoot, and at Jaffa gate I was received by the guards representing England, Scotland, Ireland, Wales, Australia, New Zealand, India, France and Italy. The population received me well." (US Library of Congress)

Australian troops, defeated the Turks at the Battle of Beersheba at the end of October 1917. Having broken through the Turkish Gaza-Beersheba defensive line, the EEF advanced as far as Jerusalem.

The Turkish forces in Arabia were gradually driven out of every stronghold, with the EEF in their front and Lawrence and Faisal's men continuing their guerrilla operations against Turkish communications, particularly the key rail junction at Deraa, during Allenby's final great offensive in September 1918. The culmination of this was the Battle of Meggido.

It was during the last stages of this two-week-long battle that Lawrence described in his famous book on the Arab Revolt, The Seven Pillars of Wisdom, an incident on 27 September when he and his Arab force were pursuing some of the retreating Turks. As the Arabs chased after the 2,000-strong Turkish column, they came upon the village of Tafas south of Damascus. The Turks had rampaged through the village, as Lawrence wrote: "The village lay still under its slow wreaths of white smoke, as we rode near, on our guard. Some grey heaps seemed to hide in the long grass, embracing the ground in the close way of corpses. We looked away from these, knowing they were dead; but from one a little figure tottered off, as if to escape us. It was a child, three or four years old, whose dirty smock was stained red over one shoulder and side, with blood from a large half-fibrous wound, perhaps a lance thrust, just where neck and body joined ... We rode past the other bodies of men and women and four more dead babies, looking very soiled in the daylight, towards the village; whose loneliness we now

An oasis pictured during the Hejaz Campaign. A hand-written comment on the reverse of the image suggests that the individual on the right is in fact T.E. Lawrence. (Courtesy of Steve and Liz James)

"Our rifles grew so hot with sun and shooting that they seared our hands."

T.E. Lawrence

Troops of the Australian Light Horse advancing, with prisoners by the wayside, during the Battle of Megiddo. Such manoeuvres were frequently supported by the Allied aircraft deployed in support of the offensive. (Courtesy of the Australian War Memorial)

knew meant death and horror." The sight was too much for Lawrence and when the Arabs finally caught up with the Turks he issued the order, for the very first time, "to take no prisoners".

The Battle of Meggido was a disaster for the Turks, as only around 6,000 men, out of a total of approximately 34,000, escaped death or capture at the hands of the EEF and the Arabs. A month after the end of the battle the Turks appealed for an armistice.

The Arab Revolt undoubtedly tied down a large proportion of the Turkish Army, troops that otherwise might have been deployed against Britain's ally Russia. Britain, though, also deployed considerable forces, including the RFC/RAF and the Royal Navy. Supporting the revolt also cost huge amounts of money as many of the Arabs had to be bribed to join Faisal's forces. It has been estimated that by September 1918, the British were spending £220,000 a month.

Victory for the Arabs meant an end to Turkish influence in the Middle East, but it did not lead to a unified Arabia. As early as 1916, Britain and France had secretly decided that in the event of an Allied victory the Arab provinces outside the Arabian Peninsula would be divided into British and French spheres of interest. Further difficulties for the Arabs arose with the signing of the Balfour Declaration which promised the establishment in Palestine of a national home for the Jewish people.

The fighting in the Middle East which began in 1916 shows no sign of abating.

ABOVE: **After the war, Lawrence's importance continued. He is pictured here walking in the gardens of Government House, Jerusalem, in company with Winston Churchill (left) and Emir Abdullah (on the right) during a conference in 1921.** (US Library of Congress)

BELOW: **The aftermath of the Battle of Megiddo, 24 September 1918 – Turkish prisoners at Beirsan, some 6,000 in all. All of the men in the foreground are officers. The commander of the Turkish 16th Division is seated with a white arm band on the right. Prisoners are receiving rations in the centre and filing off to form a convoy.** (IWM Q12977)

AMERICA ENTERS THE WAR

At the outbreak of war in 1914, the President of the United States of America, Woodrow Wilson, declared his country would remain neutral "in thought and deed". Almost all the population of the US supported that view. Yet, two-and-a-half years later, the Americans were so outraged by the conduct of the Germans, they declared war.

The Great European War that broke out in 1914 was clearly going to be an event of world-wide significance. Though the USA was determined not to be drawn into the conflict in any way, there was no doubt that it would to some degree be affected. The most immediate consequence was that US ships trying to take goods into Germany fell foul of the Royal Navy's blockade and were turned back. The Germans likewise attempted to prevent neutral ships sailing to the UK, but not having the control of the seas enjoyed by the Royal Navy, they were unable to enforce any kind of blockade. Instead when they intercepted British and neutral vessels, they sank them. It was that approach that soured US-German relations and slowly began to turn the American public against the Central Powers.

On the morning of Sunday, 28 March 1915, the SS *Falaba*, a passenger ship of the Elder-Dempster Line, was steaming fifty or so miles off St. Anne's Head, on the Pembrokeshire coast, when a lookout reported that a German U-boat had surfaced alongside. *Falaba*'s captain, Frederick J. Davies, was hailed by the commander of *U-28*, *Kapitänleutnant* Baron Georg-Günther Freiherr von Forstner; the torpedo struck the passenger ship soon afterwards. It took just ten minutes for *Falaba* to sink.

No less than 104 persons, from a total of some 160 passengers and ninety crew, perished. The Allied press was soon full of graphic accounts of the crew of the U-boat laughing derisively at drowning men and women as their craft circled around them. The *Western Mail*, for example, reported that the U-boat "circled round drowning men and women … and offering not the slightest assistance".

One of the bodies subsequently washed ashore on the Irish coast was that of Leon C. Thrasher. Thrasher, or Thresher as he is sometimes referred to, was a 30-year-old mining engineer from Massachusetts. Subsequently buried in Stradbally Graveyard in County Kerry, his death – by drowning – gained him the epitaph of being the first American victim of Germany's policy of unrestricted submarine warfare.

If the death of Leon Thrasher was the first nail in the coffin of American neutrality, others soon followed. "The attack on April 28 on the American vessel *Cushing* by a German aeroplane [and] the torpedoing on May 1 of the American vessel *Gulflight* by a German submarine, as a result of which two or more American citizens met their death," were both instances cited in a memorandum which had been drafted by President Wilson himself and sent to the German government.

Matters came to a head on 7 May 1915. The liner RMS *Lusitania* was returning from New York to her home port of Liverpool. On board were 1,198 passengers and crew, many of

ABOVE: **At 32,000 tons, the RMS *Lusitania* was the largest passenger vessel on transatlantic service at the time of her sinking. This picture shows the moment that the second torpedo struck. Note the gaping hole in the hull.** (US Library of Congress)

British Propaganda

Needless to say, the British propaganda machine capitalized on the sinking of *Lusitania*. Though America remained neutral for the time being, the sinking of the liner caused a significant hardening of opinion against Germany, which eventually led to her entry into the First World War. In this poster, published in 1915 by the Parliamentary Recruiting Committee, we can see the image of Justice holding a sword in her extended right hand. She stands above the sea in which drowning figures are visible. In the background, the four-funnelled ocean liner sinks. (HMP)

whom were Americans.

As she was sailing around the south coast of Ireland *Lusitania* crossed the path of the German submarine U-20. Its commander, *Kapitänleutnant* Walther Schwieger, could scarcely believe his luck. He fired a single torpedo which struck *Lusitania* on her starboard bow. A second explosion followed and the great liner, rushing forward at speed, began to sink rapidly, bows first.

In less than twenty minutes *Lusitania* went down. "In the twinkling of an eye the monster disappeared", remembered one of the passengers, Oliver Bernard. "What I saw in the water was … one long scene of agony … floating debris on all sides, and men, women and children clinging for dear life to deck chairs and rafts. There were such desperate struggles as I will never forget. Many were entangled between chairs and rafts and upturned boats. One by one they seemed to fall off and give up."

Of the 1,959 passengers and crew aboard *Lusitania* at the time of the sinking, 1,195 lost their lives that afternoon in the waters of the Irish Channel. Amongst the dead were 128 Americans. The incident caused »

LEFT: **Lifeboats from *Lusitania* are gathered together after the sinking. A number of these lifeboats were subsequently used at locations around Great Britain - for example at Ramsgate in Kent - in support of fund-raising campaigns.** (US Library of Congress)

LEFT: **Detail on the Lusitania Memorial which can be seen in Casement Square, Cobh, Ireland. The *Lusitania* left New York City on 2 May 1915 bound for Britain - the same day that Germany started a series of newspaper announcements stating that a war zone had been declared around the British Isles. Five days later, on 7 May, a German submarine, *U-20*, fired a single torpedo that hit the liner. *Lusitania* sank with the loss of nearly 1,200 lives.** (With the kind permission of Jim Driscoll)

RIGHT: A photograph which, purported to have been taken by a passenger on board *Falaba*, shows the moment that the German U-boat *U-28*, commanded by *Kapitänleutnant* Baron Georg-Günther Freiherr von Forstner, surfaced alongside the passenger ship. (HMP)

a huge public outcry in the United States and most people thought that America would declare war on Germany. The subject was debated by the US administration but President Wilson stuck to his policy of non-intervention, although it was a stance becoming increasingly difficult to maintain.

Once again a message was sent to the German authorities by the US administration: "It is clearly wise and desirable that the government of the United States and the Imperial German government should come to a clear and full understanding as to the grave situation which has resulted."

ABOVE: A contemporary postcard which depicts the sinking of *Falaba*. The artist has chosen to depict *U-28* as described in a number of newspaper accounts of the time - with her pennant number painted out. The actions of *U-28* on this occasion had led to the sinking of the first passenger ship during the First World War. (HMP)

Recent incidents, the communication concluded, constituted "a series of events which the government of the United States has observed with growing concern, distress, and amazement".

Just a few months later another incident caused further anger and dismay in the US. In the early hours of 12 October 1915, a British national, still wearing her nurses' uniform, was led out into a yard at the Tir Nationale Rifle Range, in the Champ de Tir, Brussels. Alongside her was Phillipe Bancq, a Brussels-based architect. Shortly after at dawn, two German firing-squads, each of eight men, were paraded in front of the pair. When ordered, the soldiers opened fire, executing both Bancq and the British nurse – Edith Louisa Cavell.

After training as a nurse in London, in 1907 Edith Louisa Cavell travelled to Brussels where she became Matron of the Berkendael Medical Institute which, amongst other things, was one of the pioneering establishments for the training of nurses in Belgium. Following the German occupation of Brussels, the Institute became a Red Cross hospital, treating casualties from both sides. Nurse Cavell had remained to continue her work – permitted to do so by the occupying German forces.

The offence for which she had been executed was in helping British soldiers who had become trapped behind German lines after the Battle of Mons, escape to neutral Holland. Clearly Cavell was guilty of aiding the enemy, as the Germans saw it, but the decision to shoot a nurse whose only crime was to help others, was met with utter revulsion around the world, including, of course, in the United States.

Whereas the Americans, many of whom had Germanic backgrounds, were not inclined to pick sides or be judgemental at the outbreak of war, such acts began to sway public opinion. Increasingly, the Germans were seen as being barbaric, a description that was promoted, if not sometimes engineered, by the Allied propaganda machine.

There were other events that roused public condemnation in the United States. Holland had managed to remain neutral and British vessels still maintained a ferry service from Harwich to Rotterdam. The ferries were slow and highly vulnerable and could not be considered vital to the British war effort.

On 28 March 1915, the Great Western Railway ferry *Brussels* was

Nurse Edith Cavell

A picture of Edith Cavell. Her trial, held in Brussels, lasted just two days. The only incriminating evidence, apart from her confession, was a tattered postcard sent, unhelpfully, from Britain by a soldier thanking Edith for her help in getting him home. The trial ended with Edith Cavell being sentenced to death by shooting - a sentence that was duly carried out by German troops on 12 October 1915.
In the months and years following her death, countless newspaper articles, pamphlets, images, and books publicised Cavell's story. She became an iconic propaganda figure for military recruitment in Britain, and to help increase favourable sentiment towards the Allies in the United States of America.
Cavell's remains were returned to Britain after the war and a state funeral was held at Westminster Abbey. On 19 May 1919, her body was reburied at the east side of Norwich cathedral. A graveside service is still held there each Octpber.
(US Library of Congress)

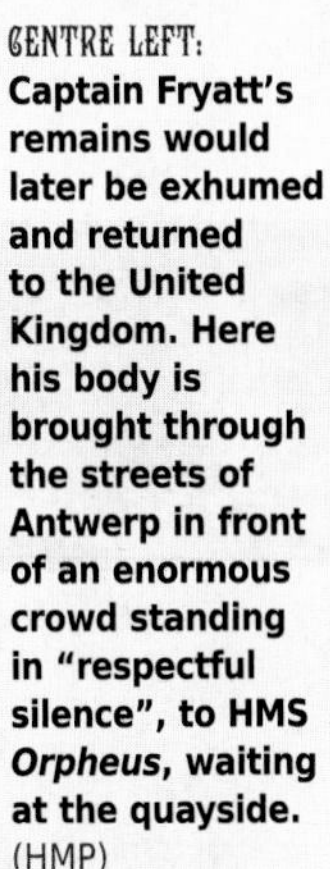

CENTRE LEFT: **Captain Fryatt's remains would later be exhumed and returned to the United Kingdom. Here his body is brought through the streets of Antwerp in front of an enormous crowd standing in "respectful silence", to HMS *Orpheus*, waiting at the quayside.** (HMP)

LEFT: **A portrait of Captain Charles Fryatt in the uniform of a Captain of the Great Eastern Railway.** (HMP)

approaching the Hook of Holland when the U-boat *U-33* surfaced in front of it and ordered the ferry to stop. "I could see it was no use trying to get away from him," Captain Charles Fryatt, the skipper of *Brussels*, explained in his report on the incident. "He could easily have torpedoed me and his speed was far greater than mine. So instead, Fryatt ordered Full Speed Ahead and *Brussels* charged straight at the German submarine.

The U-boat was forced to dive and *Brussels* made good its escape. The incident angered the Germans who were then determined to have their revenge. On the night of 22 June 1916, *Brussels* left the Hook with 100 Belgian and Russian refugees, and 390 tons of cargo and mail on board.

The Germans had been watching and waiting and shortly after *Brussels* was beyond Dutch waters she was surrounded by nine German patrol boats. There was no escape this time for *Brussels*, or indeed for Fryatt; the ferry was boarded and the crew taken prisoner. Under the German flag, *Brussels* was taken into Zeebrugge and then up the canal to Bruges. Most of the crew were taken to various PoW camps to see out the war, but special treatment was reserved for Fryatt.

An official German communiqué issued on 29 July, read: "On Thursday, at Bruges, before the Court Martial of the Marine Corps, the trial took place of Captain Charles Fryatt, of the British steamer 'Brussels' ... The accused was condemned to death because although he was not a member of a combatant force, he made an attempt on the afternoon of March 28th 1915, to ram the German submarine *U-33* ... The sentence was confirmed yesterday afternoon and carried out by shooting." Fryatt was buried in a cemetery near Bruges.

The news of Charles Fryatt's execution shocked the entire British nation and, indeed, most of the civilized world. Clearly it was the intention of the Germans to use Fryatt as an example to deter the captains of other merchant ships from trying to ram the U-boats. But their actions had the very opposite effect as it resulted in an immediate rise in volunteer recruitment across the UK.

The final straw came in February 1917 with the release of the famous Zimmermann telegram. The Foreign Secretary of the German Empire, Arthur Zimmermann, had sent a message to the German ambassador in Mexico. The telegram was intercepted by the British and decoded by Admiralty cryptographers. It read as follows:

"We intend to begin on the first of February unrestricted submarine warfare. We shall endeavour in spite of this to keep the United States of America neutral. In the event of this not succeeding, we make Mexico a proposal of alliance on the following basis: make war together, make peace together, generous financial support and an understanding on our part that Mexico is to reconquer the lost territory in Texas, New Mexico, and Arizona. The settlement in detail is left to you. You will inform the [Mexican] President of the above most secretly as soon as the outbreak of war with the United States of America is certain ... Please call the President's attention to the fact that the ruthless employment of our submarines now offers the prospect of compelling England in a few months to make peace."

The Germans renewed their campaign of unrestricted submarine warfare and in March 1917 five American cargo ships were sunk. When President Wilson asked Congress to vote for war on 2 April 1917, the result was never in doubt.

LEFT: **American soldiers pictured in trenches in France during 1918.** (US Library of Congress)

The First Blitz

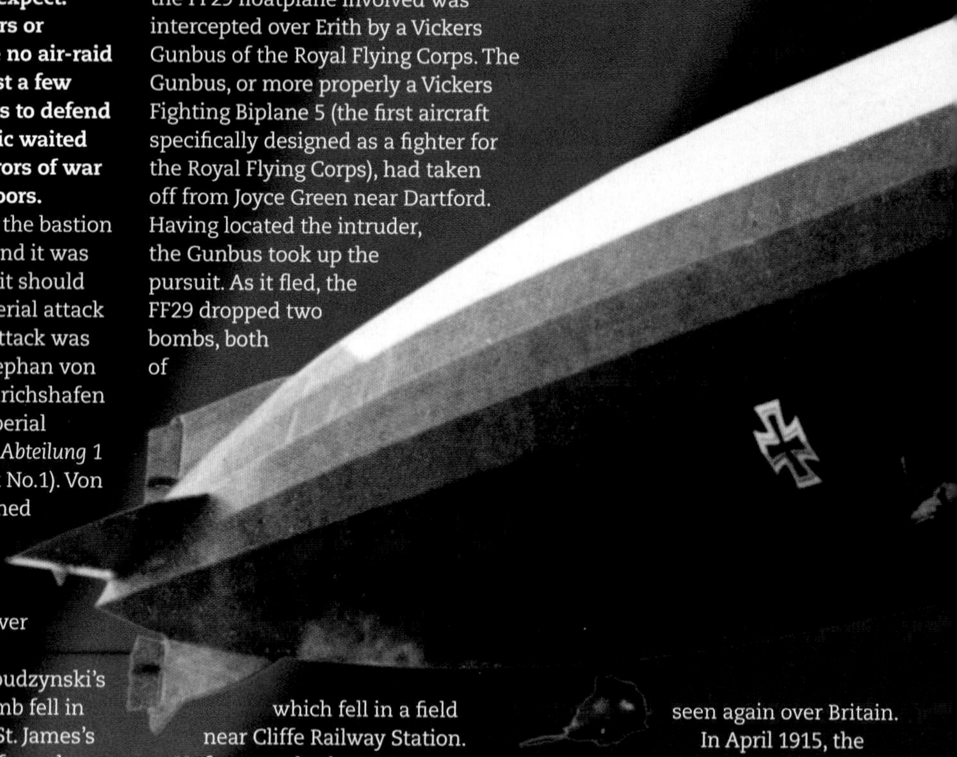

RIGHT: A view of Zeppelin *L48* in flight. This was one of the so-called "Height Climbers" which proved capable of very great altitudes, with *L55* achieving a record height for a dirigible of 24,000 feet on her way back from a bombing raid on 19 October 1917. (Imperial War Museum; Q58467)

No-one knew what to expect. There were no shelters or sandbags, there were no air-raid sirens and there were just a few modified high-angle guns to defend London. The British public waited in trepidation as the horrors of war were delivered to their doors.

Dover Castle had been the bastion of England for centuries and it was perhaps appropriate that it should be the target of the first aerial attack upon Great Britain. This attack was carried out by *Leutnant* Stephan von Proudzynski flying a Friedrichshafen FF29 floatplane of the Imperial German Navy's *See Flieger Abteilung* 1 (Naval Flying Detachment No.1). Von Proudzynski had approached Dover along the coast from the west and, at 5,000 feet, he heaved a single 22lb pound bomb over the side of the cockpit.

Unsurprisingly, von Proudzynski's aim was poor, and the bomb fell in a garden near the rear of St. James's Rectory – some 400 yards from the Castle. The subsequent explosion, leaving a crater ten feet wide and four feet deep, shattered some of the windows in the Rectory and houses nearby.

Mr. James Banks, a gardener at the Rectory, busy pruning a tree at the time of the explosion and who was blown from it branches suffering bruising, became the first ever person injured in an air raid on British soil.

This had not, however, been the first German attempt at bombing the Castle. Three days earlier, on 21 December 1914, a sister FF29 floatplane from the same unit, had also attacked Dover. The aircraft dropped two bombs – both of which fell harmlessly into the sea some distance from Admiralty Pier.

No doubt eager to build on this first ever successful air raid, *See Flieger Abteilung* 1 would return the next day. This time they were going for the big one – London's docklands. Yet again, another "first" would follow –the first ever successful interception of an enemy aircraft over the United Kingdom.

During its approach to London, the FF29 floatplane involved was intercepted over Erith by a Vickers Gunbus of the Royal Flying Corps. The Gunbus, or more properly a Vickers Fighting Biplane 5 (the first aircraft specifically designed as a fighter for the Royal Flying Corps), had taken off from Joyce Green near Dartford. Having located the intruder, the Gunbus took up the pursuit. As it fled, the FF29 dropped two bombs, both of which fell in a field near Cliffe Railway Station.

Unfortunately, the RFC crew was forced to abandon the attack when their single forward-firing machine-gun jammed. Though damaged, the FF29 was able to return to its base.

The next attacks on Britain were not delivered by aeroplanes, however, but by the much-feared, and much-vaunted, Zeppelin airships. The first successful Zeppelin raid was undertaken on the night of 19 January 1915. Conducted by the German Naval Airship Division, this attack was planned against London and the ports along the Humber. Rain and snow, with the inevitable poor visibility, resulted in Zeppelin *L6* turning back early whilst *L3* and *L4* lost their way, dropping their bomb loads upon Great Yarmouth and King's Lynn. Four people were killed and sixteen others were wounded.

Though these casualties were slight in comparison with the daily slaughter on the Western Front they shocked the nation, the newspapers describing the German action as "murderous and cowardly". The raids, though, were destined to increase in ferocity; nevertheless it was three months before the Zeppelins were seen again over Britain.

In April 1915, the north-east and eastern coasts were attacked with little damage being caused and many of the airships failing to reach Britain due either to poor weather conditions or poor navigation. The Zeppelins' fortunes, though, were about to change.

On the clear evening of 31 May 1915, *LZ38*, set off from Brussels. Flying over Margate and Southend, it headed inland to London. At 22.50 hours the airship dropped its first batch of bombs over the East End. Below, the scene was one of uncontrolled panic.

Once again casualties were not high, with seven people being killed, though the East Enders were furious. Never before had the capital of the Empire been violated in this fashion and so unique was the event that thousands paid a penny each to wander through the devastated houses where some of the victims had died.

The First Sea Lord, Admiral of the Fleet "Jacky" Fisher summed up the apprehensions of many at this time: "A Zeppelin holocaust from a ton of explosives dropped from the

clouds on to Horse Guards Parade," he feared would destroy "in one shattering explosion all the historic buildings surrounding the square with Admirals, Generals, Statesmen and Civil Servants under the ruins in one red burial tent".

In mid-1915 the German Army and Navy took receipt of larger and more powerful airships. These were 536 feet long and sixty-one feet in diameter, and were powered by four 210hp Maybach engines which enabled the great ships to climb at a rate of more than 1,000 feet per minute. Fisher's fears were obviously exaggerated, but without doubt, London would see more, and larger, ships in the sky.

Gravesend was struck on 4 June, Hull two days later and Tyneside nine days after that. Repeated attempts to reach London in early August failed, but on 10th of the month Leytonstone and Walthamstow were bombed.

September saw more successful attacks and on 13 October 1915, *Kapitänleutnant* Joachim Breithaupt commanded *L15* in a raid on the City: "At 19.30 hours we were between Cromer and Great Yarmouth at a height of 6,500 feet. The visibility was good under a starlit sky. We took our bearings, waited for full darkness, »

ABOVE: **The blue plaque in Dover which marks the spot where the first bomb dropped from the air landed on British soil.** (Courtesy of Paul Wells)

LEFT: **The damage caused to one building in Great Yarmouth following the Zeppelin attack of 19 January 1915. The original caption marked on the back states: "Mr Ellis, wounded by a bomb, and his ruined house at the junction of Lancaster Road with St Peter's Plain."** (HMP)

The Dolphin Tavern

On the night of the 8/9 September 1915, The Dolphin Tavern in Red Lion Street, London, was damaged by a bomb dropped by Zeppelin *L13* commanded by *Kapitanleutnant* Heinrich Mathy. Mathy was by then already well known both in Germany and Britain as one of the most daring and feared Zeppelin commanders. At 22.40 hours the high explosive bomb struck, and exploded, just outside the public house, blowing in the entrance and devastating the interior. The explosion and subsequent events killed three people - one of whom was Fireman Green who died as the result of severe burns received trying to put out fires in nearby houses. This interesting memento of the raid - a clock, found in the wreckage that stopped the moment the bomb hit - still hangs on the wall next to the bar. (Courtesy of Rob Langham)

A damaged building at the Royal Hospital, Chelsea, following the attack by twenty Gotha G.V. bombers on 13 June 1917. This was the first of two daylight Gotha GV raids on London. Piles of timber and brick rubble can be seen in the foreground, and the building has been damaged in such a way that it is possible to see several rooms inside it. (Courtesy of Tim Lynch)

and then steered a direct course for our objective – London. As we crossed over the coast we came under sharp fire from the batteries, and the ships were lit up by the searchlights of the coastguard and shore batteries.

"As we flew over the land we checked our position from time to time by dropping light bombs. At about 21.30 hours the Thames, with its characteristic windings, was clearly distinguishable below us. Suddenly, from all sides, searchlights leaped out towards us, and as we flew over Tottenham a wild barrage from the anti-aircraft positions began. The shells burst at a good height right in our course. I therefore rose, after dropping three explosive bombs.

"We then steered over Hyde Park, in the direction of the City. The picture we saw was indescribably beautiful – shrapnel bursting all around, our own bombs bursting and the flashes from the anti-aircraft batteries below. We flew over the City at between 9,000 and 9,800 feet and dropped twenty 110lb bombs, and all the incendiary bombs. We could see large explosions between Charing Cross Station and the Bank of England."

The airship attacks continued throughout 1915. In total there were twenty raids against targets in the UK that year and it seemed that there was little that the Royal Flying Corps or the Royal Naval Air Service could do about it. The Zeppelins were simply able to fly higher than the British fighters.

In response to the Zeppelin attacks a more concerted method of Home Defence was put together during the course of 1916. Searchlights were introduced in support of increasing numbers of anti-aircraft guns. The RFC also claimed its first victim in the skies over Britain when Lieutenant William Leefe Robinson shot down a Schütte-Lanz airship, *SL11*, on 3 September that year.

Despite the improved air defence over the UK, it was the winter weather systems that blow in from the Atlantic that were Britain's best protection against the airship raids. The Germans could never mount a continuous offensive against the UK if they limited their operations to airships.

They therefore turned to the aircraft that were now becoming available to them in increasing numbers. By the autumn of 1916, the Germans began to plan Operation *Türkenkreuz* – a daylight bombing offensive against Britain using the powerful new Gotha bombers to supplement the Zeppelin attacks.

A lone bomber had dropped six bombs on London on the night of 28 November 1916, and the success of the mission encouraged the planners to undertake an all-out offensive. With a wingspan of seventy-seven feet, the Gotha IV carried a crew of three and a load of over 600lbs of bombs, at a height of around 21,000 feet and at a speed of 90mph. It carried up to four machine-guns and, flying in formation, could easily defend itself from attacking fighters.

On 25 May 1917, twenty-three Gothas took off for a daylight raid on London. Mechanical problems led to

BOTTOM RIGHT: **The ruins of Messrs Odhams Printing Works, 93 Long Acre, London, which was bombed by two Gothas in the worst bombing incident of the war. A bomb fell on the pavement immediately under the north wall of the building and exploded in the basement. A portion of the wall was blown out and the superstructure collapsed. In addition to wrecking one half of the building, the bomb started a fire which spread rapidly until the whole building was affected. The lower storey was completely destroyed which was made more serious by the fact that the building was used as an air raid shelter and contained about 100 people when it was struck, of whom thirty-eight were killed and eighty-five injured.** (Courtesy of Tim Lynch)

TOP LEFT: **A commercially produced German postcard depicting members of ground crew bombing-up a Gotha in preparation for another attack on the UK. The Gothas carried out twenty-two raids on Britain, dropping 84,740kg of bombs for the loss of sixty-one aircraft.** (HMP)

"On 13 June 1917, eighteen Gothas appeared in formation over London in broad daylight."

some turning back, whilst poor weather forced the remainder to divert to secondary targets, namely the Channel port of Folkestone and the Army camp at Shorncliffe. In total, ninety-five people died and 195 were injured, mostly in the Folkestone area. At Shorncliffe, eighteen soldiers were killed, a further ninety were wounded.

On 13 June 1917, eighteen Gothas appeared in formation over London in broad daylight. Over ninety British fighters were sent against them but not one raider was destroyed. Flying at around 12,000 feet, the bombers dropped 100 bombs with most falling within a mile of Liverpool Street station. One struck the County Council school in Poplar, killing two children as it passed through the building before exploding in a ground floor nursery classroom where around sixty-four children were sheltering.

According to *The Times*, eighteen children were "blown into unrecognizable fragments". In all 162 people, all but four of them civilians, were killed and 432 injured. It was the highest death toll of the bombing so far.

Many people felt a mixture of outrage and fear. For the first time, children were evacuated from the most threatened areas and, as the raids continued, people were injured as crowds stampeded into the Underground whenever an aircraft appeared. By that summer, 200 fighters needed on the Western Front were tied up on Home Defence duties. Air Commodore Lionel Charlton described the raid as "the beginning of a new epoch in the history of warfare".

The Gotha and Zeppelin raids continued until August 1918. During the previous winter, the Germans also introduced the Zeppelin-Staaken R.VI – the "Giant". A four-engine bomber with a crew of seven, the Giant was capable of carrying eighteen 100kg bombs.

Nearly 9,000 German bombs of a total weight of 280 tons were dropped on British soil in fifty-one airship and fifty-two aeroplane attacks during the First World War. In all 1,412 people were killed and 3,408 others were wounded as a result of these raids, London suffering more than half of the casualties - 670 killed and 1,962 injured. There were fewer German casualties of Allied aerial bombing: just 740 killed and 1,900 wounded.

When the Second World War came, the British people had a much better idea of what to expect and this time, at least in part, they would be ready.

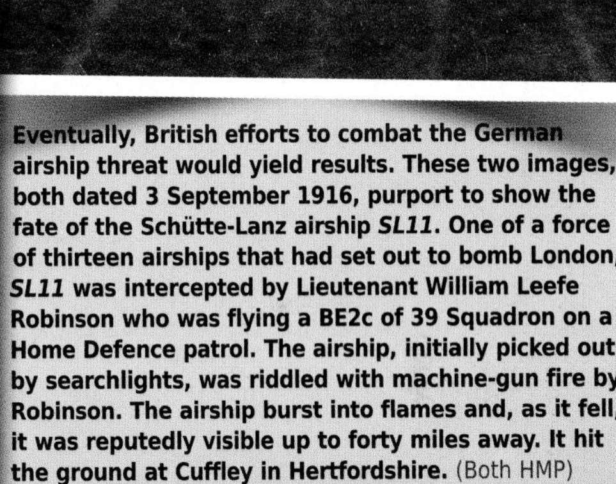

Eventually, British efforts to combat the German airship threat would yield results. These two images, both dated 3 September 1916, purport to show the fate of the Schütte-Lanz airship *SL11*. One of a force of thirteen airships that had set out to bomb London, *SL11* was intercepted by Lieutenant William Leefe Robinson who was flying a BE2c of 39 Squadron on a Home Defence patrol. The airship, initially picked out by searchlights, was riddled with machine-gun fire by Robinson. The airship burst into flames and, as it fell, it was reputedly visible up to forty miles away. It hit the ground at Cuffley in Hertfordshire. (Both HMP)

THE WORLD AT WAR

The conflict which began as the Great European War rapidly spread around the globe to become a world-wide conflagration. Africa, East and West, the Middle and Far East, all became theatres of war. In Europe itself, it was not just the Western Front that experienced the horrors of modern warfare, with bitter fighting taking place in Italy and Salonika. The conflict of 1914-1918 was indeed a world war.

The unified state of Germany had only been in existence for forty-three years when war broke out in 1914. Like so many of the European nations, this new Germany sought the prestige of an empire and quickly began to acquire territory in Africa. In 1884 Germany seized Togoland and part of Ghana to form the West African Togoland Protectorate (*Schutzgebiet* Togo). At the same time as the Germans took control of Togoland, they also took control of parts of Nigeria, Gabon, the Congo and Cameroon, which became the Protectorate of Kamerun. When war was declared in 1914 Britain immediately planned to seize these colonies.

The outbreak of war left the Togoland Protectorate unprepared, with less than 700 men, mostly natives, to defend the territory. Consequently, British and French troops occupied the Protectorate on 7 August 1914, without opposition.

It was a different matter in Kamerun where the 1,855 German *Schutztruppen* were supplemented by around 6,000 locally-raised troops. On 8 August, a mounted detachment from the West African Frontier Force from Kano in northern Nigeria set out towards Kamerun; at the same time, French troops moved from French Equatorial Africa. This British force crossed the border into German territory on 25 August. Later that day it came into contact with German troops at the border station at Tepe on the Benue River. After the skirmish, which involved fierce fighting, the enemy forces withdrew and the British occupied the station. Few casualties were suffered by either side.

More fighting, and more battles, followed and it was not until 1916 that the Allied forces finally defeated the Germans. The conflict in Kamerun cost France and Britain almost 2,000 men.

The fighting in East Africa was on a far greater scale. Around a quarter of a million Allied troops served in the East African theatre, incurring some 10,000 casualties. The Allies employed approximately 600,000 bearers throughout the course of the campaign and it has been estimated that the fighting cost the lives of 365,000 civilians.

Britain assumed that German East Africa would fall easily into their hands, attacking German outposts near Lake Victoria on 5 August 1914. Three days later, British warships bombarded Dar es Salaam from the sea. The Germans responded, with General Paul Emil von Lettow-Vorbeck leading an invasion of British East Africa.

Von Lettow's early success prompted the Allies to mount a large-scale invasion of the German territory. Two Indian Expeditionary Forces (classified as B and C, as the first Indian Expeditionary Force was sent to the Western Front), totalling 12,000 men, were assembled and despatched to East Africa. At the battles of Tanga and Kilamanjaro the two Expeditionary Forces were defeated by the numerically inferior German Army, resulting in what has been described as amongst "the most »

MAIN PICTURE BELOW: **Even during the dark days of the German's offensive on the Western Front in 1918, when the image seen here was taken on the North West Frontier, Britain's colonial wars still needed fighting. The original caption for this photograph says it all: "Numbers 6 and 7 Platoons on the piquet - our first day under fire."** (HMP)

ABOVE LEFT: **For those who fought in the so-called "Forgotten Campaigns" of the First World War, the chance of death was ever present. For this soldier from the Royal Sussex Regiment, his posting to the North West Frontier was one from which he did not return. During the First World War, ninety-one Other Ranks died or were killed whilst serving on the North West Frontier.** (HMP)

RIGHT: Gurkhas pictured having just returned from manoeuvres in early 1918. At the outbreak of the First World War the whole of the Nepalese Army was placed at the disposal of the British Crown. Over 16,000 Nepalese troops and Gurkhas were consequently deployed on the North West Frontier or as garrison battalions in India, replacing troops of the British Indian Army who were used to fight overseas. (HMP)

notable failures in British military history".

The naval war in East Africa also saw the German light cruiser SMS *Königsberg* sink the cruiser HMS *Pegasus* before the German ship was destroyed by warships of the British Cape squadron.

Fighting even took place on Lake Tanganyika itself. It was the story that inspired the Humphrey Bogart film *The African Queen*; two British gunboats were dragged overland halfway across Africa in 1915 to oppose German vessels on Lake Tanganyika in 1915.

Greater numbers of Allied troops were despatched to East Africa to try and end German resistance. Forces from South Africa and Rhodesia, led by General Smuts and including Belgian troops from the Belgian Congo, joined the Indian forces. Von Lettow continued to be successful, achieving a remarkable victory at the Battle of Mahiwa in October 1917, inflicting almost 3,000 casualties on a combined South African and Nigerian force for the loss of only around 500 men. When the First World War came to an end, von Lettow remained undefeated.

British involvement in China was, by the time of the First World War, long established. There had been trading links with the Chinese Empire for over two centuries and the British had established themselves in a number of ports throughout China. At the end of the nineteenth century the Germans had also been looking for a place where they could station their Pacific Squadron and they took control of Kiaochou Bay and set about making the village of Tsingtao into a German town. In a matter of years they had built a port suitable for the warships.

By 1914 the Germans had a strong Pacific Squadron commanded by Admiral von Spee and included such ships as the armoured cruisers SMS *Scharnhorst* and SMS *Gneisenau*. The squadron was powerful and the outbreak of the war in Europe clearly raised concerns about the squadron operating in the Pacific. Britain recognised that the port could not be allowed to provide supply and shelter for such a squadron and turned to their Japanese allies for assistance in controlling the waters around eastern China and to effectively blockade the port of Tsingtao.

Accordingly, the Japanese supplied almost 40,000 men, whilst the British deployed only the 2nd Battalion The South Wales Borderers and a half Battalion of the 36th Sikhs – in all about 1,500 men. The Germans, with just a tenth of the number of troops, held out for two months, finally succumbing on 7 November 1914.

Whilst the fighting in Arabia is well known, thanks to the exploits of T.E. Lawrence, the Middle East also saw much action in the area of Mesopotamia, known today as Iraq.

RIGHT: For the British, the Tsingtao campaign began on 22 September 1914, when men of 2nd Battalion The South Wales Borderers landed at Laoshan Bay prior to undertaking a forty-mile march on Tsingtao - the start of which is seen here. The original caption notes that "the British soldiers wearing shorts" are attracting "the noticeable interest of their Japanese allies"! (HMP)

The fighting here was for control of the oilfields of the Persian Gulf.

Though most of this region was under Ottoman control, the British Anglo-Persian Oil Company had exclusive rights to drill for oil. Shortly after the outbreak of war a fourth Indian Expeditionary Force (D) was despatched to Abadan to protect the oil fields and the refinery located there. The Anglo-Indian force found itself confronted by the Ottoman Fourth Army, with the first major engagement being the Battle of Shaiba on 12–14 April 1915.

This was a victory for the Allied troops but the Turks reversed the result at the Battle of Ctesiphon, fought between 22 and 25 November. The British Empire forces dropped back on the town of Kut, 100 miles south of Bagdad. The Ottomans surrounded Kut and the 8,000 British and Indian troops were besieged for more than four months. Numerous relief attempts were made resulting in heavy defeats for the British forces. One notable incident occurred in April 1916, when aircraft from the Royal Flying Corps' 30 Squadron dropped food and ammunition to the defenders in what was the first air supply operation in history.

British leaders attempted to buy their troops out. A team of officers, including T.E. Lawrence were sent to negotiate a secret deal with the Ottomans. The British offered £2 million and promised they would not fight the Ottoman troops in the area again, in exchange for Townshend's troops. The offer was rejected and on 29 April 1916, in what one historian described as "the most abject capitulation in Britain's military history", the garrison surrendered. Total Allied losses amounted to around 30,000 men, with a further 13,000 being taken prisoner.

In October 1915 a combined Franco-British force of two large brigades landed at Salonika (today's Thessalonika) at the request of the Greek Prime Minister. The objective was to help the Serbs in their »

LEFT: **A member of the German *Schutztruppe* in East Africa, more commonly referred to as askaris, pictured holding a German flag. The colonial force for German East Africa was established by an act of the Reichstag on 22 March 1891.** (Bundesarchiv; Bild105-DOA6369)

ABOVE: **Men from the 25th (Frontiersmen) Service Battalion Royal Fusiliers (City of London Regiment) pictured taking a rest in the bush Maktau Camp during the East African Campaign.** (Courtesy of Kevin Patience)

Within a matter of days of the loss of the SMS *Königsberg*, the cruiser's crew was back on board removing the ten Krupp guns and ammunition, together with any other useful items. In all there were eight 10.5cm guns and two smaller 8.8cm guns. The guns were taken to Dar es Salaam – during which journey this image was taken – where they were fitted with carriages and went on to see action against the Allies in East Africa over the next two years. (Deutsches Bundesarchiv)

German askaris in action during 1915 destroying a stretch of the British railway line near a location known as Maktau during the fighting in East Africa. (Courtesy of Kevin Patience)

RIGHT: An alternative method of transport used by the British on the Uganda Railway during the East African campaign – a chain drive Albion lorry that has been converted to run on the metre-gauge track. (Courtesy of Kevin Patience)

BELOW: Commonwealth troops in a trench on the Salonika front. Life in this part of southern Europe was far from easy, for this was a front where diseases such as malaria and influenza were rife. In 1916 it had been possible to evacuate the most serious cases of those suffering from disease. However, the beginning of unrestricted submarine warfare in April 1917 meant that this was no longer possible. Consequently the cases of malaria rose rapidly as the infected men were compelled to stay in Macedonia. Hospital admissions in 1917 alone were 63,396 out of strength of about 100,000 men. The men also had to cope with the most amazing extremes of temperature. (HMP)

fight against Bulgarian aggression, but the expedition arrived too late, the Serbian army having been beaten by a combined Bulgarian and German force before the Allies landed.

The Allied and Central Powers forces settled down opposite each other along what became known as the Macedonian Front which ran from the Adriatic coast in Albania to the Struma River in Greece which reached the Aegean. Though more than half-a-million men were deployed on both sides, there were no major battles until September 1918 when the Allies mounted a major offensive. At the Battle of Dobro Pole on 15 September, the Bulgarian Army was so heavily defeated that the Bulgarians sought an armistice, withdrawing from the Central Powers. Eventually Serbia was re-taken and the fighting on this front ended on 3 November 1918.

Despite the length of the campaign, and number of men involved, Salonika was widely regarded, both in Britain and in Germany, as little more than a sideshow. The military actions that did take place routinely received little attention in the press or, worse, went unreported. On the occasion when mention was made, comments were often disparaging – at one time, the men of the British Army serving in this expeditionary force were called the "Gardeners of Salonika". It has been said that people were even heard to remark that "if you want a holiday, go to Salonika".

It would be malaria that ensured that service on this "Forgotten Front" was no escape from the horrors on the Western Front. By October 1916 there had been no fewer than 162,000 cases of the disease – though effective treatment with quinine ensured that the number of deaths from malaria was limited to 821.

Italy was a member of the Triple Alliance with Austria-Hungary and Germany but when war broke out in 1914, Italy refused to be drawn into the fighting. Such an alliance was a peculiar arrangement as Austria had occupied large parts of Italy from 1714 until the Italians had fought off the Austrian yoke and achieved national unification in 1861. Italy, therefore, needed little persuasion to leave the Triple Alliance and join the Allies, which it did in 1915 under the promise of being granted some of Austria's territory after the war.

Italy opened the fighting with an attack against Austrian-held Slovenia. The Austrians, however, had strong defensive positions along the formidable Julian Alps which the Italians were unable to penetrate. Throughout 1916 this mountain warfare raged in harsh conditions and with neither side able to gain a significant advantage. The situation changed in 1917 when the Italians managed a major breakthrough and appeared to be on the verge of victory. This prompted the Germans to send forces to help their allies. The Italians were driven back and all their earlier gains were forfeited. Italy was on the point of defeat until the German troops were withdrawn to join in the Spring Offensive on the Western Front. The Italians regrouped and defeated the Austrians at the Battle of Vittorio Veneto. The latter were so badly beaten (135,000 dead or wounded and 300,000 captured) that the Austrian Army virtually ceased to exist. The Italian Front had seen the involvement of 13,000,000 men and resulted in combined casualties totalling around 3,000,000 men.

"This Senseless Disaster"

The Battle of Passchendaele

The Germans held the high ground that formed an arc around the salient which the British and Commonwealth forces had formed to defend the key Belgian city of Ypres. After many months of planning, in the summer of 1917, the start of the operations to drive the Germans from the high ground began. This was the third great battle to consume the devastated area around Ypres, the Battle of Passchendaele.

The Ypres salient protruded way beyond the Allied front line. The high ground around the salient was held by the Germans and from its flanks they could fire not just into the British lines, but into the rear areas as well. There was no escape from the German guns. The only way the shocking casualties the British were taking every week could be reduced was by seizing the high ground.

That high ground around the Ypres salient had been held by the Germans since 1914. In the intervening two-and-a-half years their defences on the ridge which arced around the salient had been rendered formidable. Any hope of assailing such strong positions required extensive planning and preparation. This began in June 1917 with an attempt to capture the Messines Ridge to the south-west of Ypres. Its capture would, to a large degree, "straighten out" the British front, bringing it almost in line with the bulge of the salient.

In order to give the attacking troops any chance of success, a huge preliminary artillery bombardment was planned along with a series of massive mines placed under the German positions which would blow the fortifications, and their defenders, high into the sky.

The Germans were aware that the British were mining under their positions and made every effort to locate them underground, but were unable to find them before the start of the great attack. For a week the British artillery pounded the ridge and then at 03.10 hours on 7 June, about an hour before dawn, the plungers were pressed. "The earth seemed to open and rise up to the sky," described Captain Greener of 175 Tunnelling Company, Royal Engineers. "It was all shot and flame. The dust and smoke was terrific. And all this debris falling back."

Greener, of course, knew all about the mines, but the infantry were only informed a minute or two before the detonations. "None of us had seen anything like it ever," reflected Rifleman Cantlon of the King's Royal Rifles. "It was just one mass of flames. The whole world seemed to go up in the air."

The infantry charged the ridge and by 06.30 hours they had taken all of the German positions on the crest. The Germans repeatedly attempted to re-take the ridge but were driven back.

The loss of the Messines Ridge was a serious blow to the German commanders who were well aware that it was merely a prelude to a far greater offensive. It was, one observer recorded, "the battle which all the world has been expecting". Despite being ejected from the Messines Ridge, the Germans were well prepared for the onslaught that they knew was imminent. >>

BELOW: A silhouetted file of men of the 8th Battalion, East Yorkshire Regiment pictured picking their way round shell craters in newly won ground at Frezenburg, 5 September 1917. (HMP)

"The whole thing became a drawn-out nightmare ... The shelling had destroyed everything. As far as you could see, it was like an ocean of thick brown porridge."

RIGHT: Men of the 16th Canadian Machine Gun Company, part of the Canadian 4th Division, hold the line in a landscape of mud and water-filled shell holes, 14 November 1917. The Battle of Passchendaele, or Third Battle of Ypres, involved troops from across the British Empire – Australia, Canada, India, Newfoundland, New Zealand, South Africa and the UK. (HMP)

RIGHT: Soldiers run for cover as a shell explodes in the area known as Glencourse Wood on 20 September 1917, the day that the Battle of Menin Road Ridge was launched. As part of this the 1st Australian Division attacked, taking Glencourse Wood with little difficulty. An indication of the stagnation of the fighting on the Western Front can be gained from the fact that Glencourse Wood was where the First Battle of Ypres had ended on 11 November 1914. (National Media Museum)

With the Germans fully aware that the British were soon to launch their attack the only way it could succeed was by amassing more guns than the enemy. Allied experiences on the Somme the previous year had demonstrated how relatively ineffective artillery fire was against barbed-wire and deep dug-outs. The Battle of the Somme had also shown that unless the enemy's defences were destroyed, the attacking infantry would simply be cut to pieces as they crossed the open ground of No Man's Land. Everything, therefore, depended on the artillery. It would have to be so powerful and so destructive that it would blow away the German defences.

This preliminary bombardment, of an astonishing 3,036 guns, began on 16 July 1917, and finished on the morning of the attack, 31 July 1917. This attack would be delivered by General Gough's Fifth Army, with some support from the Second Army and the French First Army.

The fighting raged until 10 November 1917, the men often floundering in the mud and rain, and consisted of a number of smaller battles; Pilkem Ridge (31 July to 2 August), Langemarck (16 to 18 August) and Menin Road Ridge (20 to 26 September) being amongst the early ones.

The objective on the first day was an advance in three stages to the three German trench-systems, roughly 1,000, 2,000 and, rather optimistically, 3,500 yards forward. More realistically it was agreed that a halt could be called at either of the first two objectives if this proved necessary. Gough had between 160 and 170 tanks to help break through the German defences, of which 120 would be deployed with the initial attack, the remainder being held in reserve.

On 31 July 1917, Lieutenant Robert Sherriff and his men of the East Surrey Regiment were called forward to attack the German positions:

"At dawn on the morning of the attack, the battalion assembled in

RIGHT: Troops of the Australian 4th Division, wearing gas-masks, make their way forward in an advanced trench at Garter Point during the Third Battle of Ypres (Passchendaele), 27 September 1917. The battle marked the first occasion in the war when two Australian Imperial Force formations attacked side-by-side. (HMP)

the mud outside the huts. I lined up my platoon and went through the necessary inspection. Some of the men looked terribly ill: grey, worn faces in the dawn, unshaved and dirty because there was no clean water. I saw the characteristic shrugging of their shoulders that I knew so well. They hadn't had their clothes off for weeks, and their shirts were full of lice."

Philip Gibbs was one of just five official war correspondents, and he watched the start of the Third Battle of Ypres. It is also known as the Battle of Passchendaele because the village of Passchendaele lay on the last ridge east of Ypres, five miles from a railway junction at Rouselare, which was a vital part of the supply system of the German Fourth Army and the last objective of the British and Allied armies.

"The order came to advance. There was no dramatic leap out of the trenches. The sandbags on the parapet were so slimy with rain and rotten with age that they fell apart when you tried to grip them. You had to crawl out through a slough of mud. Some of the older men, less athletic than the others, had to be heaved out bodily.

"From then on, the whole thing became a drawn-out nightmare. There were no tree stumps or ruined buildings ahead to help you keep direction. The shelling had destroyed everything. As far as you could see, it was like an ocean of thick brown porridge. The wire entanglements had sunk into the mud, and

LEFT: Men of the 1st Division pictured laying duckboards over the muddy ground in Passchendaele, 5 October 1917. (Courtesy of the Australian War Memorial; E00837)

frequently, when you went in up to the knees, your legs would come out with strands of barbed wire clinging to them, and your hands torn and bleeding through the struggle to drag them off ...

"All this area had been desperately fought over in the earlier battles of Ypres. Many of the dead had been buried where they fell and the shells were unearthing and tossing up the decayed bodies. You would see them flying through the air and disintegrating."

The British suffered shockingly high casualties as they battled first to take and then hold their initial objectives. The first phase of the operation lasted until 15 August and had been undertaken in conditions of almost continual rain – it was one of the wettest summers on record. More than 30,000 men had become casualties and little had been gained.

The conditions the men faced was described by a reporter for the *Daily Mail*, William Beach Thomas, on 2 August 1917: "Floods of rain and a blanket of mist have doused and cloaked the whole of the Flanders plain. The newest shell-holes, already half-filled with soakage, are now flooded to the brim.

"The rain has so fouled this low, stoneless ground, spoiled of all natural drainage by shell-fire, that we experienced the double value of the early work, for today moving heavy material was extremely difficult and the men could scarcely walk in full equipment, much less dig. Every man was soaked through and was standing or sleeping in a marsh. It was a work of energy to keep a rifle in a state fit to use."

As the capture of Messines Ridge had helped ease the situation in Ypres, there was no actual need to continue battering against the German positions but Field Marshal Haig was determined to carry on, regardless of the human cost. ➤➤

BELOW: Stretcher bearers struggle through the mud. One who recalled such scenes during the fighting at Passchendaele was Corporal J. Pincombe, 1st Battalion, Queen's Westminster Rifles: "Stretcher bearers coming through the mud to bring the wounded out ... doctors and orderlies working in their shirtsleeves, even in the rain ... everywhere, all over the road and shoved to the side, were broken wagons, gun carriages, and dead horses. You couldn't speak the gunfire was so terrific ... to either side there was nothing but mud, mud for miles." (HMP)

Casualties being treated on the Menin Road, looking towards Birr Cross Roads, which are located just west of the ruins of Hooge, on the morning of 20 September 1917. The wounded on the stretchers are waiting to be taken to the clearing stations; others who are able to walk are making their way west along the road as far as possible towards Ypres itself. Shortly after the photograph was taken a shell landed in this area, killing most of the wounded on the stretchers. (HMP)

example of the futility of the offensive can be gauged by the action at Glencourse Wood. That wood alone had changed hands between the British and the Germans eighteen times.

Many of the troops had adopted a fatalistic approach

with the loss of 13,000 men on that day alone. Eventually, the Canadian Corps seized Passchendaele and, on 10 November the campaign was brought to an end, the bitter battle having lasted for three months and six days.

There has never been an accurate

RIGHT: Canadian Pioneers carrying trench material to Passchendaele stop work while German prisoners carrying wounded pass by. (HMP)

He was convinced that the Germans were on the point of collapse and that by continually pushing hard at the enemy positions they would soon completely crumble.

The offensive was resumed and continued until 19 September. Despite monumental losses and despite the fact that all the effort of the last weeks had produced only limited success, Haig stuck determinedly to his strategy. An

as the only way that they could cope with the situation they faced. Captain Horridge of the Lancashire Fusiliers wrote that he could not bring himself to order his men to attack any more: "I might as well take out my revolver and kill them here, for they'd be sure to be hit the moment they went outside."

The fighting continued into October, with a large attack on Passchendaele on the 12th. It failed

figure for the number of Allied casualties, with estimates ranging from 244,897 to more than 310,000. Lloyd George wrote of Passchendaele that it was, "one of the greatest disasters of the war ... No soldier of any intelligence now defends this senseless campaign". Yet the Germans lost at least as many men and, as the German General Staff subsequently admitted, "Germany had been brought near to certain destruction".

RIGHT: Soldiers of a field artillery brigade from the Australian 4th Division on a duckboard track passing through Chateau Wood, near Hooge in the Ypres salient, 29 October 1917. The leading soldier has been identified as Gunner James Fulton, whilst the second is Lieutenant Anthony Devine. (Courtesy of the Australian War Memorial; E01220)

Timeline 1918 - Events that Shaped The First World War

January

8 The US President, Woodrow Wilson, made his famous "Fourteen Points" statement. This was the only explicit statement of war aims made by any of the nations fighting in the First World War

March

21 Operation *Michael* – the *Kaiserschlacht* or Kaiser's Offensive – began. Using a temporary superiority of force concentrated on an identifiably weak sector of the British-held Western Front, Ludendorff aimed at striking a decisive blow to shatter British military power and provoke a French collapse before American troops arrived in sufficient numbers

24 As the German offensive continued, after enduring unceasing shelling, the town of Bapaume was evacuated by the British, only to be occupied by German forces the following day. The British commander-in-chief, Field Marshal Haig, sent an urgent telegram to the War Office to request an Allied conference

26 The Allied conference demanded by Haig took place at Doullens. Ten senior Allied politicians and generals were present. The French commander General Foch was tasked with coordinating the activities of the Allied armies, forming a common reserve and using these divisions to guard the junction of the French and British armies. At a later conference he was given the title of Supreme Commander of the Allied Armies

26 General Byng's Third Army stalled the German advance north of the Somme

April

1 The Royal Air Force was created by the amalgamation of the Royal Flying Corps and Royal Naval Air Service

4 During the Battle of the Avre on this date, the Germans launched their final attack towards Amiens

5 Ludendorff halted Operation *Michael*. The Germans had captured 1,200 square miles of France and advanced up to forty miles. Over 75,000 British soldiers had been taken prisoner and 1,300 artillery pieces and 200 tanks were lost

9 The Germans began Operation *Georgette*, an offensive in Flanders which had the aim of capturing Ypres

12 Haig issued his "backs to the wall" order to the BEF

23 Carried out on this date, the Zeebrugge Raid was an attempt by the Royal Navy to block the Belgian port of Zeebrugge and prevent its use by U-boats. A smaller force also attacked the port of Ostend

29 The German offensive in Flanders ended

May

9 A second raid on Ostend was carried out by the Royal Navy. HMS *Vindictive* was sunk in Ostend harbour but only partially blocked the canal

27 German troops began the *Blücher-Yorck* Offensive aimed at capturing the Chemin des Dames Ridge, fighting which involved British troops

28 US forces made their first attack at the Aisne

June

4 Ludendorff terminated the *Blücher-Yorck* Offensive, the German advance having been halted after early gains. The French had suffered heavily, with over 98,000 casualties, whilst the British had some 29,000 casualties. German losses were nearly as great if not slightly heavier

9 Ludendorff launched yet another offensive, his fourth, this time along the Matz river

July

15 A fifth German offensive, the Second Battle of the Marne, was launched in Champagne

August

6 The Second Battle of the Marne ended in an Allied victory. The German defeat marked the start of the relentless Allied advance which culminated in the Armistice about 100 days later. Thus the Second Battle of the Marne can be considered as the beginning of the end of the First World War

8 The Battle of Amiens, the opening phase of the Allied campaign later known as the Hundred Days Offensive, commenced

26 The breaking of the German defences on the Hindenburg Line began

September

3 The Germans withdraw from Amiens to the Hindenburg Line

28 The Fifth Battle of Ypres (also known as the Advance of Flanders and the Battle of the Peaks of Flanders) – the final advance in Flanders – began

29 The German Supreme Army Command informed the Kaiser that the military situation facing Germany "was hopeless"

October

1 In the Middle East, General Edmund Allenby's forces entered Damascus

6 Germany sought an armistice under Wilson's "Fourteen Points" statement of 8 January 1918

14 Turkey requested an armistice

14 The Battle of Courtrai began. It ended on 19 October in a decisive Allied victory

23 In Mesopotamia British forces advanced from Baghdad and seized important oil fields around Mosul

29 A revolt by German Navy personnel at Wilhelmshaven quickly spread across the rest of the country

November

7 A German delegation crossed the front line in five cars and and was taken to Foch's private train parked in a railway siding in the forest at Compiègne to discuss surrender terms

9 Kaiser Wilhelm II abdicated

11 The Armistice, agreed at 05.00 hours, came into effect at 11.00 hours. The Armistice would be prolonged three times before peace was finally ratified in 1919

BACKS TO THE WALL

RIGHT: Two of the key commanders of the March Offensive – the German Chief of the General Staff, Paul von Hindenburg and his deputy, General Erich Ludendorff. (US Library of Congress)

At 09.35 hours on Thursday, 21 March 1918, one million German soldiers left their trenches to attack the British Expeditionary Force along a front of nearly fifty miles. It was Germany's last major effort to win the war, and it very nearly succeeded.

The war had dragged on towards its fourth year. There seemed little prospect of any immediate end to the ceaseless slaughter. Field Marshal Haig saw the war as a continual battle of attrition until the Germans were finally battered into submission. In Germany the economic blockade that had been imposed upon it, enforced by the Royal Navy, was slowly strangling the country. The Kaiser and his generals knew that the longer the war dragged on the greater was the prospect of an Allied victory.

Hope, however, raised its positive head when Russia, torn by revolution, sought to withdraw from the war. Germany imposed harsh terms on the Russians but these were accepted and on 3 March 1918, Russia ended its involvement in the war. For Germany this meant that all the troops that had been fighting on the Eastern Front, almost fifty divisions, were free to face the Allies in Belgium and France.

If Germany had lost one enemy, it had already made another by antagonising the United States, who had entered the war in support of the Allies. The Americans had yet to organise and ship an enough men and equipment across the Atlantic. A window of opportunity had opened for the Kaiser and his generals. Before that window closed Germany had one last chance to win the war. It would be called the *Kaiserschlacht*, the Kaiser's battle (sometimes known as the Ludendorff Offensive).

The main German attack, known as *Michael*, was directed at the British positions which stretched from the Somme to Flanders and formed the left flank of the Allied defences. It was thought that if the British line could be broken, the French would surrender. The enemy offensive began with an intense artillery bombardment by 6,000 guns.

Commissioned as a young Subaltern in the 10th (Service) Battalion West Yorkshire Regiment, Charles William Stanley Spencer, found himself in a section of front line near the French village of Havrincourt, some ten miles east of Bapaume. As early as the middle of February 1918, Stanley and his comrades knew that a big German offensive was imminent. Men were having their leave stopped, base hospitals were being emptied,

"Little field-grey figures could be seen distinctly climbing out of their support line ... Along the whole of our Company frontage, line after line of them sprang up and advanced."

BELOW: German troops on the move during the Kaiser's Offensive in March 1918. (US Library of Congress)

Soldiers from a Highland regiment wait to counter another German attack. The lack of prepared trenches and defensive features such as barbed wire would suggest that the British retreat in the face of the relentless German pressure was well underway. For a time, the Germans would achieve what they hoped the *Kaiserschlacht* would deliver - a return to a more fluid form of warfare in open countryside away from the stalemate of the trenches. (HMP)

LEFT: **An abandoned British trench which was captured by the Germans; in the background, German soldiers on horseback view the scene.** (US Library of Congress)

and ammunition dumps hastily replenished. The signs were all there.

The inactivity of the last few weeks, if not months, came to a violent end for Stanley just before 05.00 hours that Thursday morning. The bombardment "reached a simply terrific intensity with light, medium and huge *minenwerfer* trench mortar bombs raining down on us on every side, filling the trench with thick heavy gas, compelling us to put on our gas respirators at once," Stanley recalled. "Everyone felt sure that the great attack was coming at last, but there was no confusion and every man stood to his post and waited in readiness for whatever should happen next."[1]

Having not eaten since the evening before, Stanley decided to try and eat some breakfast. "The time was about 9.40am, we had had some porridge and were waiting for the bacon ➤➤

LEFT: **A German A7V tank pictured passing through Roye on the first day of the Kaiser's Offensive, 21 March 1918. This was the first time that these tanks had been deployed.** (Bundesarchiv, Bild 183-P1013-316/ CC-BY-SA)

ABOVE: **Throughout the German attacks in March and April 1918, many British units continued to resist as far as was possible. This British artillery battery, "firing from the corner of a wood during the German offensive", represents one example. The lack of gun pits would suggest that this was not a prepared position.** (HMP)

ABOVE RIGHT: **A British 60-pounder, that was captured by advancing German troops during their Spring Offensive of March 1918.** (Courtesy of Brett Goodman)

"Every position must be held to the last man: there must be no retirement. With our backs to the wall and believing in the justice of our cause, each one of us must fight on to the end."

and tomatoes that the Company cook was frying on a brazier at the bottom of the steps, when we heard a wild yell from up in the trench: 'They're coming over, they're coming over'. Grabbing our steel helmets we made a rush for the steps ... Sure enough, they were coming at last.[2]

"The bombardment had stopped and the little field-grey figures could be seen distinctly climbing out of their support line ... Along the whole of our Company frontage, line after line of them sprang up and advanced ... Their trenches must have been jammed with men, for more and more followed. Then the front waves began to advance up the slope, running a few yards and then dropping, keeping in well-extended order and making their rushes in sections, so that the whole line was never moving and exposed at once. But while they so advanced we were not idle. Every man we had, the cook, the two signallers, officers' servants, everybody, lined the parapet and, loading and reloading with desperate energy, poured streams of bullets into each enemy party as it rushed towards us." Along a front of nearly fifty miles opposite the British Third and Fifth Armies the German offensive was underway.

As the British Army had always looked to mount offensive action, it was little prepared for, or experienced in, defensive warfare. As a result the British Fifth Army under General Gough, between the French towns of Amiens and St Quentin, found itself unable to hold its line against the massive German onslaught.

"There were no dugouts in our front line," wrote a soldier of the 51st (Highland) Division, "it was very thinly held to prevent casualties. We had to huddle up under the parapet during the shelling; there was no other shelter. When the bombardment lifted, we were not attacked frontally. We were considerably shaken by the shelling. It was a moment of fear. 'What's coming out of the mist?' We fired our rifles blindly into the mist and then heard firing from our left and from the rear. We realised that we were being outflanked."

The speed of the German attack, helped by a heavy mist, completely deceived the British defenders and thousands of them were captured, particularly in the British Forward Zone of the Fifth Army's area. By late afternoon on 21 March, the southern part of Gough's line had been forced back and, in agreement with Haig, he correspondingly pulled back his divisions in the northern sector of his line. It was deemed more important to retain the integrity of his command than retain ground, which could always be re-taken later.

Gough withdrew seven miles to take up a position behind the Crozat Canal. It was the first time that the BEF had had to retreat to such an extent since the first month of the war. By midnight the Germans had taken, by direct assault and capture, just short of 100 square miles of ground previously held by the British.

General Byng's Third Army, whose defences were a little stronger than those of the Fifth Army, was able to hold back the Germans but by the evening of that first day of what became known as the Spring Offensive, Gough's entire front was on the point of collapse. In that first day of the *Kaiserschlacht*, the British Army alone had suffered 38,000 casualties and lost 138 artillery pieces. The Germans had experienced even greater losses, amounting to almost 40,000 men. Total losses for 21 March, were more than 78,000, being the heaviest losses in a single day's fighting in the entire war.

Undeterred by their losses the Germans resumed their offensive the next day. Again the weather worked in their favour, with mist concealing their movements. Once more Gough's men were driven back and that night the Fifth Army was forced to retreat even further back, all the way to the River Somme.

On the 23rd, the Germans had advanced so far that their long range railway guns started to shell Paris. The French considered pulling back to defend their capital and Haig entertained the possibility of abandoning the Fifth Army altogether and moving the Third Army to protect the Channel ports. The Kaiser, it seemed, was winning his battle.

As the Germans pressed ever southwards and westwards their communications became more extended and their advance began to slow down. "There were men driving cows," wrote one of the Germans in his diary of 28 March, "others who carried a hen under one arm ... men carrying a bottle of wine under their arm and another open in their hand ... men staggering ... men who could hardly walk ... the advance was held up and there was no means of getting going again for hours."

The difficulties the Germans were

NOTES:

1. Stanley Spencer MC, *Stanley Spencer's Great War Diary* (Pen & Sword, Barnsley, 2008).
2. The Germans "who were coming at last", were Saxons from the German 53rd Reserve Division. (Middlebrook, M. *The Kaiser's Battle*, Pen & Sword, Barnsley, 2007).

experiencing were not apparent to the Allied commanders and, with defeat staring the Allies in the face, a scapegoat was needed and Hugh Gough was the obvious victim. He was replaced on 27 March by General Sir Henry Rawlinson.

Meanwhile, Haig rushed reinforcements into the front line, including three brigades of Australians who held back the German attack at Villers Bretonneux on 4 April. With this the Germans paused to gather their strength for the final push that would see the collapse of the BEF and an end to the war at last.

Realising the predicament that the British were in, Douglas Haig, issued an "Order of the Day" on 11 April 1918, which included these memorable words: "Three weeks ago today the Enemy began his terrific attacks against us on a 50 mile front ... Many amongst us now are tired ... There is no course open to us but to fight it out! Every position must be held to the last man: there must be no retirement. With our backs to the wall and believing in the justice of our cause, each one of us must fight on to the end."

As it transpired, Operation *Michael* had already been abandoned by the Germans, who turned their attention instead to other sectors. It would be the French who would feel the full weight of the next German attack.

The great Spring Offensive had failed and it had cost the Germans some 239,000 men. The Allies lost nearly 255,000 men (British, British Empire, French and American). The Allies also lost 1,300 artillery pieces and 200 tanks.

Tragic though such casualties were, the effects were felt far more severely by the Germans who could not make up their losses. It was an entirely different matter for the Allies as already large numbers of American troops were arriving on the Continent. The men of the American Expeditionary Force, the first of whom had arrived in France in June 1917, were already making their presence felt; indeed, during the German offensive US troops were for the first time used as independent formations and had proven themselves in combat. By June of 1918, there were a million US troops in France.

The Spring Offensive was to have been the Kaiser's great march to victory, instead it set the Germans on the path to defeat.

ABOVE and LEFT: **The scale of the overall German successes during the early days of the March Offensive can be seen in these two images which both show captured British troops heading east towards captivity.** (HMP)

A British artillery position caught by the opening German bombardment of the *Kaiserschlacht*. Over 3,500,000 shells were fired by the German guns in just five hours on the morning of 21 March 1918, striking targets over an area of 150 square miles. This was the biggest barrage of the entire war and it hit all areas of British front occupied by the Fifth Army, most of the front of the Third Army, and some of the front of the First Army to the north. In total, the British suffered 7,500 casualties during this bombardment alone. The front line was badly damaged and communications with the rear areas were cut. Although the British had learned the approximate time and location of the offensive, the weight of the attack and of the preliminary bombardment still came as an unpleasant surprise. (Courtesy of Brett Goodman)

The March to V

BELOW: **In a new offensive launched on 15 July 1918, the Germans attacked the French and Allied positions around Reims. This massive assault, known now as the Second Battle of the Marne, saw forty-three infantry divisions, backed by 5,000 guns, attack the French line; British and American units were called forward to help. On 20 July the Allies successfully counter-attacked, forcing the Germans to withdraw. This photograph, taken on 20 July, shows men of the US Army Expeditionary Force crossing a pontoon bridge next to a destroyed bridge over the Marne river.** (US Library of Congress)

The Germans' March offensive had failed and by the late summer of 1918 the Allied armies had begun to advance once again. Soon, along the whole of the Western Front, British, French and American troops broke through the German positions.

"We have nearly reached the limit of our powers of resistance," wrote Kaiser Wilhelm II on Friday, 11 August 1918. "The war must be ended." Less than a month earlier the soon-to-be Marshal Foch had committed three French armies to what became known as the Second Battle of the Marne. Just 100 days later the war would be over.

At the Second Battle of the Marne, the French, supported by more than 300 tanks, had driven back the Germans and inflicted almost 200,000 casualties upon them. This was followed on 8 August by an attack by the British Fourth Army at Amiens, which saw British, Canadian and Australian troops attack in thick fog to take the Germans, for once, by complete surprise.

One of those Australians was H.R. Williams. "At zero hour the bombardment fell in one mighty blast," he later wrote. "The mist was stabbed with flashes. The rush of the shells through the air sounded like express trains passing. The earth appeared to tremble with the concussion, and when the order to move was given the officers and NCOs had to roar at the top of their voices. Company after company, platoon after platoon, moved forward into the bank of the mist."

In the centre of the attack the Australians and Canadians pushed the Germans back for almost eight miles. The reason for the depth of the British and Commonwealth armies was attributed to the mass use of transport to exploit the breakthrough, as H.R. Williams saw first-hand: "Along this road (beyond Villers-Bretonneux) no wheels had turned for many months, as it ran through German and Australian front lines. But now the scene in the bright morning sunshine made us rub eyes that surely deceived us.

"Coming along with all haste were motor lorries, loaded with ammunition, stores, and tools, horse-drawn limbers, cookers, water-carts, dispatch riders on motor bicycles, heavy guns, here and there an armoured car; mounted men regulated the traffic; and only a mile or so forward could still be heard the spasmodic rattle of machine-guns."

Such an advance on a single day by the Commonwealth forces was unprecedented. "As the sun set on the 8th August on the battlefield, the greatest defeat which the German Army had suffered since the beginning of the war was an accomplished fact," wrote Major-General Erich Ludendorff, chief of staff to Field Marshal von Hindenburg. "This was the worst experience I had to go through ... 8th August made things clear for both army commands, both for the German and that of the enemy." It was, Ludendorff said, "the black day of the German army."

The Battle of Amiens had developed, Field Marshal Haig wrote in his diary, "more favourably for us than I, optimist though I am, had dared to hope". Progress, though, began to slow over the next few days, as German reserves were transferred to the threatened sector. The battle

ctory

came to a conclusion amid the 1916 battlefields of the Somme.

Whilst to the Allies German resistance appeared as strong as ever, the enemy's morale was beginning to crack, and the fissures would be bigger than any seen up to this point in the war. Mutiny was in the air. The Germans had believed that the Spring Offensive would bring them victory and its failure, with the enormous losses which it had incurred, made it all too clear that they could not win the war. Hope – the one thing that keeps every soldier fighting – had gone.

After Amiens, the next battle was on 21 August which was launched by the British First and Third armies across the northern sector of the old Somme battlefield. Unlike that day in July 1916, the 1918 battle saw success at every point. Less than a week later the First Army, at the Battle of the Scarpe, pushed forward six miles over parts of the old Arras battlefield that the British had been unable to take in 1917. A mood of great optimism began to drive the Allies on.

Bapaume was taken, followed by an advance up to the German lines at Péronne. Here Ludendorff had ordered the construction of a "Winter Line", which, as the name suggests is where he hoped to hold the Allies until the following year. By 3 September it was abandoned as »

LEFT: **A small proportion of the artillery pieces deployed by the Allies for the opening bombardments of the One Hundred Days Offensive which began on 8 August 1918.** (HMP)

LEFT: **Troops of the 6th Battalion Australian Imperial Force pictured resting in a trench, near Lihons during the Battle of Amiens, 10 August 1918. The Battle of Amiens, which began two days earlier on 8 August, lasted four days and was the opening phase of the Allied offensive later known as the Hundred Days Offensive.** (HMP)

By the summer of 1918 the Allied supremacy in men and equipment, such as the French tank seen here (probably during the Second Battle of the Marne), was beginning to alter the course of the First World War. (US Library of Congress)

RIGHT: **German mortars captured during the fighting for the Canal du Nord. One of the mortars has been marked by the 4th Battalion, Australian Imperial Force, which captured it on 27 September 1918. Units typically chalked captured guns, mortars, and machine-guns as signs of their victories. The mortar in the foreground with the soldier is a 7.58cm Minenwerfer; the mortar in the background is a 17cm Minenwerfer 1913 short model.** (HMP)

RIGHT: **Evidence of the escalating collapse in German morale during 1918 was evidenced by the large numbers of prisoners taken each time a battle ended.** (US Library of Congress)

the Australians broke through at Mont St Quentin just north of Péronne.

The Germans soon abandoned all the territory they had won during the Spring Offensive in March 1918, and withdrew to the Hindenburg Line. These formidable defences, with concrete pillboxes, deep dugouts and barbed-wire entanglements 100 yards deep, presented a seemingly unbreachable barrier.

On 26 September the Americans and British began a series of attacks, the main focus being the sector known as the Siegfried Line. The successes of the previous weeks had been against rapidly-prepared defences where an intense preliminary bombardment had not always been necessary. The Hindenburg Line was different.

Some 1,600 guns opened fire on 26 September, starting with a new type of mustard gas on the first day followed by High Explosive on the three following days; in total, 750,000 shells were fired. Many days of hard fighting lay ahead, but it was quickly apparent that the Allies now possessed not just a morale advantage over the enemy but a numerical and technical advantage. The Spring Offensive had cost the Germans not just more than half-a-million men, it had seriously depleted their arsenal of heavy weapons. On 28 September 1918, Ludendorff told the Kaiser the war was lost and that only an immediate armistice could prevent a catastrophe.

There was good reason for Ludendorff's despair. Two weeks earlier the Austrians had made the opening moves towards seeking a peace agreement with the Allies, the Turks had been beaten by Allenby in Palestine, and Allied forces in Salonika had almost knocked Bulgaria out of the war.

All along the Hindenburg Line the Allies – mainly the British, Commonwealth and US forces – attacked. The BEF assaulted two enemy sectors, the first centred on the Canal du Nord and the second on the St Quentin Canal. The Germans had spent an enormous amount of time and effort on the construction of the Hindenburg Line and it was considered to be all but impenetrable with watercourses such as the two canals integrated into the Germans defensive scheme.

The Canal du Nord was an intimidating obstacle. Its west bank was between ten and twelve feet high and was 100 feet wide. Beyond it lay dense wire entanglements and marshes swept by machine-guns sheltered in strong trenches. On high ground overlooking the canal defences seven-and-a-half German divisions were posted with a further four in reserve. A couple of weeks later, Haig had an opportunity to inspect the Hindenburg Line: "The defence system is admirably sited and the wire is immensely strong – many belts of the thickest form of wire. Dug outs are numerous, and most of the exits are made of concrete of immense thickness."

The key to the defences, though, was the determination of the defenders and, compared with a few months before, this was fading rapidly. Haig was aware of this and he concluded his observation of the Hindenburg Line with these words: "Had the Germans been in a good state of moral [sic], the position would have been impregnable."

The morale of the Germans, however, was not good and everywhere, to a greater or lesser degree, the attackers were successful. "The enemy's defence in the last and strongest of his prepared positions had been shattered," Haig was able to write. "The whole of the main Hindenburg defences passes into our possession ... The effect of the victory upon the subsequent course of the campaign was decisive."

On 29 September 1918, the Germans staggered away from the Hindenburg Line in dismay but not, as yet, in disarray. The Germans still fought back, though they now fought alone, as Turkey, Bulgaria and Austria had finally abandoned the cause of the Central Powers.

The end for the Germans came as the Allies pushed towards the German border. For the first time since the start of the offensives in March, the Allies had a considerable numerical advantage. According to Allied estimates the Germans had been reduced to 190 divisions against the Allies' total of 221, and the average strength of a German battalion had dropped from 850 to 540.

On 4 October 1918 it happened; the Germans asked for an armistice. The German Army was on its knees, the High Seas Fleet had mutinied and Berlin was ravaged by demonstrations. The country was on the point of revolution.

The first German offer was rejected by the Allies and as negotiations continued, so did the fighting and the dying. In the month of October alone, the British Army suffered the loss of 5,438 officers and 115,608 other ranks.

On 9 November 1918 the Kaiser abdicated. As he slipped across the border into exile in the Netherlands an agreement was reached to end hostilities. At 06.50 hours on 11 November a message was sent out to all the Allied armies, whose opening words were: "Hostilities will cease today, November 11."

The virtually complete collapse of the German Army in little more than three months, after four years of bitter and determined resistance, seemed astonishing. Not for nothing did Marshal Foch declare: "Never at any time in history has the British Army achieved greater results than in this unbroken offensive lasting 116 days from 18th of July to the 11th of November."

The statistics of that run of continuous victories, which included nine major engagements, are indeed exceptional. The British and Commonwealth armies suffered some 350,000 casualties but 188,700 Germans were captured along with 2,840 artillery pieces. The French took 139,000 prisoners and seized 1,880 guns; the Americans could count 44,142 prisoners and 1,481 guns, whilst the Belgians captured 14,500 men and 414 guns. The total number of Germans killed or wounded amounted to more than 785,730.

Brigadier General J.V. Campbell VC, CMG, DSO, addressing troops of the 137th Brigade, part of the 46th Division, from the Riqueval Bridge over the St Quentin Canal, which the formation captured on 29 September 1918. The assault for the bridge began at 05.50 hours and by evening the division had captured a section of the Hindenburg Support Line. During the initial assault a company of the 6th Battalion, North Staffordshire Regiment captured the Riqueval Bridge before it could be destroyed by the Germans. (National Archives of the Netherlands)

THE GUNS FAL

The Armistice

RIGHT: **German soldiers marching back towards the Rhine in November 1918 to comply with the terms of the Armistice which stated that German forces must retire to the Eastern bank of the Rhine. Note the flowers and the occasional smiling face.** (HMP)

For days they had known that the war was coming to an end, yet the fighting, and the dying, continued until the very last moment. Nevertheless, when the guns fell silent at 11.00 hours on 11 November 1918, the war was finally over.

At 05.05 hours on the morning of 11 November 1918, the Armistice between the Allies and Germany was signed. At 06.50 hours a message was sent from Field Marshal Haig's headquarters. It read "Hostilities will cease at 11.00 hours today, November 11th. Troops will stand fast on the line reached at that time which will be reported to Corps Headquarters. Strictest precautions will be maintained. There will be no intercourse of any kind with the enemy."

Even though the war was drawing to a close the fighting continued throughout the morning. This involved Private George Price, who was a member of the 28th (Northwest) Battalion, 6th Canadian Infantry Brigade which had been detailed to occupy the village of Havre and then take up defensive positions at the Canal du Centre some four and a half miles north-east of Mons. There they were to stop and find suitable accommodation.

The Canadians took the village without opposition, but as they approached the bridge over the canal a German machine-gun opened fire upon them. Nevertheless, with the Germans holding the northern bank of the canal and the Allies the opposite side, the Canadians should have ended their advance at that point. It was now just a few minutes before 11.00 hours and the war was drawing to a close.

However, Price and three others decided to cross the canal. Precisely why they did this, with only minutes to go before the end of hostilities, is not known. It has been suggested that they may have been trying to secure billets in the houses across the canal before the ceasefire, that they were seeking out the machine-gunner who had fired at the Canadians when they approached the bridge, or were merely checking on what the enemy was doing.

Whatever the reason, the four men crossed the bridge and entered one of the houses, quite possibly the house from which the machine-gun had been fired. Inside were only the householder and his family. The Canadians moved to the next house, which again was occupied but not by Germans. The Belgians in the house warned Price to be careful but he ignored this advice.

Private George Price stepped out into the street. A single shot rang out. Price half turned and slumped into the arms of one of his comrades, Art Goodmurphy. The Canadian dragged Price back into the house. From across the street a young Belgian girl risked

SILENT

MESSAGES AND SIGNALS. Army Form C. 2123.

Prefix ... Code ... Words ... Received. From ... By ... Sent, or sent out. At ... To ... By ... Office Stamp.

Charges to Collect

Service Instructions

Handed in at YCC Office 0757 m. Received 08.11 m.

TO 19 Inf Bde

Sender's Number	Day of Month	In reply to Number	AAA
G287	11th		

Hostilities will cease at 1100 hrs today Nov 11th aaa There will be no intercourse of any description with the enemy aaa Addsd all concerned

FROM 33rd Divn

PLACE & TIME 0555

* This line should be erased if not required.

her life by running to help Price. But George Price had been hit in the heart and there was nothing Goodmurphy or the girl could do to save him. It was 10.58 hours. George Lawrence Price died two minutes before the ceasefire.

George Price was reputedly the last Commonwealth soldier to be killed in action in the First World War. His death epitomised the futility of the bloodiest conflict the war had yet known. Precisely how many people were killed or severely wounded in the war is difficult to determine. Many of the statistics that have been presented are, and can only be, estimated or approximate values, especially those regarding civilians. The usual figure given for the military deaths of the Allied Powers is 5,712,379, of which the troops of Britain and the Empire amount to 1,115,597. The UK alone suffered 886,939 military fatalities. Civilian fatalities from all causes amongst the Allies were more than 3,600,000.

Deaths suffered by the Central Powers were actually less, with a total of little more than 7,000,000. Total fatalities amongst the belligerent countries were in excess of 16,500,000 men, women and children. In addition to these shocking numbers, there was a grand total 21,228,813 military wounded.

On that Monday morning of 11 November 1918, Captain Harold Horne, amongst the ranks of the Royal Marines of the 63rd (Royal Naval) Division, found his unit near the village of Bougnies, five miles south of Mons. At 07.00 hours, less than an hour after the telegram had arrived advising them of the cease-fire, they were ordered to start advancing northwards. Needless to say, "their reaction lacked enthusiasm".

"You can imagine our feelings – four hours and then peace", Horne later recalled. Hesitatingly, the Marines followed the retreating Germans, the enemy rearguard firing occasionally to slow the British advance. By 10.30 hours the Marines had reached *Villers-Saint-Ghislain*, receiving an emotional welcome from the inhabitants.

Then, strung out in open order to cover as much territory as »

The Losses

With the Armistice and the end of the fighting in Europe, there were some 500,000 Commonwealth soldiers who were listed as "missing". This figure almost equalled the figure for those soldier casualties with a known grave.

One attempt to describe the horrendous losses suffered by the Commonwealth nations during the First World War asked the public to picture a million men marching past the Cenotaph in Whitehall, London: "Imagine them moving in one continuous column, four abreast. As the head of that column reaches the Cenotaph, the last four men would be at Durham. In Canada, that column would stretch across the land from Quebec to Ottawa; in Australia, from Melbourne to Canberra; in South Africa, from Bloemfontein to Pretoria; in New Zealand, from Christchurch to Wellington; in Newfoundland, from coast to coast of the island; and, in India, from Lahore to Delhi. It would take these million men eighty-four hours, or three and a half days, to march past the Cenotaph in London".

LEFT: **The message form announcing the ceasefire that was addressed to the 19th Infantry Brigade, 33rd Division. Received at 08.11 hours on the morning of Monday, 11 November 1918, the message states that "Hostilities will cease at 1100 hrs today Nov 11th", before adding that "there will be no intercourse of any description with the enemy"!** (Crown Copyright: With the kind permission of the Imperial War Museum, Department of Documents)

FAR LEFT: **Driven by a desire to see where a loved-one fell or was buried, after the Armistice the families and friends of those who were killed on the Western Front began to travel to France and Belgium. The development of the battlefield tour had begun. Here the sister of 27-year-old Private Norman Griffiths of the 8th Battalion Duke of Wellington's (West Riding Regiment) is pictured in front of his grave in Abbeville Communal Cemetery Extension during a family pilgrimage to France and Belgium in August 1930.** (HMP)

RIGHT: **In the armistice agreement signed on 11 November 1918, the Allied Naval Council decreed that the German High Seas Fleet should be confined to port under its supervision. On 21 November 1918, the High Seas Fleet, amounting to some seventy warships, rendezvoused with a Royal Navy escort and steamed into captivity at Scapa Flow. This image shows German warships pictured in line abreast on what became known as "Der Tag" - The Day.** (HMP)

> "At precisely 11 o'clock an officer stepped out of their position, stood up, lifted his helmet and bowed to the British troops. He then fell in all his men in front of the trench and marched them off."

possible, they moved out into the fields beyond the village. At the edge of a wood about a half mile away, German troops sent up warning flares. The Royal Marines looked at their watches. "A few seconds later we blew the whistle and stopped – in the middle of a turnip field. Shortly afterwards the Germans came out of the wood onto a side road, formed up and moved off towards Germany".[1]

Major Keith Officer, serving with the Australian Corps, was talking to an officer of the Scots Greys, when the clock chimed 11.00 hours. He later recorded this description of that momentous day: "Nearby there was a German machine-gun unit giving our troops a lot of trouble. They kept on firing until practically 11 o'clock. At precisely 11 o'clock an officer stepped out of their position, stood up, lifted his helmet and bowed to the British troops. He then fell in all his men in front of the trench and marched them off."

In hindsight, Major Officer considered that the German's actions had been "a wonderful display of confidence in British chivalry … the temptation to fire at them must have been very great".[2] The fact that Officer and his un-named companion had held their conversation in the very same building that had acted as Sir John French's headquarters during the Battle of Mons in 1914, only served to illustrate how much, (or how little!), ground had been won during the war. This was a reality that was not lost on Marine Hubert Trotman of the Royal Marine Light Infantry:

"We were still fighting hard and losing men," he recalled. "We knew nothing of the proposed Armistice." In fact, it was not until a quarter to ten on the 11th itself, as Trotman and his fellow Marines were advancing on the village of Guiry, that a runner appeared and broke the news.

"We were lined up on a railway bank nearby, the same railway bank that the Manchesters had lined up on in 1914. They had fought at the battle of Mons in August that year. Some of us went down to a wood in a little valley and found the skeletons of some of the Manchesters still lying there. Lying there with their boots on, very still, no helmets, no rusty rifles or equipment, just their boots."[3]

The war, though, was over and it was time to celebrate. Philip Gibbs, one of just five official war correspondents, was near Mons when the Armistice took effect. "All the way to Mons there were columns of troops on the march, and their bands played ahead of them, and almost every man had a flag on his rifle, the red, white, and blue of France, the red, yellow, and black of Belgium," he wrote. "They wore flowers in their caps and in their tunics, red and white chrysanthemums given to them by the crowds of people who cheered them on their way, people who in many of these villages had been only one day liberated from the German yoke.

"Our men marched singing, with a smiling light in the eyes. They had done their job, and it was finished with the greatest victory in the world."

NOTES:

1. Weintraub, S. *A Stillness Heard Around The World.* Allen & Unwin, London, 1985.
2. Arthur, M. *Forgotten Voices of The Great War.* Ebury Press, London, 2003.
3. *Ibid.*

Abbeville Communal Cemetery Extension, and the last resting place of Norman Griffiths (see previous page), as it is today - one of many thousands of sites of commemoration and remembrance from the First World War that can be found around the world. (Courtesy of the Commonwealth War Graves Commission)

The War to

The Treaty of Versailles

The final confirmation of the end of the fighting with Germany in the First World War - the signing of the Treaty of Versailles in 1919. The Paris Peace Conference opened on 12 January 1919, and meetings were held at various locations in and around Paris until 20 January, 1920. Leaders of thirty-two states, representing about 75% of the world's population, attended.
Eventually five treaties emerged from the Paris Peace Conference, each one dealing with one of the defeated powers. Each of the five treaties was named after a Paris suburb. The one which dealt with Germany was the Treaty of Versailles, and was signed in the Hall of Mirrors in the Palace De Versailles. This picture shows the various delegations signing the Treaty of Versailles in the Hall of Mirrors. (US Library of Congress)

RIGHT: **The Armistice of 11 November 1918, was welcomed in nations around the world - as illustrated by this picture of Canadians celebrating in Toronto.**

OPPOSITE RIGHT: **The victors celebrate. Here one victory parade is pictured making its way down The Mall having passed through Admiralty Arch.** (HMP)

So terrible had been the First World War that no-one could imagine the nations of Europe would ever fight each other again. That, though, depended on securing a peace that would stop all future aggression and lead to greater prosperity for all. Neither happened.

The war had been won and the Allied nations rightly celebrated. But for every victor there must be a loser, and for many of the German soldiers the news of the armistice was met with mixed emotions. "I thought the war would never end," wrote George Groz. "And perhaps it never did, either. Peace was declared, but not all of us were drunk with joy or stricken blind. Very little changed fundamentally, except that the proud German soldier had turned into a defeated bundle of misery and the great German army had disintegrated. I was disappointed, not because we had lost the war but because our people had allowed it to go on for so many years, instead of heeding the few voices of protest against all that mass insanity and slaughter."

Despite his disappointment, Groz accepted that the Germans had been defeated, but such sentiments were not expressed by all Germans, as exemplified by the words of Herbert Sulzbach who had volunteered for the German Army in 1914 and who fought until the end. "In spite of it all, we can be proud of the performance we put up, and we shall always be proud of it. Never before has a nation, a single army, had the whole world against it and stood its ground against such overwhelming odds; had it been the other way round, this heroic performance could never have been achieved by any other nation. We protected our homeland from her enemies – they never pushed as far as German territory."

It is with such words that can be seen the seeds of the nationalist movement that began to grow in Germany after the war. In the eyes of many in Germany, neither the German Army nor the German Navy had been truly defeated. The armed forces, and the people of Germany, had been let down by the politicians. This feeling that Germany had not been defeated on the battlefield was exacerbated by the terms of the peace treaty, the Treaty of Versailles, which was finally signed between Germany and the Allied Powers on 28 June 1919.

The main feature of the treaty was the insistence that Germany and her allies should accept responsibility "for causing all the loss and damage to which the Allied and Associated Governments and their nationals have been subjected as a consequence of the war imposed upon them by the aggression of Germany and her allies". Later known as the War Guilt Clause, all blame for the war was heaped on Germany's shoulders. She was forced to disarm her armed forces, accept reduced borders and pay enormous sums, many millions of marks, in reparations to certain countries that had formed the Entente powers.

There was also considerable disquiet over the subject of war crimes. In Articles 228-230 it was stated that the Allied and Associated Powers should be granted the right to bring before military tribunals people believed to have committed war crimes. The Article compelled Germany to "furnish all documents and information of every kind, the production of which may be

End War

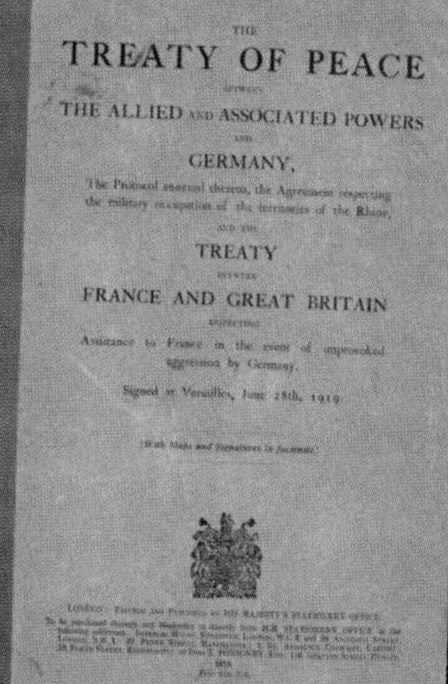

considered necessary to ensure the full knowledge of the incriminating acts, the discovery of offenders and the just appreciation of responsibility". This added further to the collective German guilt.

France, the main Power to share a common border with Germany, wanted to place Germany in such a weakened state that it would never threaten France again. It had quite the opposite effect. The Versailles Treaty's terms, especially with regards to reparations, were deeply felt in Germany. When it failed to meet its payments French and Belgian troops marched into the German industrial heartland of the Ruhr. Their intention was to forcibly extract reparations in the form of goods, particularly coal. This created enormous resentment in Germany towards the French, resentment that would not be forgotten.

That though, was in the future. The first and most immediate problem facing the former combatant powers at the end of the war was that of demobilizing millions of men. This could clearly not happen straight away and the men became increasingly frustrated waiting to return home.

It was not just the vast logistical operation of demobilization, which in itself was fraught with difficulty, but also these vast numbers of young men would have to be reintegrated into society and into the workplace. >>

ABOVE: **Luxembourgers celebrating the liberation of their country and welcoming the arrival of Allied soldiers after the Armistice in November 1918.** (US National Archives)

TOP INSET: **An English language version of the document which was intended to have helped bring permanent peace to Europe.**

RIGHT: **Following the Armistice, British, French, Belgian and American forces marched into Germany and occupied the Rhineland. The British element of the occupying force, part of which is seen here, was named the British Army of the Rhine and was based at Cologne. British troops remained on the Rhine until 1929.** (HMP)

ABOVE: **The Armistice of 11 November 1918, was signed in a train carriage in the forest of Compiègne north of Paris. That same carriage, seen here on public display in the Cour des Invalides in Paris in the late 1920s, later became the setting of France's armistice in June 1940 - Hitler specifically chose the location as an irony for the defeated French. The railway carriage itself was ultimately destroyed in Berlin during the Allied bombing of the city in the Second World War.** (HMP)

> "The 1920s saw considerable industrial and political unrest in the UK but in Germany the situation was far worse."

Almost every industry had been geared to meet the requirements of the war. Not only would many factories now have to convert to peace-time manufacturing but large numbers of companies would no longer have any business at all. Lloyd George had promised the men "a land fit for heroes" upon their return home and though there was a brief period of reconstruction after the war, soon those heroes might find themselves unemployed, even desperately poor, and sometimes deeply angry.

Nevertheless, in the British Army, the process of demobilization went surprisingly smoothly. This was mainly due to the decision by the newly-appointed Minister of War, Winston Churchill. He introduced a new and more equitable demobilization. Based on age, length of service and the number of times a man had been wounded in battle, it ensured that the longest-serving soldiers were generally demobilised first. As this was seen as being a fair system the policy was on the whole accepted by the troops.

For the soldiers from the Commonwealth, demobilization was a more problematic issue. A post-war shortage of shipping, made even more severe by dock strikes and the reluctance of shipping companies to divert their vessels away from the lucrative commercial trade, meant frequent delays and cancellations of the troop ships bound for the colonies. So, in camps around the country, thousands of soldiers waited impatiently to return to their homelands. In ever worsening conditions, their morale deteriorated with every delay, every cancellation, every broken promise.

One such camp, or "concentration area", was Kinmel Park near Bodelwyddan. Accommodating, at its peak, some 23,000 Canadian troops, it was conveniently close to the port of Liverpool from where most of the ships to North America would sail.

Conditions at the camp were poor with the men having to sleep on cold, draughty floors with little bedding. The food was inadequate and disease was widespread. But possibly the greatest cause of resentment amongst the men was the fact that post-war unemployment in Canada was very high and the country was suffering under the burden of a severe war debt. It was said that the Canadian Government was reluctant to increase the speed of demobilization because of the pressure this would exert upon the home economy. The problem for the men in the camp was that the longer they remained in the UK the less chance they had of finding a job when they finally returned home.

Little wonder then, that the growing discontent at Kinmel Park flared into violence. On the night of 4 March 1919, and throughout much of the following day, large numbers of the angry and frustrated Canadian soldiers ran riot through the camp. The camp authorities restored order with armed guards and cavalry. But in the ensuing engagements five men were killed and twenty-one others wounded. Such open anger was, however, not unusual, both in the UK and on the Continent.

Eventually, though, the armies of the combatant powers were reduced to a peace-time footing. As an example in November 1918, the British army had numbered almost 3.8 million men. Twelve months later, it had been reduced to slightly less than 900,000 and by 1922 to just over 230,000.

The 1920s saw considerable industrial and political unrest in the UK but in Germany the situation was far worse. The post-war depression experienced across the developed world, coupled with the burden heaped upon Germany under the terms of the Treaty of Versailles, lead to almost complete social and economic collapse. This paved the way for Adolf Hitler to come to power with the promise of restoring the nation's economy and, in particular, its pride.

So, far from being the war to end war, the First World War did not bring lasting peace to Europe. It merely set the scene for an even more terrible conflict that tore the world apart a mere generation later.